Wounds of the Spirit

Wounds of the Spirit

Black Women, Violence, and Resistance Ethics

Traci C. West

NEW YORK UNIVERSITY PRESS

New York and London

NEW YORK UNIVERSITY PRESS
New York and London

Library of Congress Cataloging-in-Publication Data
West, Traci C., 1959–
Wounds of the spirit : black women, violence, and resistance
ethics / Traci C. West.
p.   cm.
Includes bibliographical references and index.
ISBN 0-8147-9334-7 (cloth : alk. paper)
ISBN 0-8147-9335-5 (pbk. : alk. paper)
1. Afro-American women—Crimes against. 2. Afro-American
women—Social conditions. 3. Rape—United States. 4. Wife
abuse—United States. 5. Child sexual abuse—United States.
6. Racism—United States. 7. Sex discrimination against women—
United States. I. Title.
HV6250.4.W65 W465 1999
362.88'089'96073—ddc21   98-40142
                                 CIP

New York University Press books are printed on acid-free paper,
and their binding materials are chosen for strength and durability.

Manufactured in the United States of America

10 9 8 7 6 5 4 3 2 1

This book is dedicated to the memory of my mother, Paula F. West. The legacy of her fierce love, courage, and faith lives on in the many lives she touched.

Contents

Preface   *ix*

Acknowledgments   *xi*

Introduction   1

I   Listening to Women's Stories

1   Testimony from Nonfiction Literature   11

2   Contemporary Testimony from Interviews   30

II   Paying Attention to Women's Anguish

3   Emotional and Spiritual Consequences   55

III   Deciphering the Role of Society

4   Theoretical Resources   91

5   A Sampler of Cultural Assaults   122

IV   Garnering Methods of Resistance

6   Identifying Resistance   151

7   Maintaining the Momentum, Sustaining an Ethic of Resistance   181

Notes   *209*

Select Bibliography   *233*

Index   *245*

About the Author   *249*

Preface

Can We Talk?

Throughout my work on this project I knew that I wanted to be in dialogue with activists, academics, domestic violence practitioners, lay and clergy church leaders, counselors, social workers, public health workers, or anyone who cares about opposing violence against black women. I have been repeatedly advised against such broad intentions. "You have to choose one audience," certain experts told me. I stubbornly insisted that the nature of this topic requires that we ignore the boundaries that keep us from working together.

I know that I am taking a risk. Some suggested that I leave out the women's stories and concentrate on theory. Others gravitated toward the practical suggestions at the very end of the book and complained about the amount of cultural analysis preceding it. One person advised me to include less of the "church/religious stuff," while another commented that the spiritual and religious emphases are what is most interesting about the book.

I know that I live in a world where it would be quite unusual for a women's studies professor of postmodern feminist theory, a black church bishop, and an economically poor battered women's shelter resident, to sit down together for a dialogue and strategy session. But I maintain that we must begin to build such bridges in order to increase resistance to the violence against women in our communities. To make progress on this, we need a methodology that at least tries to blur categories like "the people" versus the intellectual elite.

My resolve (stubbornness?) is all my mother's fault. From her I learned a faith that presumes grand possibilities for social change.

Acknowledgments

In order to write this book I have benefited from the assistance of many friends, colleagues, and women whom I did not know well, but were willing to share their stories with me.

To the women who took me into their confidence and told me about the violence in their lives; and to the counselors, therapists, and shelter workers who shared their insights about their work, I express my deepest gratitude.

For their helpful contributions to the dissertation version of this project, I would like to thank Larry Rasmussen, Delores Williams, and Arthur Pressley. In particular, I cannot imagine that birthing process taking place without the tremendous support and detailed feedback given to me by my advisor, Beverly Wildung Harrison.

For their help in either reading sections of the manuscript, providing me with crucial resources, or being willing dialogue partners on particular ideas, I am extremely grateful to Amy Ballin, Annamaria Basile, Elizabeth Bounds, Jan Burdewik, Terri Green, Sara Hall, Laurel Kearns, Wendy Kolmar, Beauty Maizenaise, Joan Sakalas, Nina Schwarzchild, Faye Wakeling, Pauline Wardel-Sankoh, Jimmy Watts, Robert Watts, Elisabeth Wolf, Jennifer Wriggins, Bil Wright, and Kiki Zeldes, students in the Fall 1997 Interdisciplinary Seminar in Women's Studies at Drew University.

For her very patient and efficient low-key style that was perfect for a nervous first-time author, I thank my editor, Jennifer Hammer. I thank the anonymous reader who wrote the report for NYU Press for comments that were quite helpful, as well as the copy editors who greatly improved the readability of the text.

Finally, it is impossible to describe the magnitude of appreciation I owe my life-partner Jerry G. Watts. Among others, his contributions include editing several chapters, research assistance, intellectual mentoring, functioning as a dialogue partner on so many of the issues related to race and racism that I discuss in this book, and daily encouragement. In short, I thank him for being so very "good and nice" to me as I worked on this manuscript.

Introduction

At the core of Christian tradition is a call to morally engage this world by demonstrated opposition to social injustice and human suffering. As Beverly Harrison describes, this Christian calling means confronting "as Jesus did, that which thwarts the power of human personal and communal becoming, that which denies human well-being, community, and human solidarity."[1] In response, Christian social ethicists construct contextual analysis that names the pernicious elements of society that need to be confronted and opposed.

There is no more compelling societal problem in need of redress than black women's experience of male violence. This study arises from the fact that in the United States, white supremacy, patriarchy, and intimate violence often represent simultaneous, heinous violations of the personal and communal becoming of African-American[2] women. This book takes up the task of developing useful ways to analytically deconstruct the consequences of such violations and identify methods of resisting them.

My motivation for analyzing the problem of violence against black women stems from my personal witness of both the anguish and the resilience of black women victim-survivors. The stories of women that I have encountered over the years as a college student activist and later while working as a parish pastor and campus chaplain, have repeatedly provided the impetus for my engagement of this topic. It is by personally listening to women that I have come to recognize the specific, interwoven nature of the intimate and systemic violence African-American women face.

Intimate violence represents an alarming problem in this culture. Over the last thirty years, feminist social activists and researchers have led the struggle to broaden public awareness and promote the creation of compassionate and transformative responses to violence against women. As a result, the long tradition of silence about the prevalence, societal reproduction, and consequences of violence against women is now

1

increasingly being broken by a range of sources including self-help books, mass media talk shows, and academic studies.

Unfortunately, even recent studies too often relegate black women to the margins. The specific dynamics of black women's experiences of intimate violence are frequently either given scant attention or completely blotted out by "universally" applicable assertions that are derived from white women. In particular, the characteristics of women's emotional and spiritual trauma are often assumed to be generalizable across racial boundaries. The ways that racism violates the construction of black female identity are considered irrelevant to the consequences of intimate violence. This book challenges such generalizations and assumptions by placing the personal histories and cultural conditions of black women at its center.

In method as well as content, I address the repressive impact of omissions of, and easy generalizations about, violence against black women. Methodologically, I maintain the concrete suffering of black women victim-survivors as my criterion for evaluating the moral harm generated by intimate violence. I focus specifically on the ways in which women are compelled to assume the qualities of shamefulness and invisibility, and examine how these socially induced responses further contribute to their emotional and spiritual trauma in the aftermath of male assault. Then, by unearthing the ideologies that devalue and dismiss their personhood, I reveal further dimensions of the social constructions that compound the debilitating consequences of intimate violence.

Morally interrogating the violence against African-American women helps to unravel some of the elements that keep male violence secured within the social fabric of our culture. The moral implications of the harm to women that surface in the investigation become an index for the moral assessment of this society. This task of unraveling reveals how social norms operate as moral norms instigating, sanctioning, and augmenting male violence against black women. Deprecating social ideologies about black women spawn a collection of claims that legitimate the violence. The construction and application of these violence-legitimating claims inflicts moral harm. Exposing the way this harm is inflicted involves naming the particular demeaning and repressive cultural ingredients that abet the torment of black women victim-survivors. Note that the moral harm is doubly constituted by the damage inflicted upon women as well as by the polluting effect of intimate violence on the moral health of the broader society.

Of course, many of the consequences of intimate violence that will be described are applicable to women of other racial/ethnic groups. However, in this study I deliberately avoid making assertions about the impact of violence upon all women. Perhaps most importantly, my alternating usage of the terms "women," "black women," and "African-American women" presents the reader with the opportunity to understand the experiences of black women as appropriate and significant conveyers of women's experiences. Elsewhere in feminist literature that focuses on women, a major contention about conditions that affect women is often followed by a rejoinder beginning with the phrase, "And for black women . . ." This is usually a sensitive display of inclusivity, an acknowledgment that there are peculiar racial and gender dynamics that impact black women. Yet it is also a reinforcement of "black women" as "other," as different from the category of women that has been the subject of the rest of the study. I am experimenting with the political possibilities of placing black women's experiences as center and norm for understanding the impact of violence upon women.

The method of this study relies to a large extent upon the subjugated knowledge contained in the experiences of black women victim-survivors as a source for theorizing about violence. Incorporated throughout my analysis are depictions of violation and resistance voiced by the women I have read about and interviewed. I have drawn heavily upon their insights and the strategies they have developed. The women's testimonies shape and inform my conceptualization of intimate and systemic forms of violence, and the resistance required to defy it.

Moreover, I assume that spiritual concerns are present within and amidst all the personal and political dimensions of the experience of violence. It is an axiom of my Christian theological understanding that attention to the diverse realms of human experience is required for a full and normative vision of human wholeness. This book relies upon an ethic that is mindful of the compassionate responses that Jesus offered to individuals in need, which usually combined social critique of unjust treatment, spiritual healing, and some practical form of relief from physical and emotional torment. In Christian ethics an integrated approach to the psychological, social, and spiritual realms is needed to achieve a methodology that emulates those standards of the Gospel. Accordingly, the moral investigation of violence offered here recognizes that spiritual dilemmas and resources are not only present within psychosocial ones but also further illumine them.

Although religion provides a forum for spiritual reflection and interaction, the possibilities for spiritual expression are not exhausted by formal religious practices and beliefs. Underlying my assertion of spirituality as crucial to moral theorizing is the assumption that spirituality has both a broad definition and diverse characteristics. In this study, women's varied expressions of spirituality are included whether or not they fall within the parameters of traditional Christian religion. Apart from a relationship with God, spirituality includes a yearning and longing for connection with community, a need for meaning and purpose in life, a desire for the unconditional affirmation of one's personhood, and an appreciation for the intangible mystical wonder of being that exists in nature and humanity. My framework presupposes the importance of satisfaction of such spiritual needs. Satisfaction of them is an entitlement of human personhood. That entitlement can be denied through individual actions as well as social means that constrain and deny one's spiritual vitality. I will point out some aspects of opposition to, as well as encouragement of, women's spiritual entitlement that are manifested in the intertwined consequences of intimate and societal violence against African-American women.

Unfortunately, in our culture intimate violence occurs in numerous forms. For example, in domestic situations it may occur between siblings, an elderly parent and an adult son or daughter, a mother and a toddler-age daughter, or a lesbian couple. However, my use of the term intimate violence refers to male-perpetrated rape, childhood sexual abuse, and wife/partner battering.[3] The long-term consequences of childhood sexual abuse for adult women will be the primary focus of this book, rather than the immediate consequences for the female child.

The violence is labeled "intimate" either because of the character of the relationship between the attacker and the victim, or the nature of the act. Therefore, stranger rape would still be considered intimate violence even though the assault did not take place in the context of an ongoing intimate relationship. For sexual violation of a woman's body constitutes intimate violence regardless of whether the assault occurs within a chosen relationship of intimacy or not. But the nonsexual physical assault of a woman by a male stranger would not be considered intimate violence under my definition.

Having made clear that intimate and societal violence are understood to operate in collusion, it is also my assumption that male violence is directly spawned by a wide web of societal violence. Evidence of societal violence is continuously present in the destructive gender and race cultural cues that permeate women's experience of male violence. The term societal violence is used to capture the brutality of the systemic evils of white supremacy and patriarchy. Together they function to devalue the human worth and dignity of African-American women. White supremacy is the form of racism most commonly found actively at work in the history and culture of the United States. White supremacy includes the institutionalized dominant political, cultural, and economic power of white people, as also their disproportionate access to status through the cultural privileging of whiteness. White supremacy incorporates the notion that anyone deemed to be white, usually a person of European descent, has worth and value which is inherently superior to that of people in the society who are not considered to be white.

Patriarchy is a systematic devaluation of the worth and value of women. Patriarchy involves the political process of constructing gender supremacy from biological difference. Ideologically the transformation of male to man, and female to woman, occurs in such a way that man is prioritized while woman is rendered different (synonymous with unequal), less than, or other. Patriarchy is not primary or causal in the development of other forms of human oppression. Moreover, it not an overarching framework that adequately encompasses other forms of oppression such as class or race.[4] Women experience patriarchy vastly differently depending upon their race, class, and other social markers of identity that are different from, and interact with, their gender identity.

When referring to women who have experienced intimate violence, I have chosen to use the term "victim-survivor." I do so to rhetorically remind us of the dual status of women who have been both victimized by violent assault and have survived it. Black women are sometimes denied an opportunity to have their victimization recognized. The strength of their coping and survival abilities is commonly emphasized at the expense of an appreciation of their injury and anguish. Multiple aspects of both victimization and survival are represented in women's experiences of, and reactions to, male violence.

When examining the interpersonal dynamics of intimate violence this study concentrates on violence perpetrated by black males against black women. This book attends to some of the individualized and sociopolitical dynamics generated for women by the experience of black male assault. Issues such as whether the dynamics are similar, identical, or very different from the consequences of assault by white males are outside its purview. However, Euro-American men are of course fundamentally complicit in the structural violence of racism and sexism, which will be at issue throughout this book.

Though I focus mainly on race and gender exploitation, these categories are by no means adequate or primary for describing the range of societal problems that black women confront. For instance, economic subjugation and homophobic violence are also intrastructured hegemonic realities in the lives of African-American women. While I refer to these issues throughout the book, less attention is given to their systemic attributes and impact on women. I have simply chosen to concentrate on the relationship between intimate violence and racial and gender subjugation, and found sufficient challenge in this topic for one study.

In addition, I cannot emphasize too strongly my conviction that each woman's response to the combined impact of societal and intimate violence in her life will always be unique. I have no desire to depict a singular or "representative" black woman's experience of violence. Instead, I hope to contribute some insights into the confluent layers of meaning that may be present in a black woman's experience of male violence. In opposition to any narrow, formulaic definition, I hope to demonstrate the richly varied, complexly textured reality of violence and resistance.

I conducted interviews with victim-survivors of male violence and with practitioners who work in a therapeutic role with them. Some of my interviews are presented as qualitative case studies on violence in black women's lives. All the participants were randomly selected through informal contacts. My role during the interviews was to ask a few specific questions to help trigger the women's stories and opinions. I expressed empathy and understanding, particularly when women described incidents of violence, but primarily listened to them and refrained from entering into a dialogue. I edited the interviews so that the collection of stories presented to the reader would reflect a wide range of perspectives and experiences.

My use of both empirical and theoretical source material reflects my conviction that the "truth" of social reality can best be approached from personal reflections by individuals as well as insights from systemic social analysis. A black woman victim-survivor's narrative description of an incident of violence offers a partial glimpse of the elements of violation that ensconce her. A psychologically centered theory offers another partial glimpse of the dynamics relevant to the woman's experience of intimate violence. A feminist social scientist theorizing about the sociopoliti-

cal sanctions for violence against women that stem from patriarchal ideologies will interpret still another aspect of that same scenario of male violence. The "truth" can best be understood by gleaning insights from a
combination of these standpoints. And even then it is only possible to
achieve a fragmentary appreciation of the damage to women and the
breadth of their resistance.

The sequence of the study unfolds by first offering excerpts of testimonies about violence in the lives of African-American women from the
past and present. Selected narratives of women's stories that originate in
the time of slavery document the ongoing historical legacy of male violence against black women in the United States. In chapter 2 of this first
section, the stories of the women I interviewed also give voice to the nature and persistence of the pattern of violence in our time.[5]

In the next section of the book, chapter 3 integrates pastoral psychology and psychology literature with women's depictions of their experiences. It describes the anguish of male violence from the perspective of
the women. The chapter details how some of the common negating and
shaming community responses to intimate violence contribute to their
trauma.

The third section expands the investigation of the role of society in reproducing the violence and anguish women endure. Beginning with
some background information on the recent development of theoretical
material about violence against women, chapter 4 probes a range of theories about violence in our society, including nonfeminist, feminist, and
womanist approaches. These theories are discussed and compared in
order to ferret out an understanding of the social mechanisms that insti-
gate and sanction violence against black women. In chapter 5 I identify
some of the specific destructive ideological constructions about
women—like labeling them as liars and inherently unreliable—that contribute to the social reproduction of violence. The chapter also examines
the concrete ways that these devaluing and discounting cultural messages
are manifested in community agencies women turn to for help.

The final section explores concepts and strategies for resisting the violence. Chapter 6 begins this constructive work with a discussion about
how resistance should be defined. I address the question of how to describe the parameters and content of resistance in a manner that directly
responds to the multiple manifestations of violence against women that
have been described in the preceding sections of the book. I urge us to
cultivate the ability to recognize women's acts of resistance and then give

illustrative examples showing how anger, spirituality, support groups, and other resources are utilized by women victim-survivors. Lastly, chapter 7 considers the necessary features of an ethic of communal resistance that can fuel an ongoing social movement. The chapter describes the countercultural commitment that this ethic requires, and enumerates an array of concrete practices. I particularly stress the role that local churches can play in monitoring resources for victim-survivors and initiating violence-resistance customs.

This book has been written because of the women who struggle daily for their very lives against the multipronged societal and intimate assaults perpetrated against them. Hopefully, the revelations of this book about the nature and impact of that violence will offer support and solidarity in their resistance struggles.

PART I

Listening to Women's Stories

1

Testimony from
Nonfiction Literature

When Aisha reflected on her experience of being raped by an acquaintance as a teenager, she explained: "So, I just kept silent until I couldn't anymore, and that was like twenty something years later."[1] Her statement attests to the wounding impact of intimate violence against African-American women that exacts their silence, but ultimately evokes defiance of that silencing as well. One might easily respond with skepticism at the very idea that silence is exacted from black women. How can silence be imposed on women typically considered "big-mouthed" and aggressive? Yet for black women victim-survivors there are, in fact, multiple ways:

1/not heard. It can happen to the women in the midst of an everyday conversation. As they try to express their anguish and construct their resistance to the effects of violence, a loud, shrill cultural echo bounces back in their faces. It supplies dismissive, quick labels and familiar stereotypes that warn about "how black women do provoke you." This echo can be heard in the "jokes" or accusations by family members and friends, or may simply be present in their attitudes. It can drown out the women, making their replies to the violence inaudible.

2/not listened to. As they continue the process of finding a way to interpret their experiences of male violence, women are often encircled by hostile messages about themselves from some very authoritative sources. Persistently closing in on them are a host of public images regularly invoked by politicians and members of the news media that identify black women, especially poor black women, with distorted character traits and immorality. These sources seem to pay attention to what black women actually say and do. They quote, interview, photograph, or depict black women through "authoritative" studies. But if a woman's articulations about herself differ from those images of black womanhood, her version may be voided out, proven wrong by all that public "evidence." These public representations of her moral inadequacy give the impression that she has been seen and heard, thereby denying the credibility of her claims about her unjust treatment, and ignoring her interpretation of her experience.

3/not permitted to speak out. The rules of the abuser, the court, the church, and the racist patriarchal culture can forbid a woman to interrupt their established order by naming the torment she has endured. The punishment for disobedience of those rules can be so terrifying or shaming that she dares not violate them.

4/censored to the point of losing one's sense of self. Sometimes a woman cannot speak her truth about the violence because she cannot find her own way. She is overwhelmed by the varying and specific definitions of appropriate behavior that are given to her. Some are inflicted upon her through the psychological torture of her abuser, while others are demanded of her by her church and black community. Still other definitions, based on supposed knowledge of "the black woman's role in the black family," are projected onto her by the social worker or some other professional she seeks out for help. Any clear distinction between these external formulations and her own self-perceptions can become blurry and lost.

When women do defy such forms of tyranny, it is a noisy silence that is broken. Their defiance provides critical public witness to African-American women's self-expression and liberation. Moreover, such acts enrich the distinctive history of black women in this country.

Ever since the agonizing journey by their African foremothers to the Americas as cargo on slave ships, male physical and sexual violence has consistently been a reality in the lives of black women. The moral consequences of this intimate violence include psychosocial as well as spiritual wounds and obstacles to the wholeness and well-being of black women. Through women's stories, we can discover some of the buried truths about the harm caused by the violence and the strategies women utilize to resist it.

The Art of Learning from Women's Stories

While the analysis in this study focuses on the experiences of contemporary women, the stories from the past are lifted up in the following collage of voices. They document the ongoing historical legacy of intimate violence against African-American women. The voices from the past are needed to accompany contemporary women on their journey of recovery. The historical legacy sets the context for discussion of the experiences of contemporary women. It reminds those of us who attempt to initiate the comprehensive social change necessary to create a future with fewer victims of intimate violence, of the entrenched, structural nature of this problem.

These testimonies contribute particular perspectives for the analysis of issues of power and violence that are the wider subject of this book, helping us to recognize that these issues occur within women's lives. These voices also remind us of the diverse spectrum of perspectives on the impact of intimate violence against African-American women. In a few instances I have included secondary accounts to present women's experiences of intimate violence. Although such accounts portray the emotional and/or religious response of a witness to the violence rather than the reactions of the victim herself, they are nevertheless revealing about the impact of the abuse. Furthermore, the act of testifying on behalf of one's mother or aunt concerning the assault and disclosing its attendant suffering and/or women's feats of rebellion against it deserves appreciation. This act remains a crucial means of challenging the shame and secrecy that surrounds this subject.

The glimpses of women's experiences provided here cross historical time periods to bridge rural and urban settings, and northern and southern boundaries of the country, and highlight varied forms of intimate violence. These narratives illustrate some of the ways that male dominance and white supremacy, whether institutionalized through eighteenth-century chattel slavery or the twentieth-century justice system, compound the impact of intimate violence. Concrete insights emerge from these accounts, showing how the emotional and spiritual consequences of intimate and systemic violence fuse and collide with a woman's self-perceptions about being a woman, being black, and being a black woman.

The Peculiarities of Listening to Slave Women's Stories

The anomalous conditions of slavery that surround the earliest accounts of intimate violence against black women in the United States deserve particular attention. Slavery illustrates a unique experience of overlapping societal and individualized brutality for African-American women. As a result of being defined as property, the enslaved person suffers a kind of social death.[2] The damage to the individual's psyche and soul caused by this continuous state of social annihilation can only be approximated by those who try to understand the experience. Frequent and arbitrary physical beatings were common for many slaves. The specific focus of the slave testimonies gathered here, however, is the sexual exploitation that women experienced.

Our access to the voices and suffering of slave women is limited by the fact that few of them lived to see freedom, and of the few who did survive slavery fewer still had the opportunity to record their ideas and life histories. Later discussion in this study will offer details of the tremendous shame for women associated with sexual violation in particular. Because it was inevitable that that shame would be intensified for former slaves who disclosed information about their sexual assault(s) under slavery, there are very few first-hand accounts. Former slaves already occupied an extremely vulnerable position in their society.

Other factors also limit our access to women's own statements of their emotional and spiritual responses to the assaults. During the nineteenth and early twentieth centuries public discourse on matters related to sexuality was circumscribed by social taboos and notions of propriety and modesty for all women. Black women's willingness to discuss their sexual exploitation by white men was most likely further inhibited by common perceptions classifying those violations as odious sexual relations. The existing social and legal sanctions against miscegenation tangibly demonstrated this community sentiment.

Slave women lived with the threat of sexual violence whether they worked in the master's house or in the fields. Slave women were raped by white masters, white overseers, and black drivers. They also faced forms of sexual violence that were the peculiar inventions of the slave system. For example, as forced breeders they were made to submit to sexual relations with black slave men who were chosen by the master for breeding purposes. Another particular form of sexualized torture for slaves was the practice of whipping pregnant women and beating nursing mothers so severely that blood and milk flowed simultaneously from their breasts. Jacqueline Jones argues that part of the motivation for this type of sadistic violence by white masters stemmed from the reality that a pregnant woman signaled sexuality between husband and wife in the slave community and "symbolized a life in the quarters carried on apart from white interference."[3]

Intimate violence perpetrated by slave masters and by fellow slaves was not morally synonymous because of the obvious difference in power represented by the men involved. When slave men participated in forced breeding they were being used as instruments of violence at the behest of the slave masters. A male slave faced the brutal or even lethal wrath of the owner if he disobeyed the latter's orders. Apart from the sexual assault mandated by the slave masters, slave women's vulnerability to random acts of rape by other slaves was increased by the dearth of legal sanctions against it. Historian Deborah White does cite fragmentary court and legislative records which indicate there may have been some sanctions against the rape of girls under twelve by other slaves.[4] One can only speculate about whether there were differences in the sense of betrayal, anger, or powerlessness experienced by women when assaulted by either slave masters or other slaves.

To some degree autobiographical and biographical accounts of experience are always filtered through the lens of the anticipated audience the subject is addressing. Endemic to racial minority status in the United States must be the assumption of a white audience whenever one offers a public voice. The extent to which the need for approval or respect from whites pervades the voice of any black author cannot be evaluated with precision or certainty. Yet it is crucial to acknowledge the fact that some of the black women's accounts of violence included here, specifically some of the narratives by former slaves, were dictated to white interviewers.[5] For slaves, all whites represented an ominous, supremely controlling presence. Displeasing whites could lead to the arbitrary loss of one's children or home, to bodily brutality, even to loss of one's life, with few if any consequences for the white person. To survive, a slave woman needed the ability to anticipate the white person's response before expressing herself to the person. Moreover, most of the social, political, and economic forms of white domination that existed during slavery remained in place at the times and places where interviews were conducted with former slaves.

Thus, for some of the former slaves whose accounts are included below, we must assume that to varying degrees their presentation of self echoes off the white interviewer.[6] We can expect that the race and gender of the interviewer had an impact on what was said and heard in the shaping of the narrative accounts by former slave women. It is difficult to determine what was deleted, minimized, or overstated in women's descriptions of either the slave master's brutality or that of their male slave counterpart. However, these problems must not deter us from listening to these testimonies to the intimate and social violence that African-American women have endured through centuries of life in this country.

Legacy from the Past

"Violent degradations"

In his autobiography, former slave Olaudah Equiano (aka Gustavus Vassa) witnessed the sexual exploitation of black women aboard slave ships during the voyages from Africa.

> While I was thus employed by my master, I was often witness to cruelties of every kind which were exercised on my unhappy fellow slaves. I used frequently to have different cargoes of new Negroes in my care for sale; and it was almost a constant practice with our clerks and other whites to commit violent degradations on the chastity of the female slaves; and these I was, though with reluctance, obliged to submit to all the time, being unable to stop them.
>
> When we have had some of these slaves on board my master's vessels, to carry them to other islands or to America, I have known the mates to commit these acts most shamefully, to the disgrace not only of Christians, but of men. I have even known them to gratify their brutal passion with females not even ten years old.[7]

Ila B. Prine offered her recollection of an aunt who was beaten by a black overseer while pregnant. She voiced her feelings of rage toward this man who had abused her aunt.

> After de massa was kilt, old Miss had a nigger oberseer an' dat was de meanest debil dat eber libbed on de Lawd's green yearth. I promise myself when I growed up dat I was agoin' to kill dat nigger iffen it was de las' thing I eber done. Lots of times I'se seen him beat my mammy, an' one day I seen

him beat my Auntie who was big wid chile, an' dat man dug a roun' hole in de groun' an' put er stummick in it, an beat her for half hour straight till de baby come out raught dere in de hole.[8]

Clara C. Young spoke out about how the violence against her pregnant cousin was suppressed. From the tone of her statement describing this inhumane behavior, it seems the collaboration of a black man in this incident particularly angered Clara.

> I heerd tell one time, tho', of de hired man (he was a nigger) an' de oberseer whuppin' one of my cousins 'til she bled; she was jes' sebenteen years old an' was in de fambly way fer de fust time, an' couldn' work as hard as de rest. Nex' mawnin' afte' dat she died. De hired man tol' de rest if dey said anything 'bout it to de marster, he'd beat dem to death, too, so ever'-body kep' quiet an' de marster neber knowed.[9]

"I didn't want him, but I couldn't do nothin'"

Women who worked in the owner's house were subject to sexual exploitation by the master as well as his male children. Mary Peters, a former slave, provided an account of the gang rape of her mother which resulted in her own conception. For her part, her mother demonstrated a form of resistance just by telling others about her assault, and thereby made it possible for the crime to be known and remembered. Mary's mother also sought help by reporting the incident to the slave mistress.

> My mother's mistress had three boys—one twenty-one, one nineteen, and one seventeen. One day, Old Mistress had gone away to spend the day. Mother always worked in the house; she didn't work on the farm, in Missouri. While she was alone, the boys came and threw her down on the floor and tied her down so she couldn't struggle, and one after the other used her as long as they wanted, for the whole afternoon. Mother was sick when mistress came home. When Old Mistress wanted to know what was the matter with her, she told her what the boys had done. She whipped them, and that's the way I came to be here.[10]

Annie Young, a former slave, recalled the particularly horrific rape of her aunt by the slave master. Her aunt resisted by running away from him and by informing the slave mistress.

> I can remember once my auntie's old master tried to have her and she run off out in de woods and when he put those blood hounds or snigger hounds on her trail he catched her and hit her in de head wid something

like de stick de police carry, and he knocked a hole in her head and she bled like a hog, and he made her have him. She told her mistress, and mistress told her to go ahead and be wid him 'cause he's gonna kill you.[11]

A former slave identified merely as "Granny" by her interviewer spoke about her terror and defenselessness as a result of the physical and sexual abuse that she endured from her former owners. She referred to "Master Jesus" as a spiritual resource that helped her to endure the brutality.

"What did I do? I spun an' cooked, an waited, an' plowed; dere weren't nothin' I didn't do. An I'd be so hungry, so hungry, an I'd know dere wouldn't be nothin' for me to eat. I'd be so hungry I'd jes cry. Den dey'd whip me, oh lan's, how dey'd whip me. . . .

"Look here, ma'am," she answered, "when you see a snake in de grass, goin' along, he ain't doin' nothing, but you kill him. It was de same as dat wid me. . . . Dey could allus find sometin' dat was wrong. I useder stan' at table an' pass things, an' misses, she'd see somethin' she didn't like an' she'd nod her head. I know'd what dat would mean—one hunnerd lashes. I was scared all de time, all de time. . . .

"Granny," I said, "did your master harm you in another way?" She did not understand at once, then as she gained my meaning, she leaned over and answered, "Did you see dat girl in de house below here? Dat's my chile by him. I had five, but dat de only one livin now. I didn't want him, but I couldn't do nothin'. I uster say 'what do yer want of a woman all cut ter pieces like I is?' But 'twant no use."

. . . "Granny" I said, "how did you bear it all, how did you live?"

"I couldn't 'er done it, dear widout Master Jesus. He's held me up. I'd 'er died long ago widout him."[12]

Rose Williams, a former slave, expressed her profound bitterness about being sexually exploited through the practice of forced breeding and recounted her repeated attempts to stave off this form of violation.

Dere am one thing Massa Hawkins does to me what I can't shunt from my mind. I knows he don't do it for meanness, but I allus holds it 'gainst him. What he done am force me to live with dat nigger, Rufus, 'gainst my wants.

After I been at he place 'bout a year, de massa come to me and say, "You gwine live wit Rufus in dat cabin over yonder. Go fix it for livin'." I's 'bout sixteen year old and has no larnin', and I's just igno'mus chile. I's thought dat him mean for me to tend de cabin for Rufus and some other niggers. Well, dat am start de pestigation for me.

I's took charge of de cabin after work am done and fixes supper. Now, I don't like dat Rufus, 'cause he a bully. He am big and 'cause he so, he think everybody do what him say. We'uns has supper, den I goes here and dere talkin', till I's ready for sleep and den I gits in de bunk. After I's in, dat nigger come and crawl in de bunk with me 'fore I knows it. I says, "What you means, you fool nigger?" He say for me to hush de mouth. "Dis my bunk, too," he say.

"You's teched in de head. Git out," I's told him, and I puts de feet 'gainst him and give him a shove and out he go on de floor 'fore he knew what I's doin'. Dat nigger jump up and he mad. He look like de wild bear. He starts for de bunk and I jumps quick for de poker. It am 'bout three feet long and when he comes at me I lets him have it over de head. Did dat nigger stop in he tracks? I's say he did. He looks at me steady for a minute and you's could tell he thinkin' hard. Den he go and set on de bench and say, "Jus' wait. You thinks it am smart, but you's am foolish in de head. Dey's gwine larn you somethin'."

"Hush you big mouth and stay 'way from dis nigger, dat all I wants," I say, and jus' sets and hold dat poker in de hand. He jus' sets, lookin' like de bull. Dere we'uns sets and sets for 'bout an hour and den he go out and I bars de door.

De nex' day I goes to de missy and tells her what Rufus wants and missy say dat am de massa's wishes. She say, "Yous am portly gal and Rufus am de portly man. De massa wants yu-uns fer to bring forth portly chillen."

I's thinkin' 'bout what de missy say, but say to myse'f, "I's not gwine live with dat Rufus." Dat night when he come in de cabin, I grabs de poker and sits on de bench and says, "git 'way from me, nigger, 'fore I busts you brains out and stomp on dem." He say nothin' and git out.

De nex' day de massa call me and tell me, "Woman, I's pay big money for you and I's done dat for de cause I wants yous to raise me chillens. I's put yous to live with Rufus for dat purpose. Now, if you doesn't want whippin' at de stake, yous do what I wants."

I thinks 'bout massa buyin' me offen de block and savin' me from bein' sep'rated from my folks and 'bout bein' whipped at de stake. Dere it am. What am I's to do? So I 'cides to do as de massa wish and so I yields.[13]

Former slave Henrietta Evelina Smith told about how her great-grandmother endeavored to heal herself after she was freed. She was responding to the repeated sexual attacks inflicted on her during her enslavement.

My great-grandmother was considered pretty when she was young. She had glossy black hair and was a little short. She was brown skin and had big legs. Her master would take her out behind the field and do what he wanted. When she got free, she gave both of her children away. She had two children by him—a boy named Eli and a girl named Anna. She didn't want them 'round her because they reminded her of him.[14]

"Blame the edicts of that society"

In her autobiography, former slave Elizabeth Keckley wrote about the emotional pain which resulted from the sexual exploitation she was subjected to while she was a slave. Keckley also commented on the issue of shame and the immoral practice of raping slave girls.

I was regarded as fair-looking for one of my race, and for four years a white man—I spare the world his name—had base designs upon me. I do not care to dwell upon this subject for it is one that is fraught with pain. Suffice it to say, that he persecuted me for four years, and I—I—became a mother. The child of which he was the father was the only child that I ever brought into the world. If my poor boy ever suffered any humiliating pangs on account of birth, he could not blame his mother, for God knows that she did not wish to give him life; he must blame the edicts of that society which deemed it no crime to undermine the virtue of girls in my then position.[15]

One former slave woman explained how she fought off a white boy who tried to rape her. She was defiant about her penalty. Her account calls attention to the practice of public whippings as an aspect of the intimate violence that black women faced during slavery.

My young marster tried to go with me, and 'cause I wouldn't go with him he pretended I had done somethin' and beat me. I fought him back because he had no right to beat me for not goin' with him. His mother got mad with me for fightin' him back and I told her why he had beat me. Well then she sent me to the courthouse to be whipped for fightin' him. They had stocks there where most people would send their slaves to be whipped. These stocks was in the shape of a cross, and they would strap your clothes up around your waist and have nothin' but your naked part out to whip. They didn't care about who saw your nakedness. Anyway, they beat me that day until I couldn't sit down. When I went to bed I had to lie on my stomach to sleep. After they finished whippin' me, I told them they needn't think they had done somethin' by strippin' me in front of all them folk 'cause they had also stripped their mamas and sisters. God had made us all, and he made us just alike.[16]

One of the most detailed extant accounts of the emotional and spiritual consequences of slave sexual exploitation is found in the autobiography of Linda Brent (1818–96). Her name was actually Harriet Brent Jacobs, but she wanted her autobiography published under the pseudonym Linda Brent. Brent gave her readers a vivid account of the emotional torment she suffered as a result of being sexually harassed by her master, Dr. Flint. She made repeated and blunt appeals to her white audience and implored them to understand the unrelenting, torturous dynamics of sexual abuse for slave women. When she recounted her "shameful" sexual liaison with a white man who was not her master, Brent revealed the intention behind her actions. She was trying to maintain a measure of control over her sexuality. She also mentioned her sense of God's absence in the midst of the conditions she faced.

The narrative itself is an inspiring act of resistance both in substance and form. Brent offered a bold critique of slavery, specifically of the way it sanctioned the sexual exploitation of slave girls. With remarkable precision, she provided a detailed chronicle of her master's treachery toward her.

> He [Dr. Flint] told me I was his property; that I must be subject to his will in all things. My soul revolted against the mean tyranny. But where could I turn for protection? No matter whether the slave girl be as black as ebony or as fair as her mistress. In either case, there is no shadow of law to protect her from insult, from violence, or even from death; all these are inflicted by fiends who bear the shape of men.

Brent explained that from the age of twelve, life for the slave girl usually included sexual abuse.

> Soon she will learn to tremble when she hears her master's footfall. She will be compelled to realize that she is no longer a child. If God has bestowed beauty upon her, it will prove her greatest curse. That which commands admiration in the white woman only hastens the degradation of the female slave. . . . My master met me at every turn, reminding me that I belonged to him, and swearing by heaven and earth that he would compel me to submit to him. If I went out for a breath of air, after a day of unwearied toil, his footsteps dogged me.
>
> O, what days and nights of fear and sorrow that man caused me! Reader it is not to awaken sympathy for myself that I am telling you truthfully what I suffered in slavery. I do it to kindle a flame of compassion in your hearts for my sisters who are still in bondage, suffering as I once suffered.
> . . . By managing to keep within sight of people, as much as possible,

during the day time, I had hitherto succeeded in eluding my master, though a razor was often held to my throat to force me to change this line of policy. At night I slept by the side of my great aunt, where I felt safe.

And now, reader, I come to a period in my unhappy life, which I would gladly forget if I could. The remembrance fills me with sorrow and shame. . . . If slavery had been abolished, I, also could have married the man of my choice; I could have had a home shielded by the laws; and I should have been spared the painful task of confessing what I am now about to relate; but all my prospects had been blighted by slavery. I wanted to keep myself pure; and, under the most adverse circumstances, I tried hard to preserve my self-respect; but I was struggling alone in the powerful grasp of the demon slavery; and the monster proved too strong for me. I felt as if I was forsaken by God and man; as if all my efforts must be frustrated; and I became reckless in my despair. . . . It seems less degrading to submit to compulsion. There is something akin to freedom in having a lover who has no control over you, except that which he gains by kindness and attachment.[17]

"Everybody was afraid of him; it was like who's afraid of the big, bad wolf. Well, I wasn't."

Sara Rice knew even at the age of ten that a girl needed to know how to take care of herself in the face of sexual and physical abuse. Sara was born in 1909 and grew up in Alabama. Her autobiography includes her early life in Alabama (approximately 1919 to 1930). It discloses details about her sexual harassment as a young person by an older adult male in the church, as well as battering incidents at the hands of her first husband. Sara championed self-reliance as a primary resistance strategy. Her Christian faith also seems to have been a sustaining ingredient in her life.

So I learned not to tell things that old people did, even one time with one of Papa's friends. One of his minister friends reached out at me. I went with Papa to a meeting to represent my pastor; he was pastor of some other churches. I was filling out a little bit as a girl, and the minister of our church of Mount Zion reached at me and I hollered. I said, "you better not touch me, or I'll tell Mama." He said "I was just playing. Please don't tell your Mama." I wasn't going to tell, because I knew Mama wasn't going to let me go anywhere with him. I felt I could protect myself. I could sense things, and I figured that if he had put his hands on me like I figured he was going to do, I would have hit him just as hard as I could. That was one thing that Mama taught us. . . .

Our Sunday School teacher was a handsome young man. He grabbed me one day and kissed me, and I felt funny. I knew that wasn't right; it wasn't the way you'd kiss a child. I was thirteen or fourteen then. Finally he proposed that I go with him. He had a wife too, and I knew that was wrong. I said, "Mr. Brown, that's wrong." But he told me he loved me and was going to give me some money. . . . [After Sara successfully avoided meeting him, she said:] "Mr. Brown, if you don't leave me alone, I'm going to tell Mama. You are a man, and I am a girl, and you have a wife too. Don't ever say anything like that to me, please sir." He didn't. . . .

Jim [Sara Rice's first husband] was running around with women, throwing the money away, and jumping on me too, beating me up because I complained about his staying out all night over the weekends. . . . [After enduring a period of time that included beatings by her husband Sara describes the following incident as a climax in the relationship.] Then he jumped on me for nothing. We had some wood behind the stove for cooking. It was heavy and seasoned. He struck me. I reached over there and got a piece of that wood and hit him, with all the might and main I could give him. He fell, and it frightened me, because I thought I had killed him. But I grabbed up another piece and stood over him, just in case, I said, "you hit me again, and I'll kill you. Hitting me for nothing, and you out running around all night long." That stopped the hitting, but after that I just started turning from him. [Some time elapsed after this incident, and Sara announced to her husband that the marriage was over.] . . . I told him that was it. He said he was going to take my life. I said, "If that's God's will, let it be done." And I left. . . . Everybody was afraid of him; it was like who's afraid of the big bad wolf. Well, I wasn't. I didn't mind if he had taken my life. I didn't feel like he was going to take it. . . . It was like the hymnist: "Through many dangers, toils and snares I have already come; T'was Grace that brought me safe thus far, and Grace will lead me home." I've been through a lot of things, and nobody knew about it but the inside of the family.

A few years later, after a move to Jacksonville, Florida, Sara Rice commented on a dispute with a white woman employer in whose home she worked as a domestic worker. Sara resigned after her white employer refused to curtail disrespectful behavior toward Sara by her daughter. Sara's strategy for maintaining her self-respect in the face of racist obstacles was as follows:

With all the badness that was going on between blacks and whites my family always came out with respect, because we didn't beg people. . . . Then, if we did the best we could and we couldn't please, we womenfolks would just say, "Well, the Lord take it. If I can't please you, get somebody else."[18]

"But she was afraid even to talk with her children when he was around"

In Tennessee, during the early years of this century, (approximately 1910–20), Maggie Comer reported how her mother was terrorized by a physically violent husband (Maggie's stepfather). According to Maggie, her mother responded to the abuse with a sense of helplessness:

> [My mother] was a poor young widow with a lot of children and didn't know what to do. My stepfather was the first thing that she met, and that's the way she felt life was and had to be. And she went on with it. Whatever he did and whatever he said, she accepted. It got so he'd say "Hon, so and so." Now he had just knocked her out, but she'd say, "Whatever you say, Hon." She'd be so scared she'd say something that he didn't like or it didn't work out, and she'd get another beating. She might as well of said what she wanted to say. She was going to get the beating anyway. . . .
>
> He never played with us. He didn't even allow my mother to take up any time with us. My mother, being an orphan herself, felt the need of being with us, But she was afraid even to talk with her children when he was around.
>
> . . . He was just a mean, violent man. He didn't drink and he didn't smoke. But he was one mean man. . . . He said terrible things, terrible. "There wasn't nothing to religion! There was no God." He hated preachers. He couldn't stand the minister to come around. One minister came to the house to tell him about coming to church. He told the minister there was no such thing as God.
>
> Oh, he was the devil himself.[19]

"Now why would my husband wanna be knockin on me? I never did anything"

Living in the 1930s south, Sara Brooks expressed bewilderment about her husband's senseless brutality toward her. Sara also alluded to her dependence on prayer to help her escape from the violence.

> So when I was with my husband he didn't look after nothin and he'd fuss and quarrel all the time and you couldn't talk to him cause he'd cuss nearly every word any body said. If I tried to talk to him he'd hit me so hard with

his hands till I'd see stars. Slap me, and what he'd slap me for, I don't know. He never did accuse me of no men because I didn't have no men all the while I was married to him. . . .

Then one time he threw me out the window. Yes, he did! . . . I told him, "You should take the shoes back to the store where you got em and get a larger pair," because a growin kid don't need no shoes huggin their feet. And he said "Oh you shut up your mouth and leave it alone." . . . So he wouldn't do it and because I was askin about it, he picked me up and dropped me out the window. It was in the wintertime and the fire was in the fireplace, and as I went to reach up to get back in the house, he picked up a burning stick and burnt me under my arm. He was very cruel to me, very cruel.

. . . He was the type that liked to fight, and I didn't like to fight myself because we wasn't raised that way. I never seen my father fight my mother—I never seen him hit her in my life. Now, why would my husband wanna be knockin on me? I never did anything. If I had done somethin, it'd be different, so I don't know. But he always was mean and always fought me, and I just begin to go prayin to God—I would pray every day, "Let me get away." I wanted to get away somehow because I was gettin tired.[20]

"My God, it's terrible what something like this does to you"

In her autobiography, jazz and blues artist Billie Holiday narrated an incident of sexual assault that occurred when she was ten years old (in 1925), in Baltimore, Maryland. Holiday explained how she was humiliated by the police and punished by the courts for being a victim of rape. She was sentenced to a "Catholic institution." She remembered being cruelly punished for rule infractions while there, that were carried out in the name of God's will.[21] Later in the autobiography when she reflected on these experiences, they converged in Holiday's consciousness to form a haunting memory laced with feelings of shame and anger.

[She was lured away from home after school and sexually assaulted by the forty-year-old Mr. Dick. She kicked and scratched and screamed to fight him off.]

The next thing I knew, my mother and a policeman broke the door down. I'll never forget that night. Even if you're a whore, you don't want to be raped. A bitch can turn twenty-five hundred tricks a day and she still don't want nobody to rape her. It's the worst thing that can happen to a woman. And it was happening to me when I was ten.

. . . But that wasn't the worst of it. The cops dragged Dick off to the police precinct. I was crying and bleeding in her arms, but they made us come
along too.

When we got there instead of treating me and Mom like somebody who
called the cops for help, they treated me like I'd killed somebody. They
wouldn't let my mother take me home. Mr. Dick was in his forties, and I
was only ten. Maybe the police sergeant took one look at my breasts and
limbs and figured my age from that. I don't know. Anyway, I guess they had
me figured for having enticed this old goat into the whorehouse or something. All I know is they threw me into a cell. My mother cried and
screamed and pleaded, but they just put her out of the jail house and
turned me over to a fat white matron. When she saw I was still bleeding,
she felt sorry for me and gave me a couple of glasses of milk. But nobody
else did anything for me except give me filthy looks and snicker to themselves.

After a couple of days in a cell they dragged me into court. Mr. Dick got
sentenced to five years. They sentenced me to a Catholic institution.

. . . Things had happened to me that no amount of time could change or
heal. I had gone to jail when I was ten because a forty-year-old man had
tried to rape me. Sure they had no more business putting me in that
Catholic institution than if I'd been hit by a damn truck. But they did.
Sure, they had no business punishing me, but they had. For years I used to
dream about it and wake up hollering and screaming. My God, it's terrible
what something like this does to you. It takes years and years to get over it;
it haunts you and haunts you.

Getting booked and busted again didn't help, either. I might explain the
first rap was a freak accident. But the second was tougher. For years it made
me feel like a damn cripple. It changed the way I looked at everything and
everybody. There was one chance I couldn't take. I couldn't stand any man
who didn't know about the things that had happened to me when I was a
kid. And I was leery of any man who could throw those things back at me
in a quarrel. I could take almost anything, but my God, not that. I didn't
want anyone around who might ever hold this over me or even hint that on
account of it he was a cut above me.[22]

*"When somebody's picking at your soul with his voice, you
just naturally cover it up and try to keep it whole"*

Ossie Guffy was born in 1931 in a suburb of Cincinnati, Ohio, where
she remains. She dictated her autobiography to a white woman social
worker during the late 1960s. Her biography contains detailed accounts
of her relationships with men, including a boyfriend who physically

abused her. Because she was poor and marginally employed throughout her life, Guffy had to rely upon public assistance to provide for some of her financial and health needs. She offered a vivid account of the powerlessness that sometimes overwhelmed her in the midst of crisis.

> I guess when these social workers got trained they must have been told to always end up with "is that clear?" Maybe they didn't mean anything by it, but it sure made you feel like a dope, like you were too stupid to understand English. I just nodded again. I've heard tell that a lot of whites say blacks are sullen, but I wonder if those whites ever listen to themselves and hear how they sound. When somebody's picking at your soul with his voice you just naturally cover it up and try to keep it whole.

Ossie was in the hospital having just given birth to a new baby. She found out that one of her other children, Kim, who was being cared for by a friend, suddenly became critically ill and was downstairs in the pediatric floor of the same hospital. She argued with the hospital staff about being able to see her baby.

> I was feeling pretty weak and too tired to fight, and the tears started to roll down my cheeks. All at once a feeling that I never remembered having before rolled over me in great big waves, and that feeling was hopelessness. I could fight not having enough money, and I could fight the county wanting to break me away from my kids, and I could fight being black and letting the white folks try to make me think black, but I couldn't fight all that and fight the Lord, too. . . . I guess maybe when you're tired out and you're weak, you think things you wouldn't if you didn't feel so poorly, and maybe that's why, even while I was praying that Kim would be alright, I was sure she'd die and it would be all my fault. The county was right; I wasn't no fit mama to my kids, and now the Lord was going to make me see it, if the county couldn't. It was pride that made me think I could work and take care of the kids proper. . . . The Lord didn't hold much with pride, at least pride that ain't got no reason to be there, and like it said in the Bible, pride goeth before a fall, and I was falling.

Nero, her abusive boyfriend, was a professional gambler.

> Part of me figured I ought to hide, but another part didn't believe he meant what he was saying, and after all, it was Nero, my friend Nero who'd been so good to me. I started up the block toward him, not walking real fast, but kind of wanting to get close enough to see if he looked as he sounded and, rotten luck for me, he saw me before I saw him. With a roar, he leaped out of the dark and caught hold of my arms, twisting them behind me, and then, holding both my hands in one of his, he started hitting

me in the face with the other. He was doing it in a kind of back-and-forth rhythm and saying through gritted teeth, "Run out on me, will you? I'll teach you to run, you raunchy b-tch. They ain't never got me down, and you ain't gonna help 'em. . . . I'll fix you. I kept opening my mouth trying to scream, but the slaps was taking my breath away.

She left him after he tried to kill her with a knife when she was in her ninth month of pregnancy with his child.[23]

These stories begin to help us identify some of the ways that social and intimate violence overlap in black women's lives. These women allow us to glimpse the crisscrossing shapes and patterns that the consequences of violence can assume.

For example, Billie Holiday's personhood was dismissively treated when she was victimized by the man who sexually assaulted her at the age of ten. Then, she was "assaulted" by the punitive and humiliating response of the police and courts. Holiday's account points to the converging and lasting emotional scars from these experiences of violation. Ossie Guffy recalled the sensation of being beaten in the face by her boyfriend with repeated, almost rhythmic blows that took her breath away each time she opened her mouth to scream. This sensation was virtually mirrored in the ambushed feeling that she experienced in the hospital when her baby was dying. Ossie conceded a sense of utter defeat when apparently outmatched by the dynamics of poverty, the infantilizing white social worker, and the anger of the Lord. In her assessment, each offered reinforcing messages about her shamefulness. In another instance, Linda Brent related the emotional torture of facing childhood sexual abuse during her enslavement. She poignantly articulated the intense degradation of both slavery and sexual assault. Caught in this plight, Linda felt forsaken by "God and man."

A sense of God's disfavor seems to have evoked some of the deepest levels of despair in the women. In Ossie's case, the despair stemmed from a perception of a God who punishes poor women who persevere with strong determination against social disadvantages. Linda's story attests to a God who abandons sexually exploited slave girls.

In some instances, women negotiated the impact of intimate assault by making a deliberate effort to hide the incidents and their effects. Sara Rice boasted of her ability to control and limit community knowledge of the sexual and physical abuse she had suffered. When a pastor made sexual advances toward her, she understood the need to keep it quiet and to "take care of it" by herself. After talking about being beaten by her husband, Sara proudly explained that very few people (mainly her immediate family) had known about it. It was an act of self-censure to keep "her problems" from occupying a prominent position in the community. Yet it was also an attempt to gain a sense of control over her life in the aftermath of intimate assault.

These stories also depict an array of women's strategies to oppose male assault. Refusing to tolerate the dehumanizing phenomenon, they announce its destructive reality in the lives of black women. In response to sexual violence, the slave women ran away, physically fought back, verbally refused to submit, and appealed to their white slave mistresses for help. After gaining freedom from slavery, several reported the sexual exploitation of their aunts, mothers, grandmothers, and cousins.

In addition, spiritual resources were often a crucial source of support for women. Sara Rice had a resolute certainty that God's grace would uphold her whether facing her abusive husband or unfair treatment by racist white employers. After describing the horrors of physical and sexual assault under slavery, a freed elderly woman pointed to the sustaining power of "Master Jesus," proclaiming: "I'd 'er died long ago widout him." In addition to the comfort and strength it offered, her religious belief vindicated her in the face of societally accepted violence. One young slave woman resisted the social status which defined her as chattel and legitimated stripping her naked to be publicly whipped. Her conviction that this treatment was wrong was based on a firm understanding that God had created human beings to be equal. For Maggie Comer, her Christian religion identified her battering stepfather as evil. Thus, for some women hope and affirmation of personhood were located in their cognizance of a God of justice and goodness.

These stories of violation and resistance deserve much more attention. As our focus shifts to the present, we must remember that this legacy from the past saturates the contemporary context with constraining and liberative meanings. This legacy has played a primary role in shaping the conditions we face when seeking truthful insights into the current impact of socially reproduced violence in black women's lives.

2

Contemporary Testimony
from Interviews

Aisha was born in 1940 in the southeast.[1] Several experiences
of intimate violence are interwoven throughout her life. Her story por-
trays the assaults of poverty and racism converging with particular incidents of intimate violence. Aisha's stepfather was a sharecropper. Her
family moved on a frequent basis in response to his search for employment on farms in different parts of the southeast. Aisha had an extremely
close bond with her mother while she was growing up, and was deeply affected by the forms of intimate violation that she witnessed in her
mother's life.

Christian faith was a critical theme in Aisha's story of victimization
and survival. She explained how the experience of being raped as a young
woman and then physically abused by her husband in her later adult life,
produced "hatred in her heart." She labeled this hatred as a spiritual burden that she needed to release. During the emotional ordeal caused by a
life-threatening illness and gynecological surgery she relied heavily upon
her relationship with God. She dialogued with God to help sort out her
questions that surfaced in these health crises about her self-definition as a
woman. Later in her life, God was a pivotal spiritual catalyst influencing
her chosen vocation of ordained ministry with a focus on the empowerment of women.

"We ran away"

For a number of years, until I was six, I was an only child. . . . When I was
six, my mother had a second child who died from pneumonia and I look
back on it that was really traumatic for the whole family but for me now, in
ways that it wasn't then, because my mother left the child in the house
while she went to work for some white folks and the baby would just cry
and kick and sweat and she got pneumonia and died at three months old.

And so, you know, that's very painful but then, after my baby sister died, my mother who was in an abusive marriage took me and literally ran away from home. We ran away all stooped over, trying to keep my father from seeing us so that he wouldn't come get us and bring us back.

"I'd be her spokesperson"

Aisha talked about her bond with her mother at the age of six and seven:

Even in her relationships with men, my mother would sit down and tell me how she felt about the men. She would share this kind of information with me as young as I was. And so, I wasn't permitted really to respond but I was expected to listen. So, I usually didn't say anything back to her. I just listened. My responses came when the men came and, you know, they were acting in a way that my mother had already told me was unacceptable to her. But she didn't know how to say it because she was just a kind of a mild mannered person until she got really angry. So, I'd be her spokesperson. I would say it, I would tell them, "my mother does not like you and why don't you go home, stop hanging around this house. My mother does not want to get a bad reputation," and all sorts of stuff like that.

When her mother and stepfather were separated:

Responsibility was again on my mother and she did what she could through working in white folks' homes until the job would end and then we literally didn't have food and my mother was often too proud to say anything . . . and I would go out and get food for us. I would just tell people we didn't have food and people would give us food, you know. But mother wouldn't do that for whatever reason. It was just something in her that, I guess to her it represented failure not to be able to provide for herself and her children.

"But when it came to white folk . . ."

Now my mother resisted abuse and she would fight back when her husband abused her . . . but when it came to white folk, it was a different story . . . the white men that my stepfather worked with, would try to hit on my mother and she was somehow flattered by this instead of infuriated. . . . I remember it very well because I was angry too. I saw it. Even as a child of eleven or twelve years old, that they were just really trying to have their way with my mother . . . I think it had something to do with her own self-esteem and not having had any real attention that she wanted from men, you know, African-American men earlier in her life.

"And I couldn't defend myself"

Well, my uncle used to date a neighbor of mine who was also a friend. Much older than I but still a friend. And his wife was in the hospital and had had a baby and so forth. He was talking about taking us to the movies, taking me to the movies because I had just had a baby, but now I was able to go out. And to have a third come along, his former girlfriend came along as company. You know it was supposed to be an innocent thing where we were going to the movies. Well, when he showed up with Karen, he had this guy named Ben along with them and I said, "What did you bring him for?" I didn't like him anyway. And so, I felt that he brought Ben along to keep me occupied while he took care of his business with Karen because in the end, we never got to a movie. We went directly to some remote area. He and Karen got out of the car and went to this tobacco barn to screw and Ben drove me, I don't know how many miles somewhere else and that's where I was raped. So, anyway, he was like six feet or he seemed like six feet and so strong, and I was strong too, you know, for my size, but I weighed about ninety-eight pounds. And I couldn't defend myself. He didn't hit me. He didn't put a knife in my throat or anything, he just struggled with me until I was so tired and sore that I was limp and then he raped me. So, what made me even more confused about my own feelings and who I was in this situation was the man was actually gentle. He was more gentle than my boyfriend had ever been. And I felt like if I had responded I could have enjoyed it! So that was real confusing because it makes you think that you must have wanted it and you know, that you're even worse than you feel after such a thing has happened. And so, I just felt, I don't know how I felt. I felt so dirty because there was no way to cleanse my body.

[Afterwards,] he drove back to pick them up. And I thought, you know, I just felt sure that I was smelly, you know, and I could feel the semen oozing out of my vagina onto my clothes and I couldn't do anything about it. So, I just felt so dirty! The only place that we went after that was to some little joint . . . but I didn't drink. So I just sat there feeling humiliated. Couldn't, didn't feel comfortable to tell my uncle what had happened and I just didn't say anything. I just sat there. I just sat there. And when we got home I couldn't tell my mother because I really thought that she would have gone crazy if I had told her and I also thought that she would have made me go to court, you know, and I didn't want to do that because I had heard so many stories of what they put young women through when the women reported rape. That they would make the woman feel like a whore. I had just had a baby. [Aisha was an unmarried mother.] You know, so what was that going to do to my reputation. So, I just kept silent about it until I couldn't anymore. And that was like twenty something years later.

"God wanted me to forgive this man"

Aisha did not focus on any of her spiritual responses to the rape until twenty years later.

I didn't deal with it spiritually until God confronted me about forgiving the rapist and I thought that was incredibly unfair and there went another argument. "Tell me about that!" Well, I worked for the police department in 1981, the same year I was called [to the ministry]. . . . One night I went in to the job and I had a rape report on my desk. A nine-year-old child had been raped . . . and suddenly, I couldn't repress it anymore. It just all came back so clearly that—I was sitting there embarrassed my eyes were full of tears and I was trying to blink them back, and read the report so that I could do what I had to do and God is dealing with me about this experience way back then, saying that you've got to forgive and I'm saying, "No, I can't do that, that's not fair!" And I just went back and forth and literally, was shown things that I had done to other people during the course of time and shown how, to those individuals what I had done constituted rape in their eyes . . . one of those things had to do with having had a real brief affair with my best friend's husband. You know . . . we didn't want to continue but it happened. And she found out about it. So, God was showing me that "Hey, to her, that was a rape." . . . There were other things, more than I care to remember. . . . So, I decided that if God wanted me to forgive this man for raping me, then God had to show me how to do it, because I didn't know how to do it, nor did I want to do it.

I didn't want to do it. I did not want to do it! I thought it was extremely unfair that God required me to do it and even as I think about it now, I wonder if it was God or if it was my guilty conscience or whatever it was, because I was really trying to get my life together. It had not been all that long, maybe five years or six years since my conversion experience, and I would go to the Pentecostal Church and stand up with my hands in the air, which I love, praising God in that way, and say if I've done anything or if I have any hatred in my heart, and this was one of those times some of the hatred I had was being revealed to me. And the one thing was the rape and the other thing was the hatred that I had toward my husband for abusing me.

"The abuse started"

Regarding the abuse in her marriage:

The abuse went on for about two years. We were married. . . . We got married in 1965, and I left him in 1968. So, it went on for the duration of that period but it didn't start immediately. If I had known that he was the type of man who would fight I wouldn't have married him. But I didn't know that. And there again, I guess we can go back to black women's perceptions of themselves because society places certain expectations on young women to be married by a certain age and I was twenty-five years old and still unmarried. By this time I had two children. So, I was feeling pressures from within to get married and to give these children a father. . . . So, I didn't take the time, I didn't take the time that I really needed to get to know this man before we got married. We got married kind of on a bet. I'm serious. Kind of on . . . this pact that I had made with myself, that I wasn't going to bed with another man unless he was ready to get married. That kind of thing. And so, I didn't have sex with him. I got married.

The abuse started . . . I think from his drinking because he was like two different people when he was drinking and when he was sober. He was real quiet and easygoing when he was sober and you know, never raised any objection or hardly say anything but when he started drinking and reached a certain point, then he got extremely jealous and things that were fine before, he took offense to afterwards. So, that's how it began. Little stuff that came out of nowhere. The first time, you know, you don't know what to make of it. You're all shocked for one thing, confused, and wondering what did you do wrong and then you decide that you didn't do anything wrong and then the man comes back and apologizes and is extremely kind to you and does all sorts of things to make it up to you, and you figure it won't happen again. And as soon as you get into another social setting where he drinks beyond what he's able to handle, it happens again. I mean you're doing all the same things that you normally do when you call yourself having a good time and getting your butt kicked, not really knowing why.

So, anyway, I think it just got to a point where . . . one time when he did it, maybe about the third time, it was so bad, that I said I'm going to the police. I'm not going to take this, I'm going to the police. And I was so hurt, I mean physically injured that my children had to help me to get dressed and I found some old shades and went to the white man, that's what was so humiliating. [I] went to a white man detective to tell him that my husband had beaten me up. And so they advised me to get an order of protection and everything so, I went through that whole field and believe it or not, he didn't hit me again as long as I had that order of protection! . . . It says something to me about, hey, you can handle it when you think you're going to jail.

"The pain of so many women around me . . . was going unaddressed"

Those experiences [of abuse] have helped to shape my understanding of who God is and what God requires of women or God expects from women on many levels. For example, God does not expect or desire us to be in an abusive relationship of any kind with anyone. . . . So that's why it was important to me to have a different type of ministry than what I see being performed in traditional churches because of my own pain and the pain of so many women around me that was going unaddressed.

Well, the first thing I try to do is to help young women to feel good about who they are. I empower them in that way. And help them to know what constitutes abuse. Don't tolerate the slapping because it's not going to stop there and talk to them about issues around sexuality and just let them talk to me about how they feel too, and just listen to what they have to say. Often, if you can get young women to open up to you, you realize that they have a whole lot more smarts than we usually give them credit for having. . . . So, I always have opportunities to talk with women on that level, but I don't stop there . . . . It's just part of who I am. So, I do it in prayer meeting. I do it in my sermon. I do it just about on every level that I can think of where I have interaction with women.

"You couldn't help but listen to Malcolm"

Aisha described her racial consciousness throughout the first part of her life until she reached the age of forty:

I didn't want to be black. When I left [the south], I was sick of the signs. I was sick of the segregation and I thought coming to New York would end all that. I had heard that there were no colored and white signs in New York the way that there were in [the south]. That whites and blacks intermarried and you know, I thought this meant that all of the racism—I didn't even know what to call it then—was gone. So when I got here, I just didn't even think about being black at all, until the civil rights movement began. And, I stayed away from that a great deal, even though I did listen to Malcolm on 125th Street and 7th Avenue. You couldn't help but listen to Malcolm if you walked up and down 125th Street. So I guess in a cautious way, Malcolm X was probably the first one to raise my consciousness a little bit by the way he talked about Africa and the way he talked about black people in the United States and the charges he made against white people. What bothered me about Malcolm was the way he talked about Christianity and the way the media twisted his words to make it sound like he was sending a message of hate. So, you know, you're brought up on this love thy neighbor and God loves you, and you know, God is love and all that stuff. So, you have that deep down in your consciousness and you hear this message which on the one hand, you find very affirming, but on the other hand, it scares you a little bit because you think that it's going to pull you into this hate mode. So, there was a part of me that tried to resist what Malcolm was saying and not even consider it seriously because of that hate that they accused him of propagating.

"If I don't have these parts, am I still a woman?"

Reflecting on the anguish of major gynecological surgery, which followed her struggle with a life-threatening illness:

> The hysterectomy was because of tumors. They weren't cancerous but it still necessitated a hysterectomy. . . . So, anyway, you're faced with all this stuff and I say, now if I don't have these parts am I still a woman? I just worried God to death! I know I did. I have a walk-in closet at home so I would just walk into my closet, and stand there, and just talk to God. There I am, in the closet, asking these questions. It came to me the story of creation and how God created heaven and earth as it says in the Bible. Then [God] gave managerial powers over what was created. And so I started to look at myself as part of that creation and my own power over my life as God-given. . . . But on the question of being a woman, the Lord showed me, in that closet that if I didn't have any of these parts, I would still be a woman because of something intrinsic that God had done when I was created.

"Whatever helps me thrive is what I want to do"

So it's interesting that when these other experiences of abuse happened to me, I wasn't actively living out my faith in God. So, it wasn't like I was struggling with it while it was happening. "Lord do you really love me, if you let me go through this" came later. The theological reflection came later. But now, I know that there is no way that I would be in a relationship that, you know, that I couldn't feel that there was something of mutual giving and taking and respecting and loving and supporting and so forth. It's just not how I choose to live out my life. . . . I can love a person without allowing you to keep me in a situation of oppression and in a spirit of turmoil. I don't need that. I'm too old for that. And not only that, there is something about having a life-threatening disease that brings you to a new level of awareness and a new realization of what is really important and so whatever helps me thrive is what I want to do. So anything that's going to interfere with my thriving, then to me, that's evil, that's not of God, and should not be part of, you know, should not be in my environment to the extent that it stops me.[2]

Denise was born in 1969 in the metropolitan New York area. While growing up she was exposed to male battering incidents in her home and was sexually abused by her father. At the same time, she encountered racial animosity from whites in her community and school. Later, while attending college, Denise experienced intimidation and threats of violence because she openly acknowledged her lesbian identity. This rampant homophobia as well as white racial hostility surrounded her when she initiated her recovery process from her childhood sexual abuse. Denise accessed many internal resources to survive the effects of this barrage of assaults, including a unique spirituality based on her bond with her grandmothers.

"I didn't say the things I was feeling, but I was so angry"

In the neighborhood where Denise grew up there was

tension with blacks, Latinos, with people who do the exact same things [as whites in order to earn a living]. They come in [to the neighborhood,] having lived all their lives as a civil servant or whatever and then finally are able to own a home in the suburbs. Then there was white flight. But with the white residents who didn't want to leave, that made for a very, very volatile situation to the point of cross burnings and racial incidents that were really large. Like people fighting in the streets and things going on at the high school. When we moved there in 1979, that was at the cusp, although that wasn't happening so much in [the town where we lived]; it was happening in a couple of other surrounding towns.

. . . There was violence in my home, so that I didn't connect very much with other students. I was very much in the library a lot. I spent most of my time in the library of my high school and I had lots of problems, and when I first moved there—like, well if you're the new student, they all pick on you—but I didn't have—I mean, it just kind of spiraled for me to just [become a] completely inverted person, introverted personality—where all I did was read through most of my day. . . . But through my own hard work I got to be in the top ten of this—I was like number nine in my high school.

. . . But it caused a lot of ire amongst the white students that I got into [Ivy League colleges]. And they were absolutely livid that they didn't get into those places and they said it was all because of affirmative action and, I mean, a lot of things happened. There were a lot of incidents. They would just get all nasty about where I was accepted into college. Even though I had, you know, two summers at other universities and I did a lot of things in high school, I was in a lot of clubs, did a lot of activities, and also worked twenty hours a week after school, they still were, you know as racist as could be.

. . . [In high school,] I would sit in a classroom and they would talk about how stupid and backwardly ignorant Native American people were or African people were, and lots of times, I just kind of was, you know, totally not into—I couldn't stand up for myself the way I wanted to because I was completely just kind of silenced, just really quiet and shy, and then it just kind of imploded. So I didn't say the things I was feeling but I was really, really angry.

"Family outing"

As a young adult, Denise wrote the following poem about an excursion with her family:

> My father has been promoted
> proud new regional security manager
> all of us go with him
> to inspect the Long Island branch offices
> I am nine years old
>
> Our morning began with
> my father's fists and yells
> We are late
> because of the fighting
> But none of that matters now
> we are a happy family
>
> Down the long stretch of
> Long Island Highway
> Flanked by car dealerships,
> fast food restaurants, and mini malls
> father drives, mother navigates,
> in the back seat
> sister and I play games
>
> My father has been promoted
> and we are late because of the
> fighting but it's the last stop now
> my sister and I nag for food
> At McDonald's they are

alarmed to see Black people
even though we are a happy family

The last bank
we watch from the car my father fumbles for the keys
to the bank door
before he can turn the lock
six white cops surround our car
and him

I am nine years old
staring down the barrel of a gun
and they are warning me not to
move or they will shoot

We are late because of the fighting
Six white cops surround our car
and him
There is a gun at my father's head
he is crying now
trying to explain the situation

Over and over
he begs for his own life
provides proof that
yes, he has gotten a promotion
we are a happy family.

After telling the story of the incident referred to in the poem, Denise described her family's response:

We were just terrified and frightened and upset. That incident let me know definitively that I was a black person in America and that there is no way that it's ever going to be alright; or where it's ever going to be cozy and comfortable for me here. That racism is truly the way of the land.

"There was no room for me in that space, because there was so much going on"

My father . . . was very physically violent towards everybody in the house, especially my mother. I mean he was just a constant force of, you know, um, perpetual fear and outbursts. Or, he would just make nasty comments to people.

   And then my sister . . . she got pregnant for the first time and then subsequently married the father of the child. . . . She was nineteen and way too young to have a baby. Everybody was just like, "Wow, you have a baby now; you have to get married." . . . So she married this guy who was just like my father: abusive, horrible human being. So he was also a presence there. Just like lots of, you know, him being very abusive to my sister. . . . So there was no room for me in that space, because there was so much going on. So whatever was happening with me, people trying to beat me up or other things happening at school just kind of got lost in that. It was just me and my books for the most part.

My sister and I used to just beg [my mother] to go. We said, "Can we just go? Can't we leave? Let's go!" And she was so afraid. I mean, my mother was so desperately afraid of not having the financial resources to be able to survive out there with these two little children. And, you know, my sister and I were like: "Well, we can stand it; we're ready for anything." You know, and [my mother] was afraid. I felt totally hopeless. It's like: God, we'll never get out of this. And it was very much like—well everything that, every kind of suggestion, there was a roadblock. There was always a block. She always, always just, um, trusted people that she shouldn't have trusted.

"A positive message"

My mother always made sure that there were books in the house. As a child I thought of her as such an outgoing and dynamic figure. A person who was politically active and astute. She used to go away for weekends to writers' retreats. . . . Books being my world, I read an incredible amount and then she got to meet these people, and she'd hang out with them. . . . I totally looked up to her. You know, all kinds of things that she did despite the incredible life under my father's fist [under which] she had to live for most of that time. It was a positive message about being a woman; it was a positive message about being a black person, about being a black woman writer, [about] having that possibility, you know. . . . Because this was New York, you had black radio on at the time and so we listened to the radio shows and she said, "Sit there and [listen]." And she said, "Look girls, this is your history; this is what I lived through." You know, she'd tell us stories about what it was like to be a grown woman in the sixties, and it was really, I mean, for me that was the start of radicalization. She planted the seeds of my activism. You know, my mother . . . she's not a very radical person. She's just like this very conservative black woman from the south. That's what she is, but she inadvertently, she made a revolutionary and she didn't want to. There used to be a [television] show in New York called "Like It Is." . . . That show was amazing. And I was there [watching it] every single week. I got to see clips of Fannie Lou Hamer, and Angela Davis, and Malcolm X. I was totally fascinated always, with Malcolm X and his theories and what made him such a great warrior.

"Religion is different from spirituality"

The most spiritual moment that I can remember was when I was eighteen and my grandmother died. My grandmother's name was Denise as well; I was named after her. And when I went to her funeral and it was a small black church in rural North Carolina where my mother grew up and the choir sang. And I can feel my grandmother's presence there. . . . I'm also named after my father's mother. And I feel the most spiritual connection to them. You know, I feel them with me sometimes, during the most horrible periods of my life, I will sometimes feel them nudging me to continue on. And, that's when I feel [a sense of spirituality] most.

I was not very religious. . . . Religion is different from spirituality. As soon as the preacher started to preach—the content of his words were mostly religion; but then there is the way that he does it. You know what I mean? Like, the tenor of his voice, the kind of virtual song that is presented from the pulpit is spiritual. Religion seems to me very much prescribed and based upon a particular book and very inflexible and based on hierarchies . . . you know, everybody's got to be married and have babies. . . . It's got to be this hierarchical male/female thing.

. . . Religion is used against me. [Once] we started these little Bible study groups. . . . There was this one woman who lived in our town, who would come to our house and do Bible study with us. Once my mother got kind of an inkling that she thought I might be a lesbian, she had this woman come to our house while I was there for vacations from school. [She came to] tell me, like show me all the sections in the Bible that are all against lesbianism and homosexuality. She would just sit me down and make me read them aloud. It was just horrible. It was just like—somehow this was supposed to stop the march toward perversity—I don't know. I was thinking: "please get me out of here." That was all I could think of. This is horrible; this is so annoying and I was just trying to live through the experience. I just remember feeling really like: this is total bullsh-t. . . . I can't believe this. I know what I feel. I remember thinking that any kind of true God would not approve of this kind of activity because I was really thinking that I could not be an evil person. I knew I wasn't an evil person and I knew this was not, like, some sort of horrible, spite against Jesus or something. So I was just like, well, this cannot be of God to sit here like this.

"When racism is discussed in this country, it's discussed in terms of black males"

Being a black woman is difficult in the United States, to say the least. . . . There's this dictum, I would say, in the black community, that men come first, that black men come first, that black men are the ones that are oppressed, and the rest of us need to support them in surviving racism. Like, we don't have to survive racism, and we are somehow privileged in this country that we get all the good jobs; we get to go to college and we have it just fine here. And the poor black men are the ones that we need to somehow reach out to and help, and I don't know, sacrifice our lives for. That has always just struck me as being ridiculous. Anytime at all when racism is discussed in this country, it's discussed in terms of black males. Everyone else is a kind of fodder for their tribulations. That what I think it means to be a black woman. It's just like this kind of loss of a sense of self. You are just kind of cast away.

"I remember feeling extremely powerless"

My father was just a very physically violent person and I had to watch that [behavior with the other members of my family]. But towards me he was very sexually violent and he would constantly invade my space where I was trying to sleep. I mean, that was the most vulnerable time. . . . So, if I was trying to sleep or he would call me in when he was asleep to abuse me, and then he had—he was extremely vicious in his mind games. . . . At the same time he would say, "I love you" and then tell me how ugly I was or something like that. And he just kind of like, played with me,—as a human being. He's consistently a kind of psychologically abusive person. He'd just get to your core; you know, the thing that was the most vulnerable about you and be really mean and vicious about it. . . . He coupled his violence with psychological torture.

I totally didn't remember anything until I was starting to come out to myself [as a lesbian]. . . . I remembered him being physically violent, but the sexual abuse was just buried then until I started to tell lots of truths about [myself], to get to some of the inner parts of who I am, and that's when the [sexual abuse] started to emerge in my nightmares and dreams. They were just terribly traumatic and absolutely disturbing. And, threw me into a cycle of depression and, just self-hatred. It was just horrible. And [at the time], I was at this completely unsupportive and dangerous place to be as a black person. I was on enemy territory and to have to go through this in that kind of unsupportive space was extremely difficult. Because every day was a fight for my will to survive in that institution.

[At the time of the sexual abuse], I remember feeling extremely powerless and like,—like I could do nothing to stop what was happening. And I remember just letting it hap—not letting it happen, but just kind of like having it happen and then trying to go on with whatever I was doing—you know, whatever else was happening. I remember just making it a very—um trying to make it a normal thing. Making it like, it's not so bad; it's just, you know—I'm not going to tell anyone, it's just something that happened. I'm just going to go and watch TV now, that kind of thing. And when I started to remember, I remembered with emotion, I remembered it with the terror. That was just the absolute horror of having a flashback and just feeling like you're transported through time. Terribly traumatic.

Well, as a result of the whole thing [being sexually abused], I tried to be as perfect as possible. I did everything my mother told me to do; I did everything my father told me to do, including whatever he wanted to do to me. If he wanted me to be quiet or, you know, whatever. I never talked back. I was just very—I did everything my mother wanted and just bent completely. I was extremely quiet and shy. And, except when I was in school—before we moved to Long Island, I was much more outgoing as a student.

"It feels the same"

It feels the same. Being called nigger, being called nigger b-tch in the street and having to deal with a racist white professor at my college. I feel powerless. It feels the same as having my father do what he did to me. I start to regress. I implode. I feel the same, as if it doesn't matter what I do or say, or what I think is wrong. There is nothing that I can do.

"I think the effects go deep"

[Initially coming to grips with the sexual abuse] was a very difficult process because as I was doing it, I was surrounded by white people. There's a certain expectation that black people are sexually deviant in the first place and our sexuality is constantly under scrutiny from the minute we were brought to these shores. We are described in kind of brutish and animalistic terms. So to talk about incest is to kind of reinforce all of the notions that they already have about what black people are like. And poor black people especially . . . I was very aware of that. I was a psychology major and I'd seen these studies and be like: this is racist to its core. And that's there. It hangs in the air. I remember when I gave a presentation, it was on a panel of survivors, at my college. . . . People on the panel went into detail about their experiences, with mostly adult rape. . . . It is very clear that there are differences in how my story is going to be perceived and how the white women's stories were going to be perceived. . . . I talked about the racial considerations [that need to be recognized] when we're talking about in-cest or rape or sexual abuse where a black male is the perpetrator and how black women are just coerced into silence because of the racism that [black people are all] aware of. So instead of talking about the details of my own experience, I tried to put it back onto the audience, and say "what are you thinking?" . . . And the kind of notions that assume that lesbianism is a consequence of being abused by men. That's one of the prevailing notions too: "You're like this because of whatever your father did to you."

I think the effects go deep. I actively spend a lot of time trying to heal, continuously trying to heal. I mean the process of healing is very long. I fight with severe depression, constantly. Constantly.

What's necessary for healing is to hear what other women have to say about their experiences, specifically in a context that takes race into ac-count. People need a space to heal and time and place. I think that that's why people who have limited resources, especially, feel as if we just have to go on to the next day and that things are behind us now. And women, we say, "we've just got to move on." And I don't think that the body can do that very effectively. Eventually you're going to break down. And those are the things that are rarely talked about. The times when people just kind of like can't,—they just like stop in their living room or their kitchen floor or wherever they are, and they just can't go—can't move any fur-ther.

I think that [healing] has to be done in the company of sisters. With those who understand, who can form some sort of healing space that is safe. That is recognizable as a space where you don't have to explain your life to these people. Because I've been in so many groups and so many dif-ferent kinds of group therapy and feminist therapy sessions. [I have experi-enced] all different kinds of ways to heal from sexual violence, incest in particular. And, every time, I'm doing it in this room full of white people. I get this feeling that these women have no idea who I am. I have this reserve about talking to them because I know there are these stereotypes of what black people are like. Or like, where there's the [activity] where you have to do the art work. Where people sit there and kind of get their feelings out, but all the colors that are used to denote pain and suffering, are all the dark colors. And black is always the evil. I've had to say things in workshops or in therapy groups like: "Well, I cannot feel comfortable in this group if everybody's color schema is based on race. I can't do it." You know it took me a long time to be able to say that in a therapy session. The white women say things like: "I don't know what you're talking about. These are just the colors [that I feel]." I responded with something like: "This is too deeply embedded in America that black is related to all the bad things that happen; you're going to tell me that it doesn't have anything to do with race?" It does. And this happens to all of us, me included.

Referring to her deceased grandmothers Denise described the connection between her spirituality and the impact of the sexual abuse:

They have been very much there and helping me, to guide me through the times when I thought, why do I do this kind of work in the first place. They've been there to say: "it's okay this is the stuff that you should be doing and this is what you need to do right now." And helping me through. I've been through lots and lots of unnecessary pain associated with incest, in particular that drove me to the brink, you know, of attempting suicide, to where I was almost gone. I stumbled down a flight of stairs and that was what alerted the other people in the house until they called the ambulance. But if I had just sat down, that would have been it.

[When you have] that kind of experience of being on the brink of death, you never forget what it's like there and what happened in those spaces. At first I thought [my grandmothers] were calling me to them, and then I realized that no, they weren't calling me to them. They just wanted me to hang on a little longer, then I would see that there were other things going on, other things planned. So that was, you know,—I also saw that in that space of giving up, in the part where you're no longer ready to fight,— no longer willing or able to resist is where it's the most terrifying to me. So that moment when I was—when my heart was stopping—you know in all the time that I spent scheming about how to commit this suicide attempt, all the time that I spent in the midst of fear or hesitation and silence and inaction, were the most terrifying. And the times that I decided to live and what I wanted to do—you know, like trying to resist, being in the spaces of resistance, were the most empowering. . . . I made a commitment to myself to live and to resist this world's oppression. That is the only place that I could live. I mean, that's the only space of actually living. It is in resistance, or else I give up and that's—it's too terrifying there.

"To be silent, to be afraid, would have cost me a lot more"

I get mistaken for a gay man lots of times—just for some bizarre reason. I don't know why. [Once] I was turning left onto this street and I almost had an accident with a car full of white boys. It was really close and it was my fault. I was very apologetic but what happened was they started screaming faggot at me. I was like, "I'm not a gay man, I'm a lesbian." Then this guy got out of his car and tried to get into my car. And at that point I got out of there. I don't know what they were trying to do but they followed me screaming "faggot" and "we're going to get you." . . . I was absolutely terrified.

The following occurred at social events primarily hosted and attended by black students on her predominantly white college campus:

> If I went to a dance or something with a woman, or if I went by myself, people would physically move away from me. They would not be in my space. They would not stand next to me. So, I would dance some place with a woman and they would make a space around us. So I decided to go to all their dances so that they wouldn't be able to dance. I was just angry. I was so angry. The more I was there, the more uncomfortable and upset they were. So I was just like: "well, you're going to have to deal with me and I'm going to make you unhappy forever and ever." Or they would throw things [at me]. If there was water or something or a cup . . . at this one dance floor, they would throw ice down at me on the dance floor. Because once I started dancing, nobody else would dance . . . or some guy would or a group of guys would surround myself and the female partner and [say,] "Wouldn't you rather be dancing with us? how could you be doing this?" . . . I was very afraid. I was afraid that it would escalate. . . . they were definitely on the verge of hurting me. Um, because they felt like I was this, ah, blotch on their community or something.
>
> I remember being so-o-o angry, just really angry and out to tear that campus apart. . . . So, I'd go around with a "Queer nation" T-shirt on. I mean, not that I was part of "Queer Nation" or like I agree with their politics, it didn't matter. Whatever I could find that had queer, dyke, lesbian on it, I would walk around with it on and defy anybody to say something.
>
> I think it would have cost me a lot more not to fight back; to be silent, to be afraid would have cost me much more than to be closeted or to be scared of somebody finding out. It was a lot more liberating to just do a big "f—k you." It was a lot more liberating, you know, than it was to hide.[3]

Carey was born in 1962 in Massachusetts. She experienced childhood sexual abuse and battering by an intimate male partner. She was imprisoned for drug-related activities, and then went into recovery from a serious drug addiction problem. Her treatment for drug addiction was a turning point in her life because it provided her with her first opportunity for in-depth psychotherapy and personal reflection on her previous life struggles. Her ability to articulate and value her feelings increased as a result of her work in this program.

Carey displayed her feisty spirit through her self-reliance and re-sourcefulness when faced with a boyfriend who battered her. Similarly, in her racial attitudes her primary response to white prejudice was her self-assertiveness. Faith in God and spirituality do not appear to have been a major resource in Carey's life. In fact, she seems to convey her ambivalence about God's responsiveness to her suffering by the tone of her discussion of spirituality.

"But I can hold a lot of pain"

Well, you know, I'm the type of person where I can get hurt, but I can hold a lot of pain. You could see it too. But, no matter what—it's like if I don't want to let it go, I won't let it go until the right time. And it's—I don't know, I could just do anything. I had a lot of pain for twenty years, with my mother. . . . She—you know, I got real active on drugs, but you know, it all goes back to my childhood, you know, the way she treated me. I felt like sh-t. I mean like real dirty, and I thought, she didn't care, she didn't want me. And as I grew older, at [age] eight, she had a boyfriend and he molested me from [age] eight to twelve. . . . And because I was so aggressive then, from going through a lot, it was like, it felt good. So, I didn't tell [my mother]. And it wasn't because he said she won't believe me, or she was going to kick me out, or she was gonna beat me. He told me all of those things, but it felt good so I kept letting it happen. And even though I felt like sh-t, it was like, what else could I do?

My mother worked, we hardly seen my mother. She worked from three to eleven. So when we came home from school, she was going to work. And when she came home from work, we were asleep. . . . You only maybe seen her on Sunday. She would work overtime on Saturdays. She still do today.

[My mother's boyfriend] would come, you know, while she was at work. And we all—it didn't stop for a long time. I mean he used to take us anywhere we wanted. I mean to MacDonald's, or to get ice cream. It was like he was our very own sucker. Like, here comes Sam, we can do whatever we want, the day he comes. All of us did like that, you know. . . . He molested me and my younger sister.

"Numb feelings"

I started to have these numb feelings, you know, like I was maturing inside, you know. I didn't know it then, but I know now from treatment, like I was maturing inside. And that I could hate, and do this to men, and get what I want. I could probably say I was a devil because it made me want to like, take control, like use men. Any and all men, that's what it made me do.

[At the age of twelve,] I stopped it. Because I had—my mind had grown so much it was like—if I let him do this, then I can get this. And at twelve, I started selling my body on the street downtown. So that cut him off. And I did that, you know, for a few years. I did it for a few years. And then I went on to doin' drugs, you know, and hiding a lot of feelings, you know. Cause I was thinking about it all the time. And I'd just get high on reefer and drink a lot of liquor so that I couldn't feel it. And I had to be drunk in order to sell my body. And when I turned fifteen, I realized that when I was eight and twelve he had stuck his penis in me and I had numbed out. So, I don't remember what episode I was going through, but I remember the feeling of numbing out, of actually laying there and being—laying there and being there, but not knowing, you know, just gone, like my mind was just gone. . . . I looked at the walls, I looked around the room. Everything was just—I was not focused on what was happenin' to me at all.

I was doin' it very well. And that's how I did it on the street. You know, I would just numb out and maybe smoke a cigarette. I would actually smoke a cigarette. [The male customers] used to hate it. . . . I would just try to take whatever I could from them, you know, without givin' them anything. But, not today, I won't do that. I went through treatment and all, I was in treatment a year and I did a year after care. So, it's goin' on four years clean!

"'It'll be okay, you'll start to heal'"

Carey went to jail for a drug trafficking case involving cocaine. She was five months' pregnant at the time. After serving three and half months in prison, she was able to get admitted to a halfway house for pregnant women prisoners with drug addiction problems. Carey relates her experience with a particularly helpful counselor at the halfway house:

Being in [prison], being pregnant was like humiliation, you know. The men cops, you know, dogging you. And they tell you when to eat, sh-t, sleep—I mean it's like—I could do that, but I didn't want to do that. And I stayed to myself. I always had to keep this wall up so they would know: don't f—k with me. Just being in prison was humiliating. . . . I went once and I never went back. I'm not going back.

And I did treatment for a year. I was in therapeutic treatment. So that means that everything that happened to me when I was younger, I had to deal with. And I had blocked out my sexual abuse. For twenty years, I didn't tell nobody. And there was one woman there, I didn't know why I feared this woman, but she had come to get me in prison. . . . I saw how this woman was. That she gave out tough love. That she would break you down and she would pick you back up. I feared her to death. Cause I didn't want her to know anything about me. So she got me in group one day and it was like: "Carey, I know a lot of things happened to you, and I'm gonna be the one to get it out." And I just like—I looked at her. I said, "I'm not telling you nothin'! Nothin' about me! Nothin'! Didn't nothin' happen to me." I denied a lot of things, denied being an addict, a lot of things. I was just in denial. And she was going to work with me, you know, the next time. Yeah, she broke me down about the sexual abuse I had. I don't know how she got it out, but she got it out.

She got it out, and it was like, I just started crying. She said, "you're not going to heal until you tell us how it felt." And I was sittin' there in the chair, and the tears were just rollin' down, and I didn't want to tell all these women that it felt good and all. And I wouldn't say nothin'. Then she said, "Carey, you're not gonna heal." And I just jumped up, I said, "It felt good. It felt good." And she was like: "I know, I know." And I'm looking around at all these women, you know, they're cryin' too. And I said, "Oh, my God." I just began, you know, to pour it out. My gut seemed like there was a chip off of it now. And I just cried out loud. So she came over and hugged me, and she patted me and she looks at me and she said, "Don't worry about it." She said, "It'll be okay. You'll start to heal." Because she was sexually mo-lested. . . . That's how she knows how to take things to a certain level, be-cause she knows what you been through.

"Anything would trigger him"

Carey described her relationship with an abusive boyfriend with whom she lived prior to her arrest and treatment program experience:

And I moved in with him. . . . I mean, everything was real nice for the whole [first] year. It was real nice. And then after that it was like anything would trigger him. He would eat the last piece of cheese and then at twelve o'clock at night, he'd come in there and there's no cheese, and he'd want to fight me because there was no cheese. Anything that ran out, you know, he wanted to fight.

And if I came in at quarter to six, he was sittin' there, and he had, you know, a chop or burnt steak, or his tea or whatever. He would roll his eyes about, like, you know, "where you been? Don't you know dinner's sup-posed to be done at six." And I'm lookin at him like, "it's a nice day outside. Why can't dinner be at eight? Why can't I cook when I want?" That's what I wanted to say. I sat down and I start talking to him, and he asked me—you know, picked up a cup of tea and threw it in my face. It wasn't hot, you know, but it was warm enough to make me like hit him. Because it was like a reflex thing, for me, you know. I hit him. And we lived on the third floor, and we was fightin' in the kitchen and he tried to throw me out the window. Yeah, he tried to throw me out the window. My girlfriend was comin' down the street, and she was like: "Carey, Carey." . . . I don't know where I got the strength, but I got the strength, and I knocked him up against the window. And he looked at me like—you know, and I looked at him back, to stop, just stop. A lot of times, we fought. He would try to hit me, but a lot of times I just wouldn't let him hit me.

One night I went out, and the dog knew some one was coming upstairs, and I knew that it was after two o'clock. And he [often] said, women without a car shouldn't be out after one o'clock. And it was after two o'clock. I was comin' upstairs, and I had made it all the way into the house without the dog barking, and the dog started barking. And then he jumped up and went into the kitchen and he picked up this long knife, and he had me up in the corner. He had the knife at my throat, and I was looking at him. It was like I seen my life flash, you know, like gone. And I looked up at him and I said, "Oh no, this is it." And he said, "B-tch," he said, "where the f—k was you? If you ever come in here after two o'clock again, I'll kill you." And I said to him, "You might as well kill me right now." Cause I was outta there, you know. And I couldn't believe that he had—I mean it wasn't a little knife, it was the biggest d—n knife in the house. And I couldn't believe that he had got a knife for me . . . he let me go and he put the knife back and he slammed back into the bedroom. And I sat there all night in the kitchen. I was scared then. I was scared.

I thought about what I was gonna do. How I was gonna be able to save my kids and myself. To get outta there. . . . [So, I started] like brain washing him, and that was only the second year we was together. Like, I had to do what he wanted me to do. But in turn, I was still doin' what I wanted to do. I had to talk to him like his mother talked to him. . . . So I began keepin' a lot of things from him. Not tellin' him a lot of things. I would have dinner ready at about five thirty [in the evening], a half hour early. And the kids, I would take the kids outside, you know keep them out of the house as much as possible. Now it was about survival until I could get a section eight [note: section eight is a federal public assistance program for the housing needs of the poor]. And I had nowhere else to go. I couldn't go to my mother's, or to none of my aunts'. So I had to stay, so that meant that I had to, you know, come up with somethin' to be able to be here that long, without getting killed first.

"When I was younger, I read about God"

When I was younger I read about God. But when I got older, it was like I wasn't interested anymore. I was interested in bein' outside and stuff. And it wasn't until I went into treatment that I began studying about spirituality and God and my Creator. Because they told me that I need a higher power to help me get through this. And I didn't choose to call him God like everyone else. I called him my Creator. And that's what works for me. . . . I haven't been able to picture [God as] anything. And then it's so many things that goes along, you know, to sayin' well how God looks, you know. It's like, who really knows? So that's why I choose to say, "my creator," because it's just someone above me that I, you know, talk to. . . . I don't know if I get answers back, but I guess I do get answers back because I know that he sends 'em. . . . Sometimes I cried, "how come you don't help me when I want you to?" He does help, but not when I want. It's just not gonna be on my time, you know. I have to understand that.

"Who told you that this was your earth?"

It sucks to be black in the United States. But you know what? I'm the type of person where, when I see *Roots,* when I see posters [of what happened to black people throughout history]. I can't look at it, you know. It hurts too much inside to look at it. And then when you come out here, it's like here are all these white people out here. And I say to 'em, what the h-ll really makes them think that they're supposed to be here—that's how I am. I have been in racial contacts, but I'm like, what makes you think you're f—kin' supposed to be here, you know. Who told you that this was your earth? I look at people like that, and when I get on the bus sometimes, you know how there's the white people that's on the bus and they grab their pocketbook, you know. And those are the people I sit next to. I sit down next to 'em. And I let them know that I have just as much as they do. And I don't need anything from them. And they hate that.[4]

Each of these testimonies provides evidence, guidance, and challenges for engaging in theoretical analysis of violence against African-American women. Most importantly, these women's stories call for a constructive community response and for comprehensive social change that will reduce and destabilize the entire spectrum of assaults on them.

PART II

Paying Attention to Women's Anguish

3

Emotional and
Spiritual Consequences

The way women feel about themselves and their environment is permanently altered by the incidence of intimate assault in their lives. Deciphering the complex nature of this trauma involves naming and analyzing the emotional and spiritual repercussions of intimate violence. Naming the effects helps to break down the perception that the male violence experienced by black women is shameful and should be kept secret. Analysis of the problem signals a refusal to dismiss the anguish caused by male violence as an incomprehensible and irreducible part of women's ordeal.

Since the entire community is morally culpable for the deleterious consequences of male sexual and physical assault on women, women's anguish is a communal problem. The traumatizing impact of the violence must not be considered the isolated burden of the victim-survivor to deal with, nor seen as a merely private matter between a victim-survivor and her counselor. We all share the responsibility of comprehending the emotional torment of women. By assuming this responsibility we can grasp how we participate in socially constructing this painful phenomenon, and equip ourselves to dismantle its societal reinforcement.

There has been considerable critical discussion of the link between gender oppression and the emotional and spiritual impact of intimate violence. In the following chapters, contributions to this discussion by feminists Judith Herman, Lenore Walker, and Marie Fortune will be utilized. These three have created pioneering feminist approaches, offering some of the most comprehensively theorized and relevant material for unraveling the emotional and spiritual impact of intimate violence. Herman has provided an extensive psychological analysis of the problem of father-daughter incest and the trauma of violent assault for its victim-survivors. Walker is a groundbreaking theorist on the psychological impact of battering on women. She developed the Walker Cycle Theory of Violence now commonly used as a model to explain how battering relationships are perpetuated. In brief, the stages are 1) tension building; 2) the acute battering incident; and 3) loving contrition by the batterer. Fortune has been at the forefront in seeking recognition of a myriad issues related to Christian religious faith that arise for women victim-survivors of sexual violence.

For black women, racial and gender oppression combine to help shape the emotional and spiritual repercussions of intimate violence. Herman, Walker, and Fortune, along with many white feminist theorists working in the area of violence against women, insufficiently investigate how racial oppression influences the emotional and spiritual consequences of intimate violence. Included in the next chapter is a more specific methodological discussion of how these feminist theorists neglect the issue of racial oppression in their work (even when their stated purpose is to incorporate the social context of women's lives in their studies of intimate violence). Hence my engagement here of some of this relevant feminist scholarship necessarily involves additional analytical steps, including a critique of their silences and directing attention toward considerations related to racial subjugation. In this way I hope to contribute to the underdeveloped task of theorizing racial dynamics interactively with gendered ones when interpreting the imprint of intimate violence upon the lives of women. Another dimension of this process of racial/gender theorizing is offered in the final section. Using sources that concertedly focus on black women and intimate violence, the method of inquiry in this part of the chapter concentrates on the peculiarly amalgamated nexus of racial/gender dynamics that African-American victim-survivors encounter.

As with any life experience, women coping with male sexual and physical assault do not experience racial and gender oppression in an additive or sequential fashion. It is fallacious to suppose that one experiences abuse first as a human being, then as a woman, then as a black person, then as a black woman, then as a lesbian, and so forth. A woman's responses cannot be correlated to aspects of her social identity on a neat flowchart. Similarly, racial and gender oppression do not shape every instance of abuse with the same degree of intensity. Subjugating social norms infiltrate an individual's reality in anything but an orderly or standardized manner. To glimpse some portion of this complicated process for victim-survivors, my analysis focuses thematically on invisibility and shame as dominant features of women's experiences.

Layers of Consequences That Converge on Women

Invisibility

The struggle for visibility occurs in the community's response to the problem of intimate violence, the community's reaction to the victim-survivor, and the victim-survivor's perceptions of her own selfhood.

The context for public attention to the traumatizing effects of intimate violence is set by the sociopolitical status of women. As Judith Herman argues, the current interest in investigating the psychological trauma of rape and incest is a consequence of the most recent wave of feminist organizing. The feminist movement is responsible for the development of new language for understanding the impact of sexual assault. It can be credited with attaining public recognition for the horrendous suffering that results. As Herman writes about early feminist activists: "women found it necessary to establish the obvious: that rape is an atrocity."[1]

In order to assess both the damaging impact and the coping strategies that stem from intimate assault by males, black women must first be acknowledged as victims. There has been an astonishingly recent evolution in social recognition of women as victimized by male intimate violence, rather than as masochistic partners in their own abuse.[2] Hence the initial step in our task of unraveling the emotional and spiritual impact of abuse consists of identifying women's victimization as unwanted and undeserved agony. This rudimentary acknowledgment is necessitated by the social construction of women's gender identity as less and other—that is, as deserving of less attention and as an "other" over whose body males hold entitlement rights.

FRACTURED COMMUNITY TIES

An overall feeling of estrangement from community often results from the invisibility that the victim-survivors of intimate violence may experience. Herman describes how they feel utterly abandoned, utterly alone, and cast out of the human and divine systems of care and protection that sustain life. Thereafter, a sense of alienation and of disconnection pervades every relationship from the most intimate familial bonds to the most abstract affiliations of community and religion.[3] The intimate assault represents an attack on every valuable link between the individual and her community. In the case of an intimate assault by a stranger, a woman can feel thoroughly defenseless. Because the attack can be perceived as wholly unprovoked and random, the victim-survivor is plagued by the lack of safety that becomes an intractable part of all human contact. Especially when the assault is perpetrated by an acquaintance or family member, communal ties are severely fractured. The woman may feel that no one can be trusted. In either case, awareness of the tremendous potential for harm from others can erode every aspect of her relational life.

Devalued status based on gender and race both shape and inform the breach with community created by sexual and physical assault. With regard to domestic violence, Herman notes the covert nature of domestic captivity that ensnares women and children victim-survivors. Although they are invisible, the economic, social, and legal barriers to escape that entrap women are extremely powerful.[4] This gendered denial of rights and status compounds the breach with community. Being confined in a cage that seems invisible to everyone else nullifies a woman's suffering and exacerbates her isolation and alienation.

This kind of breach is manifest in cases of sexual assault as well. Aisha attested to this reality when she described her decision not to tell her mother that she was raped. She made this decision in part out of a fear of being forced to "go to court." She explained: "I had heard so many stories of what they would put young women through when they reported rape. That they would make the young woman feel like a whore." As a young single black mother, Aisha knew that her credibility would be especially in doubt. Community assumptions about her black womanhood can form a barrier that disqualifies her from the right to community empathy. These assumptions can also permeate her self-perceptions and deny her an opportunity for formal redress.

Race helps to define and mediate the notion of community for most women. Unfortunately, Herman neglects it in her analysis of how social isolation infuses the trauma. The relegation of blacks to outsider status is a cultural norm in the United States, and constitutes an ongoing rupture in blacks' communal relationship with the broader society. Since this ruptured condition preexists for black women when the intimate violence takes place, the sense of community abandonment may emerge as a piercing confirmation of cultural estrangement rather than a newly imposed demotion in social status. The effects of this established, racially based rift may intensify a woman's need for community acceptance and for support from other blacks. When sexual violation occurs within their families or by any member of "their" community, black women may confront the profound injury of being psychically severed from the only source of trustworthy community available to them.

Because of the ambiguities of their racial visibility, black women are on exhibit precisely at the same time as they are confined to the invisible cage referred to above. For instance, blacks are quite visible as objects for entertainment in television situation-comedies, professional sports (women to a lesser degree), or on local news crime reports (women are especially featured in welfare fraud and child abuse stories). Blackness becomes a "known" commodity through these stereotyped mass media images. One's individual identity is suffocated under a popular, generalized group definition of blacks. Contemporary cultural theorist David Theo Goldberg summarizes this concept of being "known" as follows: "Invisibility also happens when one does not see people because one 'knows' them through some fabricated preconception of group formation."[5]

In addition, the zealous use of the apparatus of the state for the police surveillance and supervision of black communities demonstrates the disproportionate attention black racial identity commands.[6] But this kind of attention merely denotes a meticulous enforcement of black subjugation. The ways in which her racial identity is treated as a known commodity may amplify a woman's sense of isolation. The alienation produced by her membership in a simplistically characterized class of objectified "others" can buttress the sense of disconnection from community already inflicted by the intimate violence.

RELIGIOUS AND SPIRITUAL CONNECTION
AND DISCONNECTION

Victim-survivors of male sexual and physical assault may feel that their needs vanish even from God's sight. They may experience a collapsed connection with divine grace—a feeling of abandonment or deliberate rejection by God. It may seem that God is not able to see a woman's woundedness and deprivation, or that God deliberately chooses to ignore them because the woman deserves to suffer. Marie Fortune suggests that Christian victim-survivors may feel left alone and abandoned by God in the midst of suffering.

If a person believes God to be omnipotent, loving and rewarding of the righteousness of good Christians, then suffering is either a sign of God's disfavor or a realization that God does not play by the rules. . . . This feeling of abandonment occurs for the victim who expected God to protect her from all pain and suffering. When she encounters suffering, she feels betrayed. The sense of abandonment by God is profound and often creates a crisis of faith for the victim.[7]

Fortune aptly describes the critical nature of the spiritual crisis victim-survivors often face. Disorientation about the essence of God and the principles that guide divine actions characterize the breach in the relationship. Fortune spells out how physical and sexual assault can appear to signal God's deliberate choice to break covenant with a woman. It sometimes destroys the trust in God which has undergirded the vitality of her faith.

However, this assessment by Fortune may need to be amended when elements of racial subjugation that affect the life experiences of black women are considered. There can be a crisis of faith subsequent to intimate assault even if one does not hold that God protects from *all* pain and suffering. In particular instances of intimate violation, the crisis of faith may certainly arise out of a dire need for God's protection. Yet, for women for whom socioeconomic and racist marginalization is a normal aspect of their daily lives, it is usually quite evident that God does not eliminate all the problems that these social realities bring. Most black women who rely on Christian faith as a primary sustaining resource do not expect that faith in God will shield them from all encounters with pain and suffering. For many of them God is a refuge in the midst of suffering, a bulwark of strength that enables them to survive in spite of overwhelming obstacles.

The fact that their faith has facilitated this accommodation to various forms of racial and economic suffering does not rule out a crisis in faith. In fact, the scope of the spiritual crisis may actually be deepened when a primary tenet of a woman's faith is that God's aid gives her resilience in the face of suffering. A perception of God's absence when she tries to cope with the oppressive aftermath of intimate violence might be even more startling and enervating than if she had begun with an assumption of God's omnipotent power to protect her from all suffering.

Women may also decide that God's apparent abandonment of them in the midst of their trauma may indeed be for a justifiable reason, and that therefore they deserve it. This "justifiable" rejection by God can be legitimated by patriarchal Christian teachings. Women who are abused can feel under constant pressure to please their abuser in a way that resembles the messages that they have learned about pleasing God. The stories of Denise and Carey offer examples of women who attempted valiantly, but to no avail, to please their abusers.

Denise described her attempt to be "perfect" in response to the sexual abuse by her father.[8] The battering of her mother and sister by their respective spouses that surrounded Denise at home, undoubtedly also contributed to the pressure she felt to assume this role of the "perfect," pleasing, family member. Similarly, Carey tried to appease her batterer through the performance of domestic chores, such as making sure that dinner was prepared at the exact time that her batterer requested it. The abusive situation can set up a dynamic whereby the victim-survivor feels that "love" can only be received if it is earned. Maybe if she is "perfect" as Denise tried to be for her father, or if the abuser is taken care of precisely the way he requests it, as Carey tried to do, the abuse will not occur. Of course, this pleasing behavior does not prevent the violence. In addition to feeling powerless, the woman or little girl who engages in it is often left with an unrelenting sense of inadequacy.

This problem may be heightened when a woman's spirituality is shaped in terms of a theological belief in a judgmental male God who calls her to an unattainable state of "perfect obedience" to "Him." The destructive emotional tether that binds a woman to the abuser in her life may be both validated and replicated in her way of imaging and relating to the Divine. God, like her abuser, is punitive and distant.[9] In this way, patriarchal Christian imagery can solidify the emotional bondage of the victim-survivor.

Desperate to break out of a sense of being in exile from God, victim-survivors may be drawn toward the widely emphasized Christian doctrine of forgiveness. They may understand forgiveness from God as a means of regaining an essential connection with spiritual and emotional support networks. If a woman has sinned against God by somehow failing to please "Him" and thereby merits the abuse, the relationship with God can only be restored through her repentance. As this reasoning indicates, reconnection with God is achieved at the price of pushing the wrongness of the violence from view as well as muting the trauma it has caused her.

Biblical and church teachings that reinforce submission to men as proper authority figures in the home can also support the idea that God sanctions the abuse of women. The husband/father is designated the head of the household in Christian biblical tradition and often heralded as such in churches. Abusers, as well as those who counsel victim-survivors, such as clergy, sometimes assert that this gives a man the right to punish his wife and children.[10] If wives are directed by the "Holy Word of God" to submit to their husbands, then a woman confronted by an abusive spouse naturally may deduce that God is unconcerned with or even condones the suffering she endures at the hands of her husband. The needs of the woman are suppressed by the message that God is concerned with the maintenance of authority and order. The significance of her distress disappears beneath the apparent collusion between God and her husband or father in maintaining her subjugation.

This pattern of torment for victim-survivors may be further reinforced by other racial and gender cues women receive. Eve, "the first woman," is reported in Christian tradition to have initiated the moral downfall of humanity because she committed the sin of disobeying "the Father." Based upon the same logic, contemporary girls and women are too often socialized to champion obedience as a primary index of good behavior. From early childhood through elderly citizenship, they receive compliments, affirmation, and reward for being a "good girl," which usually means conforming and complying with rules and authority. The opposite behavior is punished. For instance, bell hooks discusses the silencing intent of the punishments she received as a child for "talking back." She comments: "Had I been a boy, they might have encouraged me to speak believing that I might someday be called to preach. There was no 'calling' for talking girls, no legitimized rewarded speech. . . . [The punishments] were intended to suppress all possibility that I would create my own speech."[11] In this instance, communal and church traditions rationalize the taboo against female children "talking back." There are multifaceted criteria for what constitutes sufficient social compliance by girls and women, depending on the context. It is as if there is a judge of female goodness and niceness whose approval has to be won even though this judge inhabits infinite faces and venues. The nature of this coerced, boundless task of being a "good girl" abets the hostile environment created by intimate violence.

Certain racial cues can offer yet another layer in this woman-tormenting syndrome of invalidating self-expression. One aspect of racial/ethnic minority group membership includes some ongoing consciousness of a woman's marginalized racial status. Accommodation to some illusive standard of comportment that will not be penalized "in front of whites" is necessary. Especially for African-Americans, this is a daily reality for those who strive to "succeed," whether they are trying to purchase an item at a store without being followed by security personnel or hoping to gain a promotion at their workplace. To exhibit "proper Negro" behavior, a woman may continuously struggle to avoid conduct that could be considered that of the culturally "known" and scorned black. One must try not to resemble blacks who are "known" to be untidy, morally out of control, or act uppity—that is, those who challenge the authority of their betters (read whites).[12] Winning approval and acceptance from an omnipresent white critic requires concentrated, endless forethought about how to behave and appear inoffensive.

These patriarchal Christian beliefs and repressive gender and racial messages can work together against women. The unrelenting state of imbalance that they generate and the persistent lessons they teach about appropriately compliant behavior can contribute powerfully to a woman's anguish. These elements often reiterate and correspond to the type of orchestrated devaluation she reacts to or remembers from her male abuser. Especially through their insidious demands for her obedience, these religious and social prescriptions conspire to push a victim-survivor toward perpetual self-denial and abasement.

SELF-ERASURE

The suppression of selfhood is one of the most profound and complex areas in women's struggle for visibility. In response to intimate violence, women usually learn a range of methods for dissociating from the immediate incident of abuse as well as from memories of the experience. When the abuse occurs women may alter their consciousness as a form of escape, by closing down some part of their psychic selves. In the aftermath of violence, they often try to claim some part of themselves in order to survive and function with a degree of "normalcy," while rejecting other parts of themselves as related to a tainted and distorted reality. For the victim-survivor, intimate violence can establish a lifelong pattern of dutifully polarizing and silencing many of her emotional responses.

Women need to find a way to retreat emotionally and spiritually both during the actual ordeal of the assault and in its aftermath, during their subsequent attempt to cope with the damage to the self left in its wake. Victim-survivors often practice what Carey described as her ability to "numb out" when she was being sexually abused as a young child. Sometimes women may take the ultimate self-destructive step of attempting suicide, as Denise did when she sought release from the brutal emotional process of recalling repeated sexual assaults by her father.

Poet and novelist Sapphire recounts a faint memory of having the sense of leaving her body while being sexually abused as a child. She wrote these memories down in her personal journal.

> . . . and my pelvis cracks in half when his thing goes in my body. I can't breathe. I hear Daddy say, "Your mama says it's alright. Be a good girl now." My head rolls to the side and falls off into the black. My eyes close and I float up to the ceiling and from far away I see a child's bones come loose and float away in a river of blood as a big man plunges into a little girl.[13]

Sapphire's experience is a common form of body/mind splitting for sexual assault victim-survivors. Similarly, Lenore Walker reports that many battered women engage in a mild form of self-hypnosis to avoid the intensity of the pain during an attack.[14]

Acquiescent behavior, already mentioned in relation to spiritual disconnection, also exemplifies a tactic victim-survivors resort to in their suppression of the self in order to maintain their own safety.[15] In a written personal account of wife battering, one black woman, "T.," states: "I was beaten when I was pregnant; I was beaten when I wasn't pregnant. I was beaten when he was high or on drugs, and I was beaten when he wasn't. I was beaten because I didn't breathe the way he thought I should."[16] She describes one incident in which she was on her way to a church Bible study class and remembered that her husband may not have his house key. He might not be able to enter the house when he came back from work as she would not be there to let him in. She returned home immediately because she was "trying to avoid a confrontation." Unfortunately, he was already at the house and angry about her absence. Approaching her as soon as she arrived, he smashed her head with his hammer from his tool belt. In this situation, she clearly did not rush home because she believed it her wifely duty to ensure that her man was never inconvenienced. She sought to accommodate his needs because she was trying to avoid a violent "confrontation."

Women regularly develop the survival strategy of trying to predict what will appease the abuser and then act accordingly. A victim-survivor effects a pretense in order to survive. But she does so at the expense of cultivating her "true self," which remains hidden and protected. The act is costly not only because of the loss of an integrated self, but also because the woman can significantly curtail her freedom of self-assertion in so doing. Moreover, the connection to others who care and can give support may be blocked by this process.

Women have often been mislabeled as psychotic because they try to please the men who abuse them. Walker argues emphatically that, on the contrary, women's appearance of compliance and willingness to please the abuser are quite normal responses to the abnormal and dangerous situations they face. Walker's approach to the subject of women's compliance helps us understand the strategy underlying it. She suggests that compliant sex-role socialization may set up a dual dynamic between the goals of women and the means they employ. Walker and her colleague Angela Browne write, "little girls are typically taught to reach their goals by attempting to win the approval of others, adapting [to the] dominant behavior and suppressing angry reactions in favor of peace-keeping maneuvers and friendly persuasion."[17] Note that Walker does not prescribe anger as a more appropriate response for women in battering situations. Displays of anger are dangerous because perpetrators often use them to justify further violence. However, she points out how women generally learn to subvert their naturally self-assertive reactions. This sex-role socialization often meshes with the effects of intimate violence, and prompts women to be submissive.[18]

The dynamics of white supremacy in our culture can effect a similar dualistic strategy of response for blacks. As I have noted, the perception and reality of a white gaze that relentlessly judges can maintain an expectation of accommodation to proper ("white") comportment. Yet the assumption in this gaze that certain behaviors are evidence of innate black inferiority can induce a type of split consciousness. One part of the self is forced to react to white expectations because they occupy a culturally dominant power position. Simultaneously, it is a necessary and healthy survival mechanism to psychologically distance oneself from the pervasive white gaze. This protects some part of one's consciousness as an authentic "me." Protecting the self from hostile encroachment is an essential response to the permanent crisis of racism. For black women this kind of splitting behavior is analogous to and interacts with the dynamics of male physical and sexual assault described above. In both instances, such behavior subverts the growth and development of an "authentic self."

There are many other important correlations between intimate violence and a woman's social identity. For instance, in a somewhat different pattern, assumptions about heterosexuality as a universal norm for human behavior can perpetually deny value and visibility to the lesbian identity of some victim-survivors. Lesbians may find themselves continuously debating whether they should try "to pass" as heterosexuals, or risk open condemnation by the community.[19] To be "found out" and then "known" as a pervert or queer can represent a consuming fear. The ostracism based on her sexual identity or even the fear of such treatment may further intensify the breach with community wrought by intimate violence. A black woman can come under tremendous pressure to try to hide her "unacceptable" lesbian self in order to "get along" and be included. This pressure may neatly dovetail with the self-suppression in her response to her rapist or childhood sexual abuser. That is, the pressure to make a stigmatized (lesbian) part of herself disappear can work in tandem with the need to hide a disassociated "violated self" in the wake of male assault.

Finally, intimate assault produces a deep spiritual struggle alongside the emotional pain. Victim-survivors often experience intimate violence as life-threatening. Recall how Carey discussed the need for a strategy to stay with her batterer until she was able to secure another place to live "without getting killed first." The continuous awareness that death may be imminent is a fundamental spiritual crisis.[20] This spiritual crisis does not require faith in a divine supreme being. The knowledge of a mortal threat profoundly undermines the vigor and vitality which nurtures our sense of human becoming. When ties to this enigmatic internal life force that forges meaning and connection are imperiled, the hope and possibility that generate energy within the psychic self are radically attenuated. The terror that Denise described as driving her toward a suicide attempt was tantamount to spiritual annihilation. For her, the spiritual presence of her grandmothers opposed that annihilating terror. One of the most important facets of the ordeal for women victim-survivors of intimate violence, then, can be fending off ongoing spiritual destruction.

Whether through the drastic measure of attempting suicide or by slipping into a state of numbness, women learn to silence themselves. Even if understood as engagement of a healthy coping mechanism like dissociation, this silencing process constitutes a desperate response to unbearable pain and isolation. The psychospiritual consequences of assault can push women toward a disintegration and erasure of self. This potent method of psychic dismemberment can facilitate and augment women's subordination in both the private and public realms of their lives.

While male violence can provide effective, concrete lessons for women on how to mute the self, it does not perform this mission unaided. Certain Christian religious injunctions and practices overtly recommend self-censoring obedience for women which, of course, can further deepen their state of isolation. The conciliatory techniques women utilize to negotiate their devalued racial and gender status contribute to their endurance of the threats of annihilation that accompany male physical and sexual violence against them. Hence, constant subversion of self can become a normalized and necessary condition for survival. Working together, intimate and cultural assaults produce a barrage of negating and obliterating cues for the consciousness of African-American women.

Women can sometimes be completely overwhelmed by this barrage. As Denise said:

> It feels the same. Being called nigger, being called nigger b-tch in the street and having to deal with a racist white professor at college. I feel powerless. It feels the same as having my father do what he did to me. . . . There is nothing that I can do.

Shame

Shame is often a crucial ingredient in women's response to intimate violence. Margaret Gordon and Stephanie Riger found that among the worst fears women have about rape is the humiliation and stigma they expect to suffer afterward. Some of their respondents told them they would rather die than be raped and live.[21] As a response to intimate violence, shame has an especially poisonous effect.

Further analysis of intimate and societal violence enables us to understand how shame has such a profoundly invasive capacity to subsume portions of a woman's identity. While guilt is directed toward an action and can be assuaged through penalty or reparation, shame is invariably directed inward. Shame is precipitated and initiated by acts, but it can seep into our consciousness and become rooted in who we are. Thus it functions as more than simply a response to acts that we have done or endured, in the way that guilt does. Because shame has a psychic identity, it can readily merge with the social stigmas based on race and gender that are usually already at work on black women's psyches.

SHAME AND WOMEN'S SELF-IMAGE

Since a fundamental dynamic of intimate violence is the unwanted violation of the body, tactile sensations of the body significantly characterize part of women's response to, and recollection of, the episode. Shame is often connected to this kind of physical reaction to intimate assault. Recall Aisha's words about the immediate aftermath of being raped:

> And so, I just felt—I don't know how I felt. I felt so dirty because there was no way to cleanse my body. . . . [Afterwards,] he drove back to pick them up. And I thought, you know, I just felt sure that I was smelly, you know, and I could feel the semen oozing out of my vagina onto my clothes, and I couldn't do anything about it. So, I just felt so dirty! The only place that we went after that was to some little joint . . . but I didn't drink. So I just sat there feeling humiliated.[22]

After being raped, Aisha felt an urgent need to cleanse her body. Her torment was prolonged because she was not able to immediately escape the company of her attacker. Following the assault, when she had been driven by her rapist to a social outing at a bar, there was no acknowledgment of the crime that had just been committed against her. The rapist was physically present beside her. Remnants of the rape were also physically present on her body. The visceral sense of being dirtied was directly linked to Aisha's emotional sense of humiliation.

In her feminist ethical work on sexual violence, Mary Pellauer highlights the issues of shame and humiliation as crucial dimensions of the experience of assault.[23] To Pellauer, the fact that so many women feel dirty after being sexually assaulted presents an intricate set of issues that need to be disaggregated. She points to the victim-survivor's desire to wash herself as a positive expression of the need to reorder her environment. The woman wants to restore her world after it has been scrambled and fouled by violence. Pellauer observes that the "by-products of male-ejaculation left on oneself after a violent encounter are truly 'out of place' because the survivor did not consent to them."[24] The urge to cleanse oneself is a healthy recognition of the violation that has taken place.

The feeling of being dirty often incorporates major portions of a victim-survivor's self-concept. Women may view themselves as soiled, ruined, or evil. They may feel self-hatred and disgust about their own bodies as a result of sexual assault.[25] Violence that dirties the body too easily transforms the victim-survivor into an embodiment of dirtiness. The locus of the problem is transported from the act that was committed against the woman, to the victim-survivor herself. As a result, infiltrating her consciousness, and guiding and determining many of her self-perceptions, are the treacherous tentacles of shame.

The gendered nature of this destructive dynamic emerges when the shame evoked by sexual violence fuses with cultural notions about women as dirty or as temptresses. The guises that these subjugating labels can assume are varied and numerous. Women are disparaged as intrinsically dirty during menstruation, and at other times as well because of it. Vaginas are presumed to have a foul odor that constantly needs to be "freshened" and perfumed. Moreover, women are thought to have tricky and mysterious powers related to their sexuality that beguile men. When the notion that sex is a dirty secret act conflates with the objectification of women as incarnate sexuality, women are reduced to sex objects that invite dirty acts. Such deeply embedded cultural myths about women can nurture shame and self-blame in situations of intimate violence.

Pellauer points to the need to distinguish between the patriarchal "notion that women are dirty from the one that is implicit in the experience of rape survivor, that the *violence* is dirty."[26] This is an extremely delicate separation to attempt. On the one hand, identifying the violence as dirty, as Pellauer suggests, encourages affirmation and validation of the woman's interpretation of her ordeal. Her understanding of women as physically fouled by violence, as evidenced by the material by-products of sexual assault left on their bodies, seems to make this label of dirtiness manifestly appropriate. When a woman who has been raped says, "I feel dirty," her statement can be viewed as an acknowledgment of both her physical condition and a recognition of her violation.

On the other hand, the concept of dirtiness that women choose to attach to the rape experience comes prepackaged with derogatory cultural meaning. Because of sources ranging from ancient biblical injunctions about menstruation to contemporary commercial advertisements for "everyday" sanitary pads, women's vaginas are associated with uncleanness. The unpleasant, unwanted presence of the rapist's semen on a woman's body may seem to be one more instance wherein a woman is guilty of not keeping her vagina "clean." Women's open expression of sexuality is already sullied by its common linkage to immodest or whorish behavior in popular cultural definitions of femininity. Especially when she is raped by an acquaintance, a "date," or a spouse, a woman can easily equate any sexual interest or attraction she may have felt prior to the incident with the behavior of "scummy" bad girls.

Note that this connection between the aftereffects of rape and "ordinary" interpretations of women's sexuality is probably inevitable. Rape is a sexual form of violence that often does have destructive effects on a victim-survivor's sexual expression. Therefore, a woman may be unavoidably influenced by the interlocked cultural imagery of women-dirtiness-sex when perceiving herself to be soiled by violence. Gendered imagery thoroughly infuses the perception of sexual violence as dirty. The analytic strategy of separating the idea that women are dirty from the notion that sexual violence is dirty may oversimplify the problem women confront, and remain a futile gesture without the intervention of radical social change in our society.

Associating dirtiness with the violence rather than with the women may fail to remove the stigma from black victim-survivors for other reasons as well. Intertwined with the gender assumptions is racial cultural imagery that equates blackness with dirtiness, and can inform the layered social messages to women. The link with blackness supports the assumption of the women's innate racial inferiority. Blackness is commonly considered the opposite of that which is pure, clean, and innocent. When this symbolic meaning of blackness is wedded with the stereotype of black people as unkempt, unwashed, and comfortable in a squalid environment, a disparaging racial link to dirtiness is unmistakable.

The racial association with dirtiness carries still other indicting characteristics. Blackness can be a metaphorical reference to evil, ugly, and sinister qualities. These features are assumed to be present when referring to the dark or black side of a person or situation. Thus through her skin color (or racial identification), the victim-survivor of sexual assault already personifies a host of stigmas that are also commonly attributed to the violent deed done to her. Because of cultural messages about her racial (and gender) identity she can share the label of dirtiness with the act of rape. This implication may seem to make her shamefully complicit with the violence committed against her.

To be raped is to be denigrated. Denigration is a form of humiliation defined as blackening someone. The symbolic and literal meanings in our language as well as cultural stereotypes inextricably bind shame with blackness. In a culturally constructed configuration that clings to the black woman victim-survivor of sexual violence, the notion of dirtiness easily translates into a reference to blackness, and the meaning of blackness is enjoined to shamefulness. As the semen of her rapist oozes out onto Aisha's leg and she feels "smelly," "dirty," and "humiliated," there are multiple layers of reinforcing social messages supporting that labeling process.

SHAME AND SELF-BLAME

In cyclical fashion, shame generates self-blame and self-blame perpetuates the shame of the victim-survivor. Intimate violence can involve a host of complicated circumstances that may cause women to feel confused and to blame themselves. Women who were sexually abused as children may have been treated with a mixture of affection and violence by their abusers. Sometimes the only kind of "loving" attention and approval that the child received from a significant male family member occurred in the context of a sexually abusive relationship. And for women who are raped in the context of a long-term relationship with a batterer, affection often alternates with violence. The mixture of opposing affective states during the assault(s) or within an ongoing relationship with an abuser can cause the victim-survivor to feel confused. She may decide that if she feels something other than anger and disgust toward him, she is somehow partly responsible for the assault.

Psychologically, the abuse can include accusations of complicity by the abuser which may then produce self-blame in the survivor. Especially in the context of long-term relationships or during repeated assaults, psychological manipulation can be a crucial ingredient in the coercion. Batterers and perpetrators of child sexual assault often specialize in psychological torment that includes purposefully "demonstrating" to a victim-survivor that she is either a willing partner in the abuse or that she somehow caused and invited it. Here, self-blame is brought on by the methods of the attacker.

Victim-survivors of sexual violence often wonder why the perpetrator chose to assault them rather than someone else. A woman may decide that something about who she is caused her to be selected. There are particular heterosexualized gender stereotypes that can reinforce this idea and all the other forms of self-blame which preoccupy victim-survivors. Women are labeled "bad girls," *read*, "girls who ask for it" because of their clothing, their consumption of alcohol, their sexual activity, their assertiveness with men in romantic situations, their lack of assertiveness with men, and so forth. Starting from their childhood, the very fact of "being" girls and women is seen by some as exuding sexual signals that invite exploitation by men. In the context of intimate relationships with men, any request or act of self-assertion by a woman might be culturally construed as "henpecking," "bitching," and especially for black women involved with black men, "emasculation." From such characterizations of women, it can be posited that they "naturally" goad men into justifiably violent responses or retaliation.

Similarly, racialized self-blame assures women that their inherent inferiority legitimates their racial subjugation. White domination, expressed in terms of cultural marginalization and economic disenfranchisement, convinces blacks of their parasitic role in society.[27] Whites, not blacks or other peoples of color, are the agents and subjects of history. If one is convinced that in relation to the rest of the world one has not made any valuable contribution, but exists mainly as a burdensome dependent, domination seems rational. As one accepts these prevailing determinants of status and worth as just, the inevitable failure and concomitant sense of shame appear to be deserved. The presumption of black inferiority provides the rational basis for blacks to blame themselves for any social barriers that they encounter and cannot surmount. It validates the cultural inadequacy that they experience. Under the existing conditions of white domination, wherein whites are the standard by which blacks are measured, blacks are perpetually "guilty of not being white." This can make inferior status and self-blame inescapable for them.

Black women victim-survivors are sometimes held innately responsible for their racial subjugation in a fashion that mirrors and complements the self-blame induced by their experience of male violence. For example, the racialized self-blame just described can hold a poor mother accountable for the lack of quality in the health care and schools in her black neighborhood, which have frustrated the lives of her children. Such problems can be viewed as justly earned because they reflect the laziness and deficient capacities of blacks like herself. Just as the very way she breathes makes her deserving of a beating, according to her batterer, a woman's racial identity can make her deserving of any social disadvantages that harm her and her family. The beating is an articulation of her batterer's dominance, just as the unequal treatment of blacks is an expression of white subjugation. Yet for the victim-survivor of intimate violence, what identifies her as guilty, that is, what can cause her to feel shame, is the very fact that she is beaten. In the same way, the unequal treatment and status of blacks can identify them as perpetually guilty and help them to believe that they are. Said differently, the unequal treatment of blacks can become a convincing indicator of black inferiority that makes them feel ashamed, just as being beaten can make a woman shamefully decide that there is clearly something wrong with her because she continues to receive such treatment. These self-blaming phenomena can relentlessly echo off of each other, helping to deepen a woman's anguish.

Similar dynamics can be reproduced in relation to issues of sexual identity. When the meaning of a black lesbian's identity is read through the cultural norms of compulsory heterosexuality, she is perpetually condemned for being guilty of having chosen "deviance."[28] When viewed as having voluntarily made this "wrong" choice, she may be considered to be deserving of any suffering that results from the social and political repression she faces. Or at best she is seen as having "asked for it."

Epitomizing such blaming attitudes are Christian leaders who have responded to the tragic human loss and suffering AIDS has cost gay members of our communities with particularly ruthless messages that say, "You reap what you sow." This may more often be directed at gay males than lesbians. But unfortunately the AIDS crisis has led to a resurgence of public diatribes insisting that homosexuality is a dreadful sin, and to choose it is to invite trouble (even death!). The lesbian identity of some victim-survivors is viewed as inherently blameworthy because they have supposedly selected a shameful lifestyle. This designation can easily collude with the self-blame that follows from the intimate violence that has occurred in their lives. Based on their experience of violence and on their sexual identity, the women may receive tautological, tormenting cultural messages. "Bad things like male assault happen to you because there is something wrong with what you did or said to the perpetrator; there is something wrong with who you are as a lesbian, so bad things happen to you in your life."

Self-blame is often wrapped in a discrediting, slippery package called "the authentic victim." Based on some ideal of what constitutes an "authentic" rape experience, women often grapple with a sense of personal failure or self-doubt which can fuel their sense of shame. This kind of self-doubt is especially stoked by references to victim-survivors as "girls who asked for it." Also, women may believe that they should have fought harder or longer against their attacker. Children rarely fight their attackers as they are most often abused by those they already trust.

This absence of an aggressive self-defense can have a lasting, troubling effect on adults who have experienced childhood sexual abuse. The lack of brutality or sadism employed by a perpetrator during an assault may also produce self-blame. Aisha attested to this problem when she indicated that her rape experience was confusing for her because her rapist was more gentle when he entered her vagina than her boyfriend. Ironically, in circumstances of battering, women can dismiss their own victimization because they fought their abuser *too much*. Sarah, a black woman who suffered for several years in an abusive marriage, commented: "Because I fought back, I thought I was not a battered woman, just a woman having marital relations problems."[29]

In almost every instance, self-blame centers around a woman's doubt of her own experience of violence. Women know that indeed they are victim-survivors of violence, yet simultaneously they can doubt the credibility of that knowledge. The doubt is fueled by a mythical image of what an "authentic" victim "should" be. There are certain emotional reactions that she "should" have had, and particular actions that she "should" have taken during an incident of violence. Failure to fulfill the expectations within this mythical scenario means that she shares responsibility for the ordeal. Consequently *she* is shameful. The social attitudes about henpecking, emasculating, and sexually teasing women hold women responsible for intimate violence and excuse and justify the men who commit these crimes. These attitudes create and sustain the mythical scenario that women often struggle against. Sarah explains: "I came to realize that I stayed mostly because I didn't want to fail. I was already branded as 'mean' by my mother and my aunt. They told me often that it was my fault that I couldn't hold my marriage together, so I couldn't leave."[30]

SHAME AND CHRISTIAN FAITH

Androcentric Christian traditions that are restrictive, punitive, and admonishing of women regarding their sexuality can accentuate the feeling of shame and self-blame, particularly for victim-survivors of sexual violence who depend upon their Christian faith as an important resource in moments of crisis. Well-known traditions about women biblical characters such as Eve, Delilah, or Jezebel depict women as temptresses and ascribe innate seductive powers to them. These religious ideas set up an accusatory presumption about women that can also affix blame onto a woman who is sexually assaulted. Teachings that prohibit sex outside marriage and emphasize virginity and abstinence for unmarried women can cause some women to see their victimization as a sexual sin on their part.[31] Some churches enforce the idea of women's uncleanness by denying them ordination and/or access to the pulpit area in the sanctuary.

When biblical injunctions about menstruating women or Jesus's cleansing of the hemorrhaging woman are taught in churches, women, unworthiness, illness, and vagina-related "uncleanness" may all be placed in an interlocked relationship with one another. When these are left as a pile of equatable images, the message that women are somehow fundamentally tainted is communicated. All such teachings and practices can add authority to the shame-based alienation from God and faith community sometimes experienced by sexually violated women. Apart from the issue of sexuality, church teachings that advocate obedience from wives as a basis for achieving a happy stable family may compel women to assume responsibility for their own abuse in situations of spousal violence.

Aisha's story exemplifies a complex amalgam of these themes of shame, sexual sin, and violence. When she decided that God wanted her to forgive her rapist, Aisha focused on God's concern with sexual sinfulness. She was ashamed of having committed the sexual sin of adultery and was undoubtedly burdened by a sense of shame about her rape experience. Her feelings of shame together with her focus on God's disapproving concern with sexual sinfulness led Aisha to equate the actions of her rapist with her own act of adultery. Consensual sex and nonconsensual sex became interchangeable acts of sinfulness before the judging eyes of God. The interpretation of her situation through the lens of shame was perhaps key in allowing Aisha to equate being victimized by rape with her commission of adultery. Therefore, she may have sought God's absolution in order to be released from *shame.*

Christian teachings that emphasize "turning the other cheek" as a paramount virtue for believers may also influence women to view God's love and support as conditional upon their forgiveness of the perpetrator. Family, friends, and clergy often advise women that to "forgive and forget" is the only appropriate "Christian response."[32] She must forgive the abuser to be worthy of God's redeeming love, and to receive full acceptance among the faithful of the church. Jennifer Manlowe, who writes about the psychospiritual consequences of abuse for incest survivors, describes how they may seek their abusers' forgiveness. This occurs partly as a response to the guilt the perpetrator has imposed upon his victim:

> He disavows his own guilt and transfers it to the victim who is left with the feeling that it is *she* who must atone for *the offender's* behavior. His sin is now her sin. As children and even adults, many survivors turn to their

perpetrators for forgiveness. Redemption is something a survivor tries to secure by earning her abuser's love. . . . The perpetrator's shame and God's silence leave the child-victim with the sense that she is unredeemable.[33]

Whether she pursues forgiveness from God or from her abuser, the victim-survivor seeks to be cleansed of shame. She wants to restore her world and her sense of self that the shame has distorted.

The Christian doctrine of forgiveness can enforce an indiscriminate label of guilt and sin upon all the people of God. Each Christian seems to receive exactly the same requirement to forgive one another, regardless of the circumstances. The dividing lines between victim and violent perpetrator can be blurred or erased under this doctrine. Unable to extricate herself from a crime that is not hers, shame can fester and eat away at the woman's selfhood. Victim-survivors may be perpetually caught pleading in terms resembling the traditional revival hymn:

> "Have thine own way, Lord!
> Have thine own way!
> Search me and try me, Master, today!
> Whiter than snow, Lord wash me just now,
> As I in thy presence Humbly bow."

The multiedged shame that is generated in black women victim-survivors of intimate violence is a powerful covert weapon of domination. It can train women to locate deprecating social stigmas and culpability for the violence against them within their own identities. This process has a policing effect. Since the focus of the problem is gathered around the identity and actions of victim-survivors, male violence functions as an efficient tool of subjugation that teaches women to recognize their own lack of worth.

This training process constitutes a moral assault. The violations of black women collaboratively rob them of moral worth, literally demoralizing them.

Fused Racial and Gender Consequences and Women's Lives

Some of the consequences of violence in women's lives emanate from fused racial and gender expectations. Certain definitions of black womanhood can demand that a victim-survivor deny her self-interests so as to meet obligations deemed more important, usually to her racial group, family, or male abuser. Our understanding of some of the emotional and spiritual struggles that result will be enriched by the analysis of theorists and practitioners[34] who attend to these fused racial and gender patterns, together with more insights from women's own testimony.

TRYING TO ALWAYS BE THE STRONG BLACK WOMAN

For most black women, the concept of "the strong black woman" occupies the status of both enduring cultural myth and realistic depiction of relatives, friends, and some aspect of self. Sometimes victim-survivors sacrifice their legitimate needs for safety and well-being by internalizing this concept. They neglect the nurture and development of their selfhood in order to give priority to the protection and care of others. Sometimes the goal of perseverance for its own sake wholly overwhelms a healthy perspective on self-care. The cultural ideal of persevering regardless of the obstacles becomes a straitjacket that functionally mutes women's perceptions of their fundamental rights to personhood.

Dr. Anderson is a psychology professor and therapist who has practiced in public and private settings for over twenty years and specializes in black family issues. In my interview with her, she analyzed the cultural messages that often serve as a basis for women's attempts to be "strong" enough to endure abusive relationships. She explained:

> As black women, we are taught a couple of different messages. One is that we're meant to struggle. The other is that we're supposed to try to maintain control at all times, of all things. And that we can, and I mean this is really the fantasy—that we're supposed to parent the world. We are often parental children starting from a very young age. So, we want to fix it. We want to change it. We want to make the situation better.[35]

This psychosocialization which creates an obligation and duty to persevere against all obstacles, can help to entrap women in relationships with violent men. Aisha, who was handed adult responsibilities during childhood, illustrates Dr. Anderson's point about this tendency. At the age of six or seven Aisha was her mother's spokesperson rejecting the male suitors that her mother wanted to be rid of. And she asked neighbors for help when the family was desperately in need of food. From this early age, she was taught that it was her role to manage family troubles. A girl/woman's duty to bravely face struggles and crises often becomes a normalized understanding of black femalehood. As this expectation is supplemented by a sense of obligation to also solve problems and control their consequences, victim-survivors may be caught in a vicious trap. The anguish that ongoing intimate violence causes a woman may appear to be just one more struggle she is obliged to face.

The cumulative effect of the family demands in a woman's life can also lead her to set aside her own needs in the aftermath of male assault. As director of a sexual assault crisis center in Los Angeles founded specifically to work with black women, Monica Williams was quoted on her views about the racial diversity issues that have arisen in the anti-rape movement.[36] Based on her work with sexually assaulted black women, Williams commented as follows on their need to be perpetually "strong":

> I think our image has always been of being strong and persevering and you can take it all, and it doesn't make a difference, and I started to notice that most of the women who were assaulted, that it wasn't a priority for them, that they couldn't see that they were hurting too.... Usually their first concern was their children, or their home or their husband, or how'm I going to make ends meet.[37]

This notion of indefatigable strength can obstruct black women's acknowledgment of the ways that they have been emotionally hurt by male violence.

Basic issues of economic survival are also often entangled with black women's experience of intimate violence. Women may indeed recognize that they have been psychically damaged by an intimate assault. Yet they may decide that they must prioritize their needs. Their need for self-care in response to male physical or sexual assault may seem like a lesser concern when measured against other urgent problems. Williams noted that basic survival was frequently the most pressing problem of victim-survivors she worked with. Being beaten and/or raped was merely part of a larger list of problems her clients faced, leading them to say "by the way," not only do I have job, money, and food needs, but I was also assaulted.[38] Another rape victim-survivor described her frustration with her therapist, who seemingly failed to understand the primacy of her financial crisis:

> It seemed like all she was concerned about was the fact that I got raped. Hell! I know that was important, but that bastard got my last twenty-five dollars. That was all the money I had, till payday. I can deal with the rape later, but I won't have a job if I can't get back and forth to work.[39]

The crisis of violence that confronts victim-survivors such as this one is comprised of competing needs. In addition to the intimate violation, the injurious assault of socioeconomic deprivation also deserves recognition and demands redress. Perhaps part of the reason why the damaging effect of intimate violence is less important for these women is that the link between social and intimate violence is ignored by the responses they are given. Their testimony also illustrates the joint workings of social and intimate violence in perniciously reinforcing women's sense of obligation to struggle, to maintain their composure, and to persevere regardless of the cost.

In work related to this theme, Gail Wyatt presents data on black women's tendency to sacrifice their own needs for professional help in the aftermath of male assault, so that their families' financial needs can be met. In her study she examines the differences between the experiences of 126 African-American women and 122 white women in reporting and disclosing incidents of rape and attempted rape.[40] She found that African-American women reported incidents to extended family members more often than their white peers did. White women utilized friends and authority figures such as teachers, doctors, school counselors, or therapists significantly more often than African-American women.

The reasons why some had not disclosed the incident of abuse at the time it occurred also differed along racial lines. African-American women were slightly more likely than white women to cite fear of the consequences as their reason for not telling anyone when it occurred, while white women more often than black women reported fear of blame as the reason. Wyatt reasons that one explanation for this difference "apparent in the responses of the African American women" was their acute awareness "of the financial hardships their families would suffer if a stepfather or mother's boyfriend were to leave the house."[41] Again, lack of socioeconomic privilege and resources can work in conjunction with the trauma of intimate assault to silence black female victim-survivors. But also note that this process is cemented by the inculcation of a sense of hyperresponsibility for the stability of the household in the socialization of young black girls.

Victim-survivors who have been battered may also make their concern for family preeminent. These adult women may place the same emphasis on trying to act responsibly toward their adult extended family members as do black girls who are sexually abused. "T.," a victim-survivor of battering, explained that she did not tell her parents and brother about the abuse she endured because she needed to protect them. Her batterer threatened that if she told anyone about the abuse:

It would be my fault when they [her parents and brother] ended up dead and, unfortunately, I believed him because I knew what he was capable of. So out of a warped sense of responsibility (trying to protect those I loved) I took the abuse. . . . I also knew if they had any idea of the torment that I was going through they would have killed him and I would have that to live with. So being raised to fight my own battles and to be independent, I didn't seek help until I could no longer take it.[42]

Her torment was secondary to the protection of her family. Even when surrounded by potentially supportive relatives who might decidedly side with them against the abuser, women can be thoroughly convinced that "independence" and responsibility require that they singlehandedly take care of the situation.

Stifling spiritual dynamics can accompany this emotionally debilitating barrage of factors that women face. Reverend Frame is the director of a battered women's shelter that predominantly serves poor women of color (about 40 percent of whom are African-American).[43] In my interview with her, she explained that as a result of cumulative assaults on their selfhood some of the women she worked with have evolved to a point where their "spiritual person was not articulated, not developed." When Reverend Frame hears a woman ask, "Where is God?" an array of betrayals may have prompted that question. God, community, and intimate partner may all seem to have participated in betraying the woman's trust. Reverend Frame suggested that rejection by a violent spouse, and the stigma of receiving public assistance and lacking a formal education often combine over a long period of time "to anesthetize women's emotions." In the face of this onslaught, numbness represented by a "strong, tough" demeanor can become a permanent coping mechanism.

Sometimes religious faith can send a contradictory messages to women who face domestic violence. The church may be one of the few outlets that allows and affirms women's self-expression. At the same time, as already noted certain restrictive church practices and teachings about women in the Christian faith deny that right to freedom, and can be interpreted as directly endorsing male violence. In Kesho Yvonne Scott's *The Habit of Surviving*, Marilyn, one of the women whose life struggles she records, poignantly spoke to this contradiction. Caught in an abusive marriage, Marilyn said: "I turned to God." She became actively involved in her church and developed an exciting outreach ministry. She commented enthusiastically, "I felt that my church was calling black women to play an important role in the ministry. I felt we had a real heavy-duty part to play in international affairs."[44] The more successful and fulfilling her ministry became, the more the beatings by her husband escalated. She admitted that she felt "perplexed" about trying to live in accordance with biblical scriptures that exhort: "Whatever the man does, a woman should accept that. You are supposed to take it. Even when he is physically beating your -ss."[45] As this example illustrates, religion sometimes offers a peculiar form of spiritual torment, freeing and entrapping women simultaneously.

The Need to Maintain "Honorable" Families

The absence of fathers in black families also generates shame and self-blame in black women, and contributes to the impact of violence. Women may feel pressured to stay in a relationship with an abusive man because of the stigma of being a single black mother. Anna Carlson was an incest survivor and staff member at a battered women's shelter.[46] She described how a legacy of absent fathers had burdened her family with a multigenerational sense of shame. In Carlson's view, this legacy helped to perpetuate the intimate violence in her own childhood home. The parents of Carlson's mother were unmarried. Carlson's mother often expressed her anger about having had to grow up with "the dishonor of not having a father," because her mother had chosen not to marry. Apparently this grandmother of Carlson's had refused a marriage proposal from Carlson's grandfather. Influenced by her own childhood wounds of shame, Carlson's mother remained with Carlson's father who was a batterer and a sexual molester of their daughter (Anna). Carlson's mother wanted her children to have a father in order to be spared the "dishonor" that she had suffered during her childhood.

In her work at the battered women's shelter, Carlson heard her black women clients express hopes for family life that sounded familiar. She discovered that their concerns about having fathers in the home resembled the sentiments articulated by her own mother.

> [The women have] lots of feelings like . . . I don't want my children growing up without a father. And white women have the same issue, but they don't have it in the same way. It's not so urgent. I mean, I hear white women saying, "I don't want my children to grow up without their father." *Their* father. . . . For black women, it's: "I don't want my kids to grow up without *a* father." You know?[47]

While such statements could indicate grief or sadness about the possibility of their children missing out on having a father, they may also point to the dishonorable status of the black "female-headed house-hold."[48] Households headed by black single mothers are considered the opposite of a normal, healthy family environment, that is, a white, male-headed, two-parent, socioeconomically advantaged family.[49] The status, worth, and hence self-esteem of women is too often directly linked to having a male partner. As Dr. Denson, a clinical psychologist in a public hospital, commented, "[for black women], there's no pride in being able to say that you're a single parent especially if you had a mate and the marriage did not continue."[50] In addition, in the statements that Carlson observed in the shelter, the women may be assuming the responsibility for keeping a father in their children's lives. The woman may internalize the fact that the children are separated from their father as her failing or shame, rather than the fault of the batterer.

Black women also receive a variety of cultural messages in black communities about diminishing their expectations of family life. These messages excuse men who batter and encourage women to remain with them. Women's desperation is fueled by reminders about the shortage of men and the fact that there certainly are not enough "good ones" to go around. Dr. Anderson noted that friends and family members sometimes dismiss domestic violence for these reasons, offering victim-survivors retorts like: "You've got a man, you should be thankful and try to keep him," or "at least he's a good provider." She added that an especially unfortunate message sometimes passed down to girls is that "All black men are no good anyway, so what did you expect?" These messages may cause women to have minimal expectations of positive treatment. They generate more self-doubt in the struggle for self-esteem, especially with regard to a sense of entitlement. Most importantly, women who are in a desperate crisis—in a violent situation—are encouraged to feel even more hopeless. This dismal portrayal of social realities trivializes the intimate violence and accompanying emotional anguish that black women may endure, even making them seem inevitable in heterosexual relationships. The trauma of the victim-survivor may be deepened because she is confronted with the culturally constructed choice of either being a stigmatized single black mother (or single woman) or being grateful for an abusive man.

NEEDING TO GIVE PRIMACY TO THE
SUPPORT OF BLACK MEN

The vicious presence of racism in the lives of black male perpetrators emerges as another inhibitor to self-care by black women victim-survivors. Evelyn White is an author and advocate for black women's health care. She argues that black women's awareness of the systematic oppression of black men through lynchings, imprisonment, unemployment, and the ever prevalent "rape" charge causes women to feel obligated to be understanding and forgiving of black men.[51] There are cultural cues that foster the notion that because of the racist oppression suffered by black men, a sacrificial role is demanded of black women. "Betty," a victim-survivor of a clergy batterer, explained: "He felt that he was very oppressed as an African-American male. . . . It was really, really hard for him to get a job and to be able to keep that job. And that partially it was the fault of society. And if I was a strong woman I should hang in there and help him."[52] In this instance, the abuser unabashedly used the concept of his social oppression to reinforce his victimization of her. Under this twisted logic, strong womanhood is defined as "helping" your husband by staying with him and enduring his violent assaults.

Further verification of the key role that concern for the sociopolitical plight of black men plays in the emotional dilemmas of black women is offered by practitioners who work with victim-survivors. For instance, Dr. Anderson found the relentless racism in the lives of male perpetrators an unfortunate excuse for domestic violence that often needed to be countered in her treatment of women victim-survivors. Dr. Denson contended that in her work with victim-survivors of battering, many black women felt pressured by

> the idea that black men are angry. That they have good cause to be angry. Historically, because of the role that they were forced to play during slavery times, they weren't given the chance to really be responsible. The black [woman's] guilt is that if we as black women will not support them emotionally and stay with them, what does that say about our respect for our race. So there are people who do feel that the best thing is to remain in the relationship with the angry black male that is abusing her. The rationale is that it's not really me he's beating. He's frustrated. . . . It's not his fault.[53]

It is clear that racism plays a complicated role in the responses of black women to male assault. Women's bodily harm and anguish at the hands of angry males can be considered a justifiable symptom of racism. When a woman's injury and terror are measured in relation to a man's anger—purportedly the result of white racist treatment—she presumably matters less. Anna Carlson summarized this form of erasure with the comment: "One thing that is unfortunate for a lot of black women, like myself, [is that] it's hard to get validation of our experience [of abuse] because we always have to jump to protect the black man, which is not the black man's fault, or our own fault, but has to do with living in racist America."[54]

As for the women, terrific damage to their psyche and soul may occur as a result of these racial politics. Andrea Benton Rushing explains the fears that developed for her because she was raped by "a brother." Her account of being raped by a stranger offers emotional and political insight, as well as searing, vivid images. "My core is cracked when the rapist is a man my politics have taught me to call brother,"[55] Rushing explains. As a university professor she made a conscious effort to maintain her ties with the black working class she had come out of, and to resist the cultural loss and breach that could easily have developed. As she comments: "Now the class chasm has opened and I, of all people, feel muscles from my shoulders to my toes cramp in the presence of dark men whose body language, attire, or accent echo the rapist's. Ashamed of my fear, I hate the rapist for changing me."[56] The onslaught of racism combined with class prejudice against nonelites often draws *women* to seek the sustenance and protection of communal solidarity in black communities. For some, even those who have acquired access to the elevated class status that higher education offers, the need for this supportive link is not diminished. Rather, it may be heightened. As Rushing explains, women may undergo a complex mixture of loss, fear, and shame when intimately assaulted by someone they expect and desire to be a communal ally and "brother" to them. A woman's "core is cracked" as the personal and political framework that grounds her identity is violated.

RACIAL RESPONSIBILITY AND SHAME

Because of the pressure of trying to always be the strong woman and giving primacy to the support of black men, the mere admission of pain may seem shameful for victim-survivors. Rhonda Brinkley-Kennedy, psychologist and clinical director of a sexual assault center in south central Los Angeles, asserts: "We have women who are walking around, especially African-American women, with so much pain they don't even know they have because we have carried the weight of the world for so long that our attitude is 'get over it.' The women come in and they feel ashamed for feeling pain."[57] Under the terms of a subcultural norm that they are supposed to struggle and manage "the weight of the world," it is not just unfortunate that women are unable to "get over it" when they are raped. The pain that persists for black women can represent a shameful signal that they have failed to meet the standard expectations of black womanhood.

It is common for black victim-survivors of intimate assault to combine a sense of obligatory racial responsibility with self-censorship. In response to her battering male partner, shame may fuel a woman's racial guilt, which in turn supports the appropriateness of her repressing her needs. A distorting, subordinating blend of racial and gender assumptions may be embedded in her reactions. Shame can inhabit these complicated dynamics in the following manner. Black men are victimized by the racism of whites in their daily lives. They may experience anger and shame about their inability to prevent this onslaught. Black women observe both the assault of white racism and the powerlessness of their men. They feel protective and responsible for assuaging the debilitating impact of white supremacist social violence upon the men. Either before an episode of violence—perhaps during a period that Lenore Walker calls the tension-building stage in her cycle theory of violence—or after the violence has erupted when a woman may be trying to understand how she may have "caused it," she may see herself as reproducing the shame that the man has experienced due to white racism. Any violation of his patriarchal authority may seem to mimic the shameful violation that he endures from whites.

In short, it appears that she disrespects him just as "the white man" does, and thus provokes his anger. The violence against her is justified by her alleged participation in shaming him, that is, by denying him his "rightful" patriarchal authority as a man. The act of calling in "white authorities" for assistance can be seen as the consummate expression of betrayal of him, because this action confirms her collusion with white racism in the "emasculation" of black men.[58] Of course, this rationale is based on the androcentric definition of racism referred to above, wherein women are mere appendages to the black man's subjugation. Hence she has committed the supremely shameful act of betraying the whole race, because she is working with "the white man" to bring down the black man. In taking this self-protective step, she may risk or bear deep intragroup shame.

The combined onus of shame and racial responsibility can surface in other ways when women's victimization is exposed "in front of whites." For instance, Aisha had to confront her own sense of racial pride when she decided to go to the police after being beaten by her husband. Recall that the beating was so brutal that she had to have her children help her to get dressed to go to the station. She recounted: "I found some old shades and went to the white man, that's what was so humiliating. [I] went to the white man detective to tell him that my husband had beaten me up." Even when one has a woman-centered perspective on racism, shame can be evoked in relation to women's racial identity. A *woman's* sense of independence from whites or her self-esteem about the integrity of her black family can be injured. Reporting perpetrators to white authorities can invite racial stereotyping and exploitative judgments by whites. To expose oneself to that kind of treatment is humiliating.

In another instance, for a woman to describe incidents of childhood sexual victimization by a black perpetrator to a white audience is to risk being considered a shameful traitor to her racial group. Denise pointed out that if she were to speak to a white group about being sexually assaulted by her father it would probably reinforce stereotypes of black depravity that many whites already have. When she gave a presentation on a panel alongside white women sexual assault survivors, she found it necessary to edit her disclosure. She excluded the details of her own abuse in an attempt to circumvent the slightest tendency by members of her white audience to make pejorative racist assumptions about black sexuality. She did so out of a sense of responsibility to her racial group.

Similarly, she was afraid of compounding the stereotype that incest "causes" lesbianism. Myths that lesbianism is rooted in a psychological disorder and that all lesbians innately hate all men could be summoned by the image of a lesbian revealing childhood sexual abuse. In the process of deciding how to divulge the assaults by her father, she had to negotiate her role as an ambassador of blacks and of lesbians, in front of an ignorant and/or hostile audience. She battled against the stigma of shame that is attached to aspects of her identity by the dominant cultural ethos and against her own fears of confirming that stigma. Yet even while carrying out this valiant struggle for dignity, Denise was compelled to enter into the logic of her subjugation and edit her presentation. Unfortunately, even her most sophisticated efforts at tailoring her speech could not ensure that racist and homophobic assumptions by her audience would be averted.

Any act of speaking out about intimate violence involves the risk of generating racial shame. In her study about black women and incest, Melba Wilson writes about the political risks and taboo-breaking that are necessary for black women who disclose their experience of incest. Because she is an incest survivor herself, she struggles as an author with her own fears about reinforcing negative white stereotypes. Wilson reveals her process of self-scrutiny:

> Why tell, because it's just going to mean that we confirm their worst expectations of black people as sexual animals? Why tell and bring shame on to the family, the community? . . . I was afraid, too, that the physical pleasure which if I am honest, I have to admit was part of it, meant that if I looked too closely at myself and the incest, I would somehow find that the stereotype of loose sexual morality might after all apply to me. I know, of course, that it does not.[59]

Demeaning racial and gender ideologies work together in the creation and maintenance of the stereotype of the sexually promiscuous black woman who will "spread her legs" for anyone. Wilson demonstrates how this mythology can haunt the survivor, and become especially troubling for her when she has ambivalent feelings about the nature of the assault that include her own pleasurable sensations. She must struggle against internalizing this moral castigation.

Women who enjoy success in the "public domain" and whose family of origin is quite proud of that success, are also vulnerable to special fears about public shaming.[60] In her study of incarcerated battered black women, Beth Richie shares an interview with a woman who was "the prize child" of her family, and who held "a good job." The woman explained to Richie that the extended family "loved to come to my house and see how well I was doing."[61] For this victim-survivor, the worst aspect of the domestic violence involved the disgrace of revealing to her family that she was being battered. She admitted that when her parents found out about the battering: "I thought I was going to die from humiliation, not the abuse."[62]

Disappointing her family of origin who took pride in having a "happy and successful" African-American woman daughter or sister, places an especially heavy burden of shame on some women. The ever present gaze of whites and the constant struggle to ward off their devaluing perceptions of blacks lurks in the not-too-distant background of this sense of shameful failure. Consequently, these women are under pressure to keep the violence "private" in order to maintain their status as an example who disproves white assumptions of black inferiority.

These multivalent assaults on women mercilessly attack their sense of self. As Sarah writes,

> I did not think he was a god, but I was writing on the wall "Sarah is nothing. Sarah is nothing." I had no explanation for why I did that until now. I was in a war with no allies—no one to come to my defense.[63]

PART III

Deciphering the Role of Society

4

Theoretical Resources

Male violence and the accompanying terror and agony that women victim-survivors must cope with is neither an inexplicable nor an aberrant phenomenon. It is a problem that society has helped to create and sustain. In order to both adequately account for and develop a morally nuanced response to it, we need to use an analytical method that goes beyond the isolation of specific acts and focuses on the motivations of, and effects on, individual women. The task of sorting out the intricate ways our society invents and perpetuates the anguish of black women victim-survivors represents another key step in the process of recognizing the violence that besieges them.

It is therefore important to critically interrogate macrolevel, theoretical understandings of how male violence against women is socially instigated, sanctioned, and reinforced. In this chapter, several arguments about this process will be presented within a series of thematic groupings. Collectively they will enrich our insight about the social origins of male violence. Moreover, these conceptual approaches offer differing interpretations of the racial and gender dynamics that define the impact of male violence on black women. I examine these varying interpretations in order to identify those which are theoretically helpful for the development of our analysis. We need a nuanced, feminist, and antiracist understanding of how and why particular cultural norms reproduce the women's trauma.

Tracing Recent Theoretical History

Mediated Visibility in Violence against Women Literature

Accounting for the root causes of violence against women in our society is one of the most difficult tasks initially undertaken by "second wave" feminists. Unlike other women of color, black women have been included in some of the early theoretical literature on violence against women generated by the 1970s women's movement. Many writers sought to conceptually identify the existence and prevalence of systemic instigators of male violence. One of the earliest feminist approaches describes black women's victimization in the context of white male patriarchy. In her pioneering 1971 article, "Rape: The All-American Crime," Susan Griffin argues that rape is beneficial to the ruling class of white males. Griffin equates the rape of women with the rape of Viet Nam, the raping of black people, and the rape of the earth. "The white male ethos" consists of combined sexist and racist elements and creates fictive presuppositions which intensify the trauma of women of color. Griffin notes that "if white women are subjected to unnecessary and often hostile questioning after having been raped, third-world women are often not believed at all. . . . Third world women are defined from birth as impure. Thus, the white male is provided with a pool of women who are fair game".[1] As an example of this, she mentions Billie Holiday's mistreatment by legal authorities after she was raped. Hence white patriarchy generates conditions conducive to the sexual violation of "third-world women" as well as the state apparatus that legally legitimates those acts of violation. As a result, sexual assaults are rendered morally neutral, and black women's objections to this victimization are discounted.

What is a feminist framework for understanding the black male rape of black females? Is the problem still related to white male patriarchy? Lynn Curtis addresses this issue when she discusses "forcible rape" in her 1975 study, *Violence, Race, and Culture*. She focuses primarily upon male offenders. But she offers a perspective that avoids the silencing of what she terms "black-black patterns of rape." Curtis argues that the rape of black women by black men is a symbolic expression of the white male hierarchy.[2] In a later study of women rape victims, Joyce Williams and Karen Holmes articulate a similar notion about the reproduction of violence by black males against black women. They argue that "in raping minority women, minority males frequently are doing no more than imitating the White males."[3]

Feminist authors such as these see violence against women as the patriarchal terrorism of white male elites being waged either directly against black women or by proxy by black men. Black women are the victims of white male elites, and/or the victims of the victims of white male elites. Locating the genesis of violence against women within this hierarchy of oppression is a common formulation in early, second wave, women's movement literature. It provides a condensed evaluation of the plight of black women. It simply points to their pitiable position below multiple layers of subjugation. In this schema, the weight of the social hierarchy perpetuates and compounds the trauma of black women victims. The nature of their victimization and its attendant anguish are made visible only in relation to the primary reference point of the white male.

In Susan Brownmiller's landmark study of rape, *Against Our Will*, the voices and experiences of black women are given more detailed attention.[4] She documents the legacy of the sexual exploitation of black women in antebellum times by slave masters and in the postbellum period by the Ku Klux Klan.[5] Brownmiller also gathers the contemporary testimony of several black women from a range of socioeconomic backgrounds and ages. Their testimony demonstrates the racial/gender dilemmas that black women confront when treated despicably by the police. For instance, two of the women's stories illustrate the contrasting emotional consequences of sexual assault by a stranger. One reflects a woman's pride in fighting off an attacker and another gives evidence of a woman's resultant fears of all black men.

Brownmiller's racial analysis in this volume is deeply flawed. In her discussion of the Emmett Till case, Brownmiller equates the patriarchal power of the 1950s south, white male legal authorities, and lynch mob participants with black male teenagers who were the potential and actual victims of lynching. She collectively interprets their motives as "group-male antagonisms over access to women."[6] Similarly, in her discussion of the southern 1930s case of the Scottsboro boys, she compares the subjugated status of the white women accusers with that of the black men accused of assaulting them. Brownmiller describes both groups as "the movable pawns" of white men.[7] These preposterous claims are made with regard to two of the most celebrated and egregious examples of white supremacist assaults on black men carried out in the name of protecting white womanhood.[8]

The subtlety of Brownmiller's overall analysis in *Against Our Will* obviates any accusation that she envisions a simplistic social hierarchy, such as those espoused in other early theoretical discussions of the origins of sexual violence against women (e.g., Curtis 1975; Williams and Holmes 1981). However, in her discussion of the Till case she places black men and white men on par in the patriarchal hierarchy. And her examination of the Scottsboro case places white women and black men on the same rung of the social ladder. These formulations may serve a feminist theoretical agenda that concentrates on maintaining the understanding of white women as victims of white male patriarchy, but they belie the potent realities of white supremacy that also grant white women privileged social status over black men. This privileged status is particularly potent when black male sexual violation of white women is the contested issue. Brownmiller does lambaste the pernicious terrorizing of black men in the south. Yet she makes an equivocating bid for a sympathetic understanding of the vulnerability of white women. Perhaps unwittingly, she adds to the legacy of defending white womanhood at the cost of minimizing both the importance of white supremacist attacks on black males and of white female collusion in those attacks.

At one point in her book, Brownmiller extrapolates from her own feelings of vulnerability and rage at being whistled at by men on the street. She describes her gradual emancipation from smiling and accepting insults on the street from black men. Apparently she had been reacting in this way because of her own feelings of white guilt. The process of being liberated from this response to street harassment gives her a new sense of empowerment:

> And did not white women in particular have to bear the white man's burden of making amends for Southern racism? It took fifteen years for me to resolve these questions in my own mind, and to understand the insult implicit in Emmett Till's whistle, the depersonalized challenge of "I can have you" with or without racial respect. Today a sexual remark on the street causes within me a fleeting but murderous rage.[9]

Here Brownmiller describes her own negotiation of the burdens that white women must bear with regard to southern racism. This analysis presents a thoroughly individualized and acontextual interpretation of the social significance of sexual harassment. The argument entices the reader to view Susan Brownmiller's feelings when she walks down the street as ubiquitous and representative of all (white?) women. Within the logic of the narrative, the reader is compelled to understand that if it feels the same (to Susan Brownmiller) to be whistled at by a black man as it does by a white man, it *is* the same. Brownmiller has become liberated from the white woman's burden of having to recognize the legacy of white supremacist violence leveled at black men on behalf of white women. She can now ignore this reality that often clouds confrontations between white women and black men. She can feel free to express her legitimate rage at being whistled at by black men. She transports this "liberated" viewpoint back to 1950s Alabama, to boldly unearth the insulting nature of Till's behavior. Via Brownmiller's ubiquity, we are led to understand that the sociopolitical and individual significance attached to Brownmiller's plight when whistled at, applies to (white?) women anywhere, in any time period.

White-woman centered analysis about violence against women, like Brownmiller's discussion of Emmett Till, creates an ideological tradition that affects subsequent dialogue when the topics of feminism, rape, and race are broached. It inadvertently helps to set up conditions that invite the subversion of black women's experiences of male violence, even the ones highlighted in Brownmiller's book. Their testimony can now too easily be hidden behind the urgent task of battling racist white feminist disregard for the plight of black men.[10] To be associated with any feminist analysis of rape is to be tainted by the assumption that Emmett Till's whistle is an exercise in patriarchal privilege tantamount to any white man's. Equating the status of black and white males in this manner makes Emmett Till, in the words of Angela Davis, "almost as guilty as his white racist murderers."[11]

Brownmiller's theorizing has yet other implications for interpreting the specific experience of the women victim-survivors of sexual violence. Under this notion of patriarchy as equally upheld by and rewarding of black and white males, black and white *women* may be seen as wholly analogous victims of male violence. This notion allows their experiences to be viewed as different in form, but basically the same in substance. Thus, the white privilege of white women who are sexually assaulted, is absurdly deemed inconsequential. Even though Brownmiller helped to identify the historical legacy and contemporary incidence of violence against black women, she also contributed to the erasure of their experiences. She did so by promoting a theory of male dominance that discounts the salience of racial stratification.

Black Consciousness Literature and Shameful Black Women

How does the centering of internal black community dynamics in discussions of intimate violence shape the analytical recognition of black women's trauma? Black women's experiences of male violence have been included within studies that reflect the black consciousness movement and the burgeoning feminist movement of the 1960s and early 1970s. Sociologists Calvin Hernton, Robert Staples, and Joyce Ladner provide some of the first examples of scholarship representative of this period, attempting to focus on the sociocultural conditions affecting black women. These authors have widely differing approaches. Hernton concentrates on sexuality; Staples offers a comprehensive description of social conditions that are distinct in black women's lives; and Ladner restores a humanized and wholesome portrait of poor black femaleness. Like the white feminists considered above, they focus on sexual violence.

The concerns of the women who are victimized by violence do not fare well when sexual violence is analyzed as merely an aspect of the way sexuality can be politicized. For instance, Hernton is particularly concerned with untangling some of the interlocking dynamics of sexuality and race. In his volume *Sex and Racism in America*,[12] he examines "the sexualization of the race problem." In *Coming Together*,[13] Hernton analyzes the dynamics of black sexuality, emphasizing the distortions inflicted by white supremacy. He acknowledges the brutal atrocities of sexual assault by white men that black women have suffered historically. Due to this history, he theorizes that the personality of the "Negro woman" has been permanently distorted.

In a curious combination, Hernton condemns the sexual exploitation of black women, but then also assigns black women a pathological unconscious desire to be exploited. He postulates that despite the cruelty and humiliation involved, black women may be waiting and hoping for the sexual advances of white men.[14] He describes a similar unconscious need that black women have toward black men. He writes: "[M]aybe the women yearn to be raped, to be *made* by fierce black men, literally assaulted with a big black weapon, to within inches of their lives."[15] In the religious arena, Hernton declares that the sexual exploitation of women parishioners by black preachers is a rampant problem in the black church. Yet black women are depicted as willingly submitting to sexual exploitation (*consciously* seeking it), because they worship and love the black preacher. According to Hernton, women are sexually and financially generous, giving "not only their good loving but their hard-earned money, even the money that their husbands and boyfriends have slaved long hours to earn."[16] Hernton argues in a decidedly sexist fashion that derides women and nullifies consideration of them as the subjects of (clergy) exploitation. In instances of sexual assault, although he acknowledges the authenticity of women's victimization, he attributes to women a masochistic desire for it which effectively undermines their victim status.[17] This viewpoint presents the emotional life of women as significant, yet intrinsically distorted. It seems as if the paradigm of sexuality and race which frames these arguments dictates the portrayal of black women as entirely driven by desire, including the desire to be sexually assaulted and exploited.

Attributing a causal connection between the psychological distortions women supposedly exhibit and the violence committed against them may be part of a larger pattern in the diagnosis of gender issues in black life. Black female culpability in the alleged dysfunctionality of black communal and family life is a long-standing theme in sociological analysis as well as national politics (which will be discussed further in the next chapter). In *The Black Woman in America*, Staples inserts his views on the subject by providing a general report on the status and role of black women in America.[18] In this text, he seems sympathetic to the dual burden of racism and sexism confronting black women. Staples identifies sexual violence as a significant part of the black woman's reality, but he treats it as primarily a problem of lower class life that may sometimes be enjoyed. As illustrative of the supposed sexual culture of lower-class girls, he presents the following interview with a seventeen-year-old unwed mother.

Q: How old were you when you had your first experience?

A: I think 14 years.

Q: Were you satisfied?

A: I was pissed off.

Q: Describe it in detail.

A: He was about 22 years. It was at his house. I was just talking to him (visiting). He just decided he wanted to screw. And he kissed me which was O.K. but he forced himself on me.

Q: Did you enjoy it after he started?

A: I didn't enjoy it at all. It bothered me for sometime. I get scared of dudes sometimes. Plus when I was 10 years old my uncle tried to rape me.

Q: What about birth control?

A: I don't use birth control.[19]

The insensitivity of the interviewer in failing to offer any validation of the unwanted, undeserved nature of the violence she had endured, undoubtedly caused further anguish for this young woman. The experience of the sexual assaults evidently had long-term traumatic consequences for her. These are unacknowledged by the interviewer and ignored by Staples in his discussion of it in the book. This "objective" treatment in the overall study insidiously fosters indifference to the anguish of women and girls who have suffered violent assaults.

Staples finds the crime of rape troublesome to identify since "often a girl leads a man to believe that she will have sexual relations with him but protests when he reaches the point of penetration. Sometimes she wants to be taken in a violent way," while at other times it may be "forcible intercourse."[20] Although Staples finds it difficult to consistently identify it, he labels rape as primarily spawned by the conditions of lower-class life. Therefore, he does acknowledge sexual assaults by black men as constituting a troubling issue for some black women. In addition, he unambiguously stresses the gravity of the problem of sexual harassment and exploitation that many black women report about their encounters with white men. However, within black relationships sexual assault is considered an unfortunate problem complicated by various forms of blameworthy female behavior, particularly evidenced by the poor. He especially stigmatizes poor black females by the allegation that the victim sometimes invites the sexual violence committed against her.

Joyce Ladner offers a markedly different emphasis from Staples's view of black lower-class life. In her pioneering study, *Tomorrow's Tomorrow*, Ladner examines the race and gender consciousness of poor black girls.[21] Her study attempts to refute the negative portrayals in social science literature of poor black girls as merely pathetic pathology-ridden creatures. She stresses the coping and resisting behavior of girls who have been sexually assaulted. Ladner argues that rape is a socially generated problem over which the wider society must exert control.

> For example, an eight year-old girl has a good chance of being exposed to rape and violence . . . and neither parents nor community leaders have the power to eliminate this antisocial behavior. The community power base still lies outside its borders. In a similar manner, many children are forced to go hungry, without shoes and clothing and an adequate home to live in because of the powerlessness of their parents.[22]

Ladner wants to assure us that the problem of violence is not internal to the black community. Within this argument and throughout the rest of the book one finds an apologetic aimed at disputing racially based victim-blaming ideology.[23] To eliminate sexual violence within the black community one must understand how societal power is structured in relation to that community—how it is withheld from that community. The problem of assaults on black females by black males is simply part of the broader black community's struggle for empowerment and self-definition.

The negotiation of shame and stigma dominates these theoretical attempts to locate the blame for the problem of sexual violence against black women. Sometimes the authors appear to support claims about the shameful characteristics of black females, and at other times they seem to try to refute them. But in each instance they insufficiently unearth the distinctive truths of black women's experience of male violence. Hernton's dismissal of women's victimization, Staples's conditional acknowledgment of the sexual assault of some women, and Ladner's defensive analysis primarily geared toward racist stereotyped notions of the black community inadequately deduce how male violence against black women is socially produced and reproduced. Most distressingly, Hernton and Staples accept a rape myth that has profoundly traumatizing effects for victim-survivors, one that holds that rape is something women may (secretly) desire. When these racially based frameworks include male violence against women in their research, they fail, in differing degrees, to appreciate the gendered inequalities and devaluations that inform black women's experiences of male abuse. These accounts expound and contest depictions of black culture, yet they probe male violence (to the extent that they even acknowledge it) only within the parameters of their racially bounded exegesis.

Nonetheless, these discussions deepen our understanding of the construction of ideologies about black women. They elucidate how such construction is burdened by a lens of white domination that judges and measures the worth and value of black humanity. In addition, these authors collectively help us to recognize the need to consider independent black cultural dynamics. Such dynamics originate from a coalescence of subcultural and mass cultural influences that cannot be simplistically reduced to a mere imitation of whites, and that profoundly shape women's experience of violence.

Analyses that link poverty and intimate violence (such as Staples's) can also create the impression that rape and incest are "natural" occurrences in the lives of poor black women simply because they occur frequently. Such arguments can be read as relocating the responsibility for such acts from male aggressors onto an amorphous and impersonal factor called "poverty." In so doing, the difference in social power between poor black men and poor black women is ignored. Poverty is undoubtedly a wretched condition for both, but it does not confer gender equality. Moreover, this depiction trivializes the emotional and spiritual trauma that results from male assaults as an unfortunate and inevitable consequence of ghetto life. Ladner does note the devastating effects of male violence but rather than dwelling on those effects, she chooses to emphasize the resourcefulness and determination of girls to overcome such "obstacles."[24]

The cumulative impact of these approaches is somewhat analogous to the way Denise described being psychologically tormented by her sexually abusive father. She explained how "he would say, 'I love you' and then tell me how ugly I was or something like that. And he just kind of like played with me—as a human being." Methodologically, these theories explicitly affirm black community life, and black women in particular. It is as if the women are told "I love you," because they are embraced and recognized as crucial members of society. This is an assertion of "love" that undermines their marginal racial status. On the other hand, they are found blameworthy or minimally affected by the violence. That is, a woman who is seen as inviting the violence in the first place, or a violated girl who survived but could not primarily display an ability to overcome its consequences, is a blemish on the black community—is "ugly." Such arguments toy with women's humanity to the extent that they offer any compromise on a woman's moral right to have both the violent victimization and the full extent of the resultant trauma unconditionally recognized and opposed.

Combing Current Theoretical Resources

In addition to specifying the origins of male violence, we are also challenged to discern the social mechanisms that allow for its continual reproduction. We would no doubt be better prepared to interrupt its cycles if we were able to locate the routine factors upon which it depends for sustenance. Are the patterns that perpetuate the violence limited to conventional black heterosexual couple behavior? Are they fed by the general breakdown of orderly conduct in the family? Are they entrenched in a societal consensus defining women as objects that are always available for men to dominate? Or can other models provide more accurate answers pinpointing how and why violence against women persists?

I have created thematic groupings to both magnify the differences between some of the current theories about violence and more easily distill their particular insights into the social reproduction of violence against women. The clusters of theories are labeled social displacement, social disorder, cultural victimization, and cultural obstruction. These divisions are meant to convey analytically useful groupings of authors who share similar basic assumptions. They do not represent rigid categories nor do they preclude any overlap of ideas between them.

Analytical clues which focus on the violation and torment of black women, *without* shaming or diminishing their personhood, are of supreme moral importance. They supply evidence of the moral significance attributed to women's experiences within a diverse landscape of current strategies, and expose the struggle still needed to increase that attribution.

Nonfeminist Investigations of "Everyday" Structural Support for Intimate Violence

SOCIAL DISPLACEMENT

Determinations about a man's proper role in the family and what a man needs in order to assume that role can be key to judgments about why he would engage in improper violent behavior. Yet this set of concerns may allow us to lose sight of women's right to violence-free lives no matter what the social circumstances of their battering male partners. Social displacement theories of violence focus on domestic violence in black families by exploring the ways that black families, and black men in particular, are severed from healthy communal bonds. They name particular socioeconomic factors that cause black males to feel stressed and disconnected from society. Such factors may subsequently lie at the root of their violent behavior toward their female partners. These paradigms consider the inability of black men to enact traditional male roles in the family as a particularly salient instigator of violent behavior. This inability is directly related to the stress of economic displacement that many black males face.[25]

In the social displacement approach presented by sociologists Robert Hampton and Richard Gelles, the structural relationship of black family members to their community is seen as a core contributor to violence against black women.[26] Drawing upon a national study on domestic violence, Hampton and Gelles collected data on a representative sampling of black couples for the purpose of addressing the prevalence of spousal violence in black families.[27] Their study examines the incidence and risk factors for black spousal violence. Citing the dearth of literature on black women and spousal abuse, their investigation highlights the psychological distress black women experience as a result of abuse.

Hampton and Gelles identify factors such as unemployment and the short time span that a family may have spent in a community as structural barriers that have a significant relationship to family violence.[28] Unemployment is a structurally induced economic problem for black men. A family unit residing in a community for a brief time is culturally isolated from family and other supportive networks.[29] According to Hampton and Gelles, such structural and cultural problems lead to violent maladaptive behavior by males, which then causes severe psychological distress for their women victims. "Maladaptive behavior" or violence grows in "the place" where healthy communication patterns would develop were it not for certain circumstantial, impeding factors.

According to Hampton and Gelles, depression, stress, and somatic disorders are central aspects of women's trauma resulting from male abuse. In sum, at the root of domestic violence are culturally and structurally marginalizing conditions which help to generate certain violent behaviors in men and have brutal, agonizing consequences for women. The acknowledgment of women's trauma is quite helpful, yet its moral significance may be diminished by the main premise of the theory. The trauma is understood as a mere consequence of the primary issues of the men's social displacement or the family's displacement in an unfamiliar community. However, if the premise was changed so that the torment of women was shifted into the foreground, issues such as men's lack of employment might be seen as mere excuses.

In another approach that fits under the category of social displacement, criminologist William Oliver formulates a theory about domestic violence that emphasizes the connection between constricted black male role fulfillment and destructive intrapersonal black male-female dynamics.[30] Because black men are structurally inhibited from traditional role fulfillment they develop destructive cultural patterns. The displacing and dysfunctional structural and cultural mechanisms of society augment violence against women. In other words, intimate violence occurs as a result of racially based structural displacement and subsequent dysfunctional cultural adaptations to that displacement.[31] Oliver argues that specific definitions of black manhood, "the tough guy" and "the player of women," have evolved as alternative images for black males as a result of racially based structural barriers that inhibit their success through conventional avenues of society. Oliver advocates the adoption of an Afrocentric cultural ideology as a remedy to nurture more positive images for black males and foster healthier male-female relationships.

In Oliver's view, conflictual male-female dynamics fueled by the cultural displacement and alienation of males directly relate to the differential structural impediments that white racism creates for black males and females. Accordingly, the structural barriers of white racism and the institutionalized patterns of discrimination place black males at a greater disadvantage than black females for successfully fulfilling their respective "traditional roles."[32] Black males are displaced from their traditional roles since their high unemployment rate denies them the esteem by which males are valued in our society. However, black females fulfill traditional role expectations for women because they are able to have and care for their children. This configuration of structural barriers feeds and supports the "interpersonal conflict" between black men and women, which precipitates "male versus female" violence:

> In most incidents involving the male versus female dyad, black males will respond with violence toward females who they perceive as trying to control them, make them look bad in the eyes of others or manipulate them. Hence, when black males engage in violence against black females, it is because they have defined the situation as one in which the female's actions constitute a threat to their manhood . . . issues related to maintenance of the tough-guy image are predominate with respect to the intrapersonal decision to use violence.[33]

The particular behavior of black females, which is interpreted as a threat to black manhood, reenacts the devalued status that males encounter outside the domestic arena. According to Oliver, the male who initiates violence simultaneously assumes a defensive posture toward his mate and the rest of the world.

The troubling androcentric nature of Oliver's analysis reinforces the relevance of Denise's comments about black women and the black community. She said: "There's this dictum, I would say in the black community, that men come first, that black men come first, black men are the ones that are oppressed. . . . Everyone else is a kind of fodder for their tribulations. That's what it means to be a black woman. It's just like this kind of loss of a sense of self. You are just kind of cast away." Her testimony reminds us of the emotional and spiritual price that this kind of male-oriented framework can inflict upon women victim-survivors.

Moreover, in the comparison of male-female fulfillment of traditional roles proposed by Oliver, the social construction of those roles is presumed to be equatable. In fact, females are even posited as being more successful than males at social role fulfillment. This premise of social displacement theories (articulated most explicitly by Oliver) is, to say the least, highly contestable. For example, the value that society places on women's child-rearing labor is assumed to be on par with that placed on "men's work." Furthermore, the value of black women's production of children is assumed to be of equal worth and status as white women's production of children. Both assumptions are quite refutable and reveal the lack of attention in this theory to understanding how women's worth and value is socially constructed. Also, Oliver constructs male and female roles through an objectivist lens that involves an uncritical assimilation of what constitutes the "traditional male role." A thorough investigation of the social implications of measuring men's worth through their work is missing. Consequently, he presupposes that the fulfilled traditional male role does not significantly encourage violent behavior.

Together with Hampton and Gelles, Oliver interprets woman battering as a manifestation of the social displacement experienced by African-American men. In both approaches, barriers such as unemployment are proven to correlate with domestic violence against women. But does the existence of these barriers make black male responses to them inherently rational? Under the terms of this explanation, it might become acceptable to assert that sometimes men batter their female partners because they are unable to fulfill the male role of breadwinner of the family.

Whether based on environmental circumstances or other factors, one embarks on a dangerous slippery slope when one identifies "reasons" for the violent behavior of certain males that deny their individual moral agency. There are an infinite number of "reasons" that might make a man feel he "has to" batter his partner, but no discrete reason accounts for the widespread cultural phenomenon of male violence. These sociologists leave unanswered the question of what generates and feeds this particular culturally invented activity of men beating up on their female partners. Even if men are, seemingly, responding to stresses such as unemployment, why do they choose *this* mode? There are many, many alternatives a batterer could choose!

Finally, this rationale for violence in social displacement theories conjures up the myth that "certain men," for example black men, are most prone to committing intimate violent acts against women because of the structural displacement they encounter in society. Within the terms of this logic, intimate violence can be mistakenly understood as the exclusive problem of the economically and socially marginal. Are we to assume that employed white family patriarchs do not ever batter their female partners because they have no reason to do so?

SOCIAL DISORDER

If the right of black women to be liberated from victimization by violence is one's primary starting point and goal for analyzing societal patterns, social disorder theories may be as unsatisfying as social displacement approaches. Social disorder theories attribute the problem of violence against women to the general social breakdown of order in families and communities. In this paradigm, which revolves around the theme of social disorder, the erosion of institutional and informal communal support for the maintenance of social order increases the rate of all violence, including intimate violence. For those who subscribe to this type of analysis, normative proposals to alleviate problems such as intimate violence involve repairing some of the "broken" functions that disorder family and community life.

Richard Gelles and Murray Straus, social scientists who specialize in studying family violence, offer a social disorder theory about how the breakdown of social control helps to foster violence in the family unit. In *Intimate Violence*, Gelles and Straus discuss the findings from their 1985 Second National Family Violence Survey.[34] They designed their study to measure the alterations in the frequency of violence toward children and between adult partners since their First National Family Violence Survey in 1975.[35] *Intimate Violence* is also a qualitative assessment of the causes and consequences of family violence. For Gelles and Straus, violence against women is one feature of family violence that exists alongside others. They point out that violence against women and children, which is the focus of their study, occurs too frequently in families, "but the most common form of intimate violence is between siblings. The most difficult to treat may be the abuse of the elderly. The most overlooked may be the violence directed at parents by their adolescents."[36] Although their study of intimate violence analyzes its causes, and the impact upon women as well as the social responses to it, the issue of race is generally absent from their discussion. Although they collected data on race, differences in the experiences of women related to racial background are not investigated in their book.

In their version of the social disorder framework, it is the absence and breakdown of social controls which significantly contribute to family violence.[37] Social attitudes that reinforce the inequality of smaller versus bigger family members and public acceptance of the idea that the privacy of the family is sacrosanct, are presented as examples of the deterioration of social control. Apart from social attitudes, certain family structures can also erode essential mechanisms of social control. For instance, Gelles and Straus argue that features in the structuring of the family like high degrees of emotional intimacy and spatial contact between family members may be key contributors to the causes of violence. Higher degrees of social control are viewed as the necessary solution to the breakdown that can degenerate into violence. Yet how would one ensure that the interests of women are guarded and well served by increased social control over the family and community? Black woman-empowering values seem neither crucial nor explicit ingredients of whatever it is they assume has broken down within the family. Nor are such values deemed important in a healthy, wholesome family structure. *This* "absence" in their reasoning is quite worrisome.

Whereas Gelles and Straus focus on the family unit, Deborah Prothrow-Stith's analysis centers on the community as the primary determinative social unit. A medical doctor and public health researcher, Prothrow-Stith treats the problem of violence in the context of public health. She focuses on urban youth violence.[38] She gives particular attention to black urban youth and the influences that place them at especially high risk to be victims or perpetrators of violence. Life-threatening risks that face African-American girls are minimally considered. However, to help stem the catapulting wave of violence in urban communities, she suggests prevention strategies that mainly seek to change the attitudes of these youth about lifestyle options and that increase self-awareness in the family, and in the educational and community environment.

Violence in poor urban communities is fostered by conditions that can be addressed and improved. Prothrow-Stith explains that city resources tend to go to affluent neighborhoods. Services such as garbage collection, fire fighting, and emergency medical care are notoriously unreliable in very poor neighborhoods.[39] Unsatisfactory city services combine with a lack of civic and charitable organizations in socioeconomically poor communities and emotionally troubled families. This dual shortage foments conditions which perpetuate and worsen the problem of violence.

By implication, this theory brings to light the desperation and hopelessness for the poor black female victim-survivors of intimate violence that may be created by society's blatant neglect and abandonment of poor black communities. Addressing the problem of adolescent rape, Prothrow-Stith writes, "It would appear that some young men routinely push, shove, and slap young women into having sexual relations . . . young women desperately need to be informed about their choices so that they can exercise true rather than pro forma choice" about sexual relations.[40] In addition to educational programming that directly addresses the problem of sexual assault, Prothrow-Stith suggests that the overall problem of violence in the community be addressed by enriching and strengthening community services and resources.

In social disorder theories, male violence against women is collapsed within the broader framework of other types of violence in the family or community. This melding process distracts from the clarification of the issue of violence against women because it obscures recognition and analysis of the gendered aspects of social control or social breakdown. The particularity of women's anguish that results from male violence can be minimized or totally effaced from the spectrum of moral concern. At best, it is seen as an unfortunate by-product of a disordered family or community. Moreover, consideration of how violence against women may help sustain male social control of women and thus help maintain a patriarchal social order is inconsequential in the work of theorists like Gelles and Straus. For them, violence against women is merely one form of the breakdown of social control. We are led to believe that this breakdown signals the disintegration of some preexistent ethic of nonviolence toward women. But what if violence against women is a "normal" part of the social order sanctioned by the cultural value of male dominance? Fundamental sanctions for male violence emanating from male dominance and white supremacy will not be disrupted, as these theorists contend, when social controls are restored and increased.

For theorists like Prothrow-Stith, social strategies that broadly affect the community are presumed to have an impact on the particular problem of violence against women. Furthermore, her assertion that education about choices and options for alternative modes of behavior would lead to fewer sexual assaults presupposes that rape is "chosen" because individuals get caught up in a subculture that encourages and legitimates rape. She assumes that those who are given the broadest exposure to a wide range of healthy cultural options for intimate behavior would "choose" neither to rape nor to be raped. In her approach, the only factors relevant to sexual assault against women seem to be those generated by customs of the poor, urban, black subculture. Like social displacement theorists, she emphasizes the peculiarity of disordering structural barriers and social conditioning in the subculture where the violence takes place.

The propositions in social disorder and displacement approaches are reminiscent of Carey's assertion that anything could trigger the violence of her abusive partner. Her testimony illustrates the absurdity and danger of an emphasis on what triggers the batterer. She said, "It was like anything would trigger him. He would eat the last piece of cheese and then at twelve o'clock at night, . . . he'd want to fight me because there was no cheese." Social disorder and displacement theorists lead us to believe that frequent family moves, male unemployment, the close spatial proximity of family members, or chronically inadequate city services and community resources can trigger intimate violence. Carey's story challenges these theorists to focus their concern on the impact of violence on women and girls. Recall that on one occasion, when Carey came home very late at night, her intimate partner put a knife to her throat. She said, "It was like I seen my life flash, you know, like gone." When he finally released her and went back to sleep, she sat there in the kitchen for the rest of the night. "I was scared then. I was scared." The theorists miss the urgency of women's predicament by making role fulfillment by males or the restoration of control and order to the community and family their primary goals. That women are the chosen targets must be made paramount in analyses of men's violence against them, because it is these women's dignity, human rights, and very lives that are at stake.

Feminist and Womanist Resources for Conceptualizing Instigators of Violence

In contrast to social displacement and social disorder theories, feminist theories problematize gendered violence more explicitly as a consequence of the varied patterns of male dominance in our society.[41] Male dominance is not restrictively understood as a subcultural phenomenon, but is presumed to be universally operative within society. Hence in most feminist discussions of violence against women, it is assumed that men assault women because they can.[42] Male violation of women is a "right" possessed by all men in our society. Elizabeth Stanko writes, "the fact that all men do not exercise this right is irrelevant to the power afforded to men *as a gender* over women *as a gender*."[43] She explains that the physical and sexual abuse of women is so often characterized as "typical male behavior" that it comes to be seen as a natural right. Consequently, the humiliating and terrifying anguish that it causes women is often ignored. To account for factors that act as guarantors of male physical and sexual violence against women and girls, some explanations emphasize women's victimization at the cultural level, while others stress the cultural and material conditions that obstruct women's agency in their resistance to male violence.

In several feminist theories of violence against women, issues pertaining to race are minimally theorized. Therefore, the implications of racial and power dynamics for the social reproduction of violence against women are not analyzed or clarified. Writers who concentrate on the cultural victimization of women are especially wanting in this area. They insufficiently investigate the differential societal sanctions for male violence that depend upon the race of the victim and the race of the male who exercises the gendered "right to violate." Because they do not consider the sociopolitical manifestations of race, the lack of uniformity in the way violence impacts women is often theorized in an inchoate fashion.

The neglect of issues of race can be further illustrated by returning to the feminists who research the complex psychological and faith-related impact of intimate violence (referred to in the previous chapter). The methodology of these authors usefully pinpoints the types of distortions found in white feminist violence against women literature. Avoiding the pitfalls of some of their racial parochialisms means taking a few more steps toward a paradigm that simultaneously attends to racial realities in its method and directly seeks the empowerment of black women in its goals.

Feminist and womanist scholars who treat cultural and material conditions as the prime purveyors of violence against women present a wide breadth of relevant instigators of violence, within woman-centered analyses. Womanist religious theorists who place the concerns of black women at the center of their scholarship distinctively emphasize the cultural and spiritual dimensions of the problem when tracing the roots of violence against black women. They interpret, critique, and draw from black church and black community resources to depict the struggles and creative survival tactics of women. However, to merely locate a black-woman-authored analytical discussion that focuses upon black women victim-survivors must not be mistakenly seen as a sufficient goal when the subject is violence against women. The objective to be reckoned with here is how to give theoretical precedence to women's right to have lives free from the torment of intimate violence and how to expose the cultural obstructions which deny that right. The ongoing challenge for all concerned feminist and womanist thinkers is to identify the societal inhibitors that victim-survivors face without becoming a contributor to those inhibitors, as a theorist.

THE CULTURAL VICTIMIZATION OF WOMEN

A categorical assertion of the patently disadvantaged status of women lies at the core of certain feminist analyses of intimate violent assault. Victimologist Emilio Viano and legal theorist Catharine MacKinnon represent divergent approaches on the spectrum of such feminist theorizing. Viano characterizes patriarchy, ageism, and racism as comparable manifestations of social hierarchy, while gender hierarchy clearly has primacy in MacKinnon's theoretical formulations of society. Yet both account for violence against women by describing the nature of women's victim status within our culture. Male violence is generated principally by the gendered hierarchical ordering of society that defines all women in a subordinate victim role.

Feminist theorists such as Viano who offer cultural victimization explanations of violence against women cluster their ideas under a paradigm that concentrates on domination. Viano specializes in the field of victimology, bringing together practical and theoretical concerns about the roots of violent and victimizing behavior in our society.[44] The reproduction of violence is linked to social hierarchies that society creates to exploit differences and to subdue and oppress those deemed to be inferior. He asserts that every society identifies certain groups as weaker and thus as appropriate objects of hostility. The fact that women constitute such a group in this society is at the root of the preponderance of male violence. Male violence against women exemplifies the cultural value that accepts "violence in our society as the legitimate and necessary means of enforcing compliance and of solving conflicts."[45] Varying forms of sexual and physical assault against women are "expressions in different degrees, of the subordinate roles and of the low status of women in society."[46]

MacKinnon's radical feminist theory on violence against women contains assumptions about gender hierarchy similar to Viano's, if not more rigid. Her argument emphasizes the cultural valuation of sexualized violence. MacKinnon contends that gender, constructed as male dominance, is one form of a sexualized hierarchy.[47] Although she does not elaborate on other kinds of sexualized hierarchies, she stresses the fact that gender not only encodes male domination but also incorporates a sexualized, erotic component to female subjugation. Thus, she asserts that "forced sex as sexuality is not exceptional in relations between the sexes but constitutes the social meaning of gender. . . . To be rapable, a position that is social not biological, defines what woman is."[48] In MacKinnon's framework male dominance and sexualized violence against women are conflated within the construction of gender. In this fundamental respect, her thinking presents a vivid contrast to social disorder and social displacement theories. The degree to which community ties and services are improved for families or employment opportunities for males increased is irrelevant, because it is the social construction of gender that sanctions violence against women.[49]

The premise of theorists such as these is plain: the reproduction of violence against women stems from male dominance that is inscribed throughout the social order. The resulting victimization of women is steeped in an ideological legitimation of violent behavior toward women. Thus, the trauma of a woman victim-survivor of male violence is reproduced through her social definition as subordinate object. Since women can be defined as appropriate objects of male violence, the meaning of womanhood can signify an invitation to violate. This places a woman in the position of perpetually inviting male violence by reason of her social definition. It locates responsibility for violence within a woman's selfhood, thereby reinforcing messages of shame and self-blame for women victim-survivors. When consigned to the status of "rapable object," an intrinsically shameful identification is imposed upon women.

The discrete "categories of dominance" or uniform definitions of the social construction of gender posited by these theorists neglect important realities like the one represented in Carey's assertion: "Who told you that this was your earth?" Carey reported that this was her attitude in certain public situations, as when she defiantly sat down next to a white woman who, at the sight of Carey, grabbed her own pocketbook, clutching it close to her body. These two women certainly negotiated something about their identities that extended beyond gender constructions. At the same time, more than "race" was at issue in their confrontation, which raises questions about what it means to be "seen" as a woman. The clash centers upon how the constructed meaning of the stranger's white womanhood as well as Carey's black womanhood was acted out on this public bus.

This example illustrates how the fusion of racial and gender social meanings violates the depiction of women's victim status provided by these feminist theorists.[50] When womanhood is defined by an exclusive emphasis on gender hierarchy, the fusion of racial and gender social meanings that are especially obvious in certain interracial encounters between women cannot be accounted for. Since such racial/gender realities are not reflected in these feminist theories on violence against women, the full implications for black women's experience of violence are obscured.

White Feminist Racial Distortions

Even feminists who focus solely upon the social norms and barriers that affect women's responses to violence back away from the incorporation of racial analysis. This "tradition" in white feminism requires special attention beyond basic assessments like "they leave out our experience," or name-calling that arrests dialogue like, "they're just racist." What are some of the specific characteristics of the exclusionary methods these authors employ? What is the apparent rationale for the "whiteness" of white feminist discussions of violence against women?

It seems especially contradictory when issues related to race are neglected in the work of authors like Herman, Walker, Fortune, and others who focus on the psychological and faith-related consequences of intimate violence. In the feminist dimensions of their analysis, they explicitly promote the idea that the manner in which social status and role are culturally defined for women has a striking impact on their emotional and spiritual responses to male violence. In fact, in their depictions of women's victimization, Walker and Herman are sometimes criticized for overstating the traumatizing effect of psychosocial factors.[51] Walker points out that "analysis that does not pay attention to the social context will be more likely to lead to erroneous conclusions about the psychology of women."[52] Yet these authors neglect the potent influence of racial cultural norms in shaping the social context of women victim-survivors.

Some feminist theorists ignore issues of race altogether. They intentionally include black women in their studies about violence and, on the basis of similar replies from their respondents, assert that women's emotional and spiritual reactions are generalizable across racial and ethnic boundaries. Others refer to race only in relation to black women, and then mainly with regard to the sociological barriers they face when seeking help in the wake of intimate violence. In every category, the authors universalize the consciousness and gender subjectivity of white women. Ignoring or diminishing one's own racial identity as a determinative feature of the social context is an inherent aspect of white privilege in U.S. culture. Blindness to the ways that race mitigates the impact of intimate violence for white women victim-survivors inevitably leads to the neglect of the way race impinges upon the emotional and spiritual experience of black women. Hence, white women's identity, which gives minimal consideration to racial factors, is standard and normal in many white feminist analyses.[53]

Issues that might arise if black women and their experiences of racial oppression were considered remain unexplored in many religious feminist analyses of intimate violence. For instance, the implications of racial oppression for black women victim-survivors of violence would have altered the previously mentioned discussion of dirtiness by Pellauer or the argument by Fortune about how women feel abandoned by a God who is supposed to alleviate all suffering. When issues related to the dynamics of racial subjugation are omitted, it is reasonable to assume that these theorists intentionally offer an analysis relevant only to white women. Do these authors want to explore those dilemmas related to spirituality, Christian faith and traditions that arise exclusively for white women victim-survivors of violence? When references to race are left out altogether, it is impossible to know how they are defining the racial context of their work. Of course, if one assumes that whiteness is the universal norm for the psychospiritual journey of all women, references to race may seem unnecessary. Note that it would be just as erroneous to suggest a uniform "white woman's experience of violence" as it would be to point to a singular "black woman's experience." Ignoring the issue of race muddles and truncates our understanding of the variegated roles that racial identity might play in women's reactions to intimate violence.

Sometimes a white feminist author may overtly state that she intends to base her study upon Euro-American women's experiences of violence. Thus, Herman consciously leaves black women out of her study on incest. She explains why she limits her study to white women:

> We made the decision to restrict the interviewing to white women in order to avoid even the possibility that the information gathered might be used to fuel idle speculation about racial differences. White people have indulged for too long in discussion about the sexual capacities, behaviors, and misbehaviors of black people. There is no question, however, that incest is a problem in black families, as it is in white families.[54]

Herman goes on to cite black women authors such as Maya Angelou and Toni Morrison as daring contributors to the public discussion of incest. Certainly, the task of writing about white women and their experience of father-daughter incest is crucial. Herman advances the cause of race-conscious feminist work by a frank admission of her deliberate decision to focus on white women. Still, she might have discussed issues of race relevant to white women's consciousness. Unfortunately, she does not reveal her reasons for this omission. Whiteness comprises a key factor in the socialization of white women. It constrains, enhances, or in other ways definitively informs their affective experience of violence.[55]

However, the rationalization given for the decision to focus solely on white women is nothing short of incredible, given the topic and emphasis of Herman's scholarship. It is quite perplexing that Herman justifies the omission of black women victim-survivors from her study by deferring to the potential for public misinterpretation. What makes this so unusual is that Herman reiterates throughout her many writings, including this one, the necessity for public attention to and concern for the needs and treatment of survivors of violence. In fact, an overriding quality of her work is the careful, scholarly analysis which exposes the trauma of victim-survivors of violence and offers therapeutic responses to that trauma. To Herman, one of the essential contributions of feminist activists and scholars has been the act of exposing the prevalence and traumatic impact of intimate violence for women in defiance of the preponderant male supremacist social attitudes that suppress, excuse, and trivialize the problem. In light of this commitment, is it conceivable that Herman would decide not to interview *white* women survivors of incest in order to avoid being publicly misrepresented by people with stereotyped views of female sexuality? To allow societal bias to silence the voices of women survivors of intimate violence and prevent their victimization from being analyzed is completely contrary to the guiding convictions of Herman's scholarship—except when it comes to black women. The possible distortion and misinterpretation of feminist research is unavoidable, particularly when women and sexuality are mentioned together. It is appalling and tragic for feminist researchers to allow the existence of demeaning cultural ideology to negate the dire necessity of addressing the problem of sexual violence in the lives of black women. To ignore the trauma and treatment needs of black women victim-survivors of violence on these grounds is to respect racist ideology, rather than to broach the imperative task of challenging it.

Black women survivors of intimate violence are deliberately included in the research of some feminist theorists (such as Walker), but still fare poorly in discussions of the impact of racial subjugation on their psychosocialization. Walker includes black women, as well as Hispanic, Asian, Native American, and Pacific Islander women in her study of the psychosocial dynamics of battering that led to the development of her cycle theory of violence. Based on this inclusion, she asserts that "anglo and minority women alike told similar battering stories and experienced similar embarrassment, guilt and inability to halt their men's assaults."[56] She seeks to dispel racist myths that identify battering as a "minority group problem." Walker asserts that the experience of violence was comparable across racial and ethnic boundaries. Her theories about the psychosocial consequences for women are based on this assumption. Unless the category of race is directly interrogated in the research design or the interpretation of the data, it may be misleading to minimize its importance for women's experience of violence. Again, the assumption of the minimal significance of race in psychosocialization is steeped in the presuppositions of white privilege.

Some theorists who include black women in their work on the psychological and spiritual dimensions of male violence seem to commodify race as a social problem for black women that is separate from the emotional and/or spiritual crisis that all women share. "Race" is problematized as a black woman's issue. The influence of racial oppression within the dynamics of intimate violence that black women encounter is considered primarily in terms of sociological barriers. They raise important problems related to racism and community services such as battered women's shelter services or the police.[57] Yet, with this caveat about the sociological barriers that black women face, the ensuing psychological and theological claims of these authors assume the psyche of black women to be almost identical to that of white women. Little room is allowed for the possibility that those barriers significantly influence the emotional and spiritual impact of violence, creating configurations of anguish and coping that may not fit the model that the theorist has designed. The complexity of black women's emotional life is denied.

These may all seem like plausible strategies for demonstrating sensitivity to blacks: the complete omission, the deliberate exclusion of them for their own sakes, the incorporation of black women assuming their sameness with all women, the inclusion of race issues as institutional barriers black women confront. Unfortunately, each of these methods muffles or erases to differing degrees black women's trauma. The rationality of white domination has such a firm grip upon the collective consciousness of our society that it can seem nearly impossible to free ourselves of it. Feminist research must develop a stance that is at least antagonistic to it. Since placing women's emotional and spiritual realities within a social context is a significant contribution of feminist scholarship, social categories beyond gender that shape and inform women need also to be explored.

Feminist theorizing about intimate violence must include a discussion of race without further buttressing white domination. This task may be laden with pitfalls. Nonetheless, it also holds the promise that our perceptions of the cultural victimization of women that leads to the violence against them will be sharpened.

THE CULTURAL OBSTRUCTION OF WOMEN

Racial considerations tend to occupy a more prominent position in discussions of violence that emphasize a broad range of comingling factors obstructing victim-survivors. Feminist theorists who emphasize the cultural victimization of women focus on isolating male dominance as an accepted cultural expectation that instigates and legitimizes violence against women. Other feminists concentrate on features of the culture that obstruct women's agency in their attempts to resist male violence. The approach of cultural obstruction theorists highlights varied systemic factors in the organization of our society that function in partnership with male dominance ideology.

These theorists insist that women's victimization by male dominance is generated by forces located outside women's identities. Activist and writer Ann Jones blames "our society's habitual pattern of male dominance" for the perpetuation of woman beating.[58] However, she is less interested in devising a theory about the ideology of male dominance than in illustrating the victim-blaming institutional barriers that sanction woman beating. She criticizes the very term "battered woman" on the grounds that it emphasizes a woman's situation as the victimized object of another's actions while obscuring the woman's subjectivity and agency. Because it is crucial to retain women as subjects and not to relegate them to the exclusive role of objects of male dominance, Jones adamantly refrains from labeling women as victims.[59]

Women are seriously impeded by the ways that violence against them has become publicly accepted. Although the forms that this acceptance assumes in public consciousness and practices will be detailed in the next chapter, I would like to preview the significance of the concept here. The way male violence is depicted as a type of love by mass media opinion-shapers ranging from news journalists to self-help pundits, has a numbing effect. The public becomes inured to the peril that woman battering bodes for women. In her study of sex crimes, Jane Caputi discusses the dangerous effects that the cultural mixture of sex and violence has had on perpetrators. She quotes one Viet Nam veteran recalling the dramatic sense of power this combination gave him.

> I had a sense of power. A sense of destruction . . . in Nam you realized you had the power to take a life. You had the power to rape a woman and nobody could say nothing to you. That godlike feeling you had was in the field. It was like I was god. I could take a life. I could screw a woman.[60]

Our society encourages males in an inability to distinguish sexual intercourse with women from the violent assault of them. The cultural reinforcement of notions that conflate sex and violence, or loving behavior and violence fuels the attacks which ensnare women victim-survivors.

Social tolerance for this violence is also demonstrated by the ways in which community institutions that are supposed to provide help, fail to do so. Citing case after case, Jones stresses the need to examine the myriad impediments to women's survival that are constructed by state and social agencies whose mandate is to assist women assaulted by men. She explains the systemic "buckpassing" that perpetuates the problem of male violence:

> Police say there's no point in making arrests when prosecutors won't prosecute, and prosecutors in turn say they can't prosecute when (a) police don't arrest, or (b) judges won't sentence anyway. Judges say that women

waste the court's time. Blaming the victim allows everyone in the system to pass the buck; and buckpassing conveniently enables individuals within the system to acknowledge the problem without doing anything about it.[61]

The victim-blaming practices of these officials maintain the violence against women. We shall return to these arguments by Jones in a later discussion of women's resistance.

Apart from certain cultural ideological and institutional impediments, the material conditions of women's lives also militate against women contending with male violence. Susan Schecter, an activist and teacher, traces the history of the battered women's movement in the United States from the 1970s. Offering a socialist-feminist analysis that links economic and cultural factors, she describes the collaboration between male dominance and other systemic oppressive forces such as capitalism and racism in the reproduction of male violence. Especially important is Schecter's insistence on the need to include the contribution of capitalism to the perpetuation of male violence against women. Certain material preconditions must exist to end this violence. Schecter explains: "these conditions—shelter, adequate jobs, incomes, free health care, affordable housing, and child care—are essential to allow women independence from violent men and to enable all people to live decently . . ."[62] The material conditions of women's lives are inextricably linked to the reproduction of male violence. Under capitalism "the home" is cordoned off as a privatized sphere where women's dependence upon men to maintain decent material conditions for themselves and their children helps to impede their escape from male violence.

Since this analysis pays attention to concrete social arrangements which prevent women from being free of violence, it is especially amenable to considerations of race. Schecter avoids the usual practice of relegating all discussions of race to the category of institutional confrontations commonly faced by black women in the wake of male assault. Without overgeneralizing, she suggests some features of the impact that racial and power dynamics can have upon *white women* as well as women of color. These dynamics impact their access to resources, feelings about reporting their abuser, and the types of abuse they might be likely to experience. She argues that institutional racism and class discrimination make it difficult for women of color and poor women of all races to be taken seriously and to find help.[63] The sex role socialization of white middle-class women, that often affords them more opportunities to live out the feminine ideal calling for dependence on men, can poorly prepare them to survive on their own to escape battering.[64] In this view, ideologies of race, gender, and class collude to erect salient obstacles that can impact all women's struggles to escape domestic violence.

Both institutional and material facets of the culture assist in the reproduction of male violence by obstructing women's acts of resistance to violence. The agony for women who have been beaten by men is reproduced by a cultural bias that holds women responsible for being assaulted by men. This bias is structurally enacted by official agencies of law and medicine that respond to women victim-survivors. Furthermore, the emotional and spiritual trauma of male violence is compounded by interlocking socioeconomic structures and ideologies that functionally debilitate and disempower women. In this feminist approach, society's accountability for the intimate violence that women face is proven by analyses of the cultural obstructions embedded in the conditions of women's lives.

Womanist approaches direct attention to cultural obstructions that exist specifically as a consequence of black community realities. Religious sociologist Cheryl Gilkes uses the term "cultural humiliation" to denote a major component of racial oppression which inflicts damaged and conflicted inner visions in black women's embodied selves. She acknowledges the harmful personal consequences that physical assaults wreak upon women. But she places that fact within the understanding that "the culture's approach to African-American women, their images, and their lifestyles has been a central thrust in the continued humiliation of the entire African-American community."[65] According to Gilkes, historically molded assaults on black women's lives and bodies have produced a "racialized sexism" which compounds "our own community's ambivalence about the meaning of being Black and female in America."[66] As this careful rendering of context by Gilkes makes evident, key to an analysis of violence against women is their placement within the broader landscape of cultural meanings that are internal and external to the black community.

Perhaps because these womanists write against the background of a history of exclusion from white feminist and black male religious thought, they are particularly attentive to method and the ways that it can distort knowledge. Ethicist Toinette Eugene specifies that in deciphering sexual violence against African-American women, the method must recognize "the convergence of racism, sexism, classism and heterosexism" as the contextual reality of African-American women's lives.[67] Adding further methodogical clarity, Eugene explains that a womanist definition of sexual violence includes recognition of it as "a violation of one's psycho-spiritual-sexual integrity."[68]

Appreciation of the integrated and multifaceted impact of sexual violence provides the deepest insight. Though offering a different model, theologian Delores Williams also emphasizes the context for analysis of domestic violence against black women by describing three levels. She insists that the long history of national violence directed at black women and men be taken into account (national level). This should be considered alongside the violence that women have encountered while working in the homes of white employers (work), as well as that which they have faced within their own homes and communities (home).[69] This tiered contextual approach captures both the historical distinctiveness and breadth of domestic violence relevant to black women.

For womanists, violence against women within black communities must never be separated from an understanding of violence against the community. Ideological and material assaults and humiliation of the black community constitute essential cultural obstructions helping to generate the violence women face. As Eugene notes, healing from the violence and the promise of a just future lie in "love of Black women, Black children and Black men—the community—and the Spirit."[70] Healing is linked to community bonding.

There may be some risk in this choice by many womanists to focus so heavily upon women's linkage to black communities. A primary identification with the black community may be a problematic prescription for some black women victim-survivors. For them, deep antagonisms toward church and community might be a consequence of the responses they received to their victimization, which may in turn have decentered their relationship to black communities. This possibility would seem to land them outside the central healing possibilities envisioned here.

Attention to assaults on black communities from the outside should not preclude explicit identification and confrontation of the male-violence-sanctioning attitudes and practices within the community. Activist and author Frances Woods crafts a direct challenge to black communities and churches that is simultaneously an entreaty and a sharp critique. She decries the silencing of violence in the church context, explaining that "the legendary strong Black woman has become the personification of the permissible victim."[71] Like other cultural obstructionist theorists, she names specific attitudes that reflect public tolerance of intimate violence. She charges men in black communities and churches with viewing the battering or rape of women "as simply a hazard of being female."[72] The fact that the clergy often fail to condemn violence against women helps to perpetuate it. The "abusive behavior, which we call taboo is not the real taboo; speaking the truth about the abuse is."[73] The internal dynamics of church culture can create an informal ban·on women's revelations about the violence they face in their homes.

In alignment with other cultural obstructionists, womanist analysis of male violence holds black women's cultural context fundamentally responsible for the violence. They insist on the link between violence against the black community and the violence against women perpetrated by black males. Again, in this emphasis there may be a tendency to omit or minimize the peculiar status and interests of black women that impede the prospects of a communal ethos that is fully unified in its joint struggles. Communal dissension and rift could be a necessary part of the process of authentically confronting the issue of black male violence against black women. Nevertheless, religious womanist theorizing contributes desperately needed articulations of how to identify the social contexts that perpetuate the violence black women encounter. They rightly insist on a highly complex method of analysis that includes multiple sites such as work, home, and public contact with white males. And they usefully point to multiple buttressing, intersecting realities like heterosexism, cultural assaults on the psyche related to the way black women's bodies are imaged in the culture, and black-woman-as-permissible-victim ideology.

This process of cultural permission-giving for sexual and physical male violence that repeatedly, deeply wounds a woman's body, dignity, and spiritual wholeness undermines the morality of the entire society. Realigning and reforming systemic power, whether it is rooted in the police, the media, or the black clergy will be inadequate without a new moral vocabulary for marking status and worth. The moral transformation that is needed must dislodge the ideological and institutionalized support for male violence within black communities and the broader U.S. culture, while appreciably affirming the entirety of black women's personhood. Yet for this transformation to occur we must be as precise as possible about identifying those violence-affirming cultural elements that need to be dislodged.

5

A Sampler of Cultural Assaults

Certain ideologies and cultural myths about black women require closer examination. They must not be comfortably regarded as remote diffuse ideas that merely float in the air, occasionally landing in particular academic treatises which discuss them (like some of the works mentioned in the previous chapter). On the contrary, these cultural messages are articulated in a variety of public settings and manifested in specific encounters within the lives of victim-survivors. As we have seen, in the aftermath of male assault a black woman's self-perceptions as well as her reading of the significance of each aspect of the assault is (largely) filtered through cultural lenses. When she reflects on it, she struggles between resisting and absorbing the cultural meanings attached to this experience. The struggle varies with the circumstances of her assault and the elements that configure her personality or compose her individual biography. Yet, in every case, her trauma is deepened by the diverse and deprecating cultural messages that assail her. These messages take the shape of particular, erroneous, public beliefs about victim-survivors, as well as institutional barriers confronting them. These barriers inhabit a diverse assortment of public and private agencies including the police, religious institutions, and even battered women's shelters.

Guises That Ideology Assumes

The ideological assumptions that will be interrogated consist of ideas that contribute to the image of African-American women in our society. These assumptions can take the form of direct assertions about black women, claims about women in general, as well as racial characterizations of blacks. Each type of ideological claim retains the capacity to legitimate male violence against black women and nurture myths that invalidate their experiences of victimization. To identify some of these ideological constructions entails sorting through an array of popularly held beliefs, images projected in the media, and publicly propagated political commentaries and social teachings. The formulations which will be examined below assert that women make false claims about intimate assault; black women are often in need of black male beatings; male violence is romantic and sexually alluring; and finally, that black women are particularly blameworthy for setting up the dynamics that cause the male violence committed against them.

Women as Liars and as Inherently Unreliable

Cultural myths that impugn women's credibility are a particularly disturbing source of anguish for women victim-survivors. Martha Burt, a social science researcher, categorizes a series of rape myths that contribute to the cultural sanctioning of this crime and to the agony of women. Her conversations with women callers when she served as a volunteer on a rape crisis hot line form part of the basis for her analysis of how damaging these myths are for victim-survivors. One of the myths in Burt's typology is the belief that many women falsely accuse men of rape. She argues that "many people believe that women lie, 'crying rape'" to cover up an out-of-wedlock pregnancy, or to get at a man who has jilted her or refused her advances. Also in this category are myths that hold that women's rape claims are "sheer fantasy, or wishful thinking."[1] In a recent manifestation of this last type of myth, antifeminist polemicist Katie Roiphe asserted that women college students falsely accuse men of rape as a clever, calculated way of calling attention to themselves "out of a desire for dates."[2]

Women who accuse their fathers, uncles, brothers, or other male relatives of sexually assaulting them as children, often have to contend with the counteraccusation that they have invented the story in the service of some vindictive motive.[3] Women who report the violent behavior of their male partners without physical evidence of bruises or supporting witnesses are likely to be accused of lying or exaggerating. For one black woman victim-survivor accused of murdering her batterer, the darkness of her skin color was a variable in denying her the help she requested from the police. She explained that the police were summoned to her house numerous times after beatings by her male partner, but they discounted the degree of violence that she was experiencing partly because she was dark-skinned and did not show bruises as readily.[4]

Women who are not credited with being obvious and intentional liars are often seen as emotionally unstable by nature, and thus as unreliable informants about their experience of violence. As Burt comments, the view of women as naturally inclined to be "subjective" is "the most damning in a society committed to science and objectivity."[5] Consequently, the assumption that women are ruled by emotions and subjectivity undermines a woman's testimony when her version of an assault is directly pitted against a man's. Whether because women are considered to be manipulative liars or just inherently unreliable, the reality of male violence is denied by these intransigent cultural myths.

Another variation on myths that attack the credibility of women's testimony about sexual violence involves the misnaming of rape as consensual sex. Psychoanalytic literature has provided "scientific" justification positing the willing participation of women and little girls in their own sexual assault.[6] Feminist researchers have pointed out ways in which this literature has offered as plausible the notion that the severe emotional problems of little girls are responsible for their initiation of and participation in the sexual assaults perpetrated against them. In flagrant victim-blaming fashion, girl victims of sexual assault, even some as young as five years old, have been described in psychoanalytic literature as very attractive, charming, appealing, submissive, and seductive.[7] For instance, in her study of child sexual abuse, psychiatrist Lauretta Bender writes: "It seemed evident that some children had used their charm in the role of seducer rather than being innocently seduced."[8] Moreover, the psychiatric categorization of women who have been battered by men as "masochistic" or as suffering from "borderline personality disorder" implies an emotionally sick collusion in their own abuse.[9] Some mental health clinicians prefer these designations for women instead of recognizing emotional trauma as a normal response to violence and danger.[10] When the anguish of victim-survivors is interpreted as psychotic behavior, it becomes a scientifically validated method of community dismissal.

One specific ingredient in the process of being disbelieved is the dishonoring of women. As Judith Herman describes with regard to sexual violence, discounting women's testimony of male violence signifies the social production of dishonor in victims. Herman explains that when conventional attitudes fail to recognize most rapes as violations, "women discover an appalling disjunction between their actual experience and the social construction of reality. Women learn that in rape they are not only violated but dishonored."[11] Because the community response of disbelieving women can provide pivotal reinforcement of a victim-survivor's shamefulness, it constitutes a core component in a process of communally shaming women. Moreover, denying the reality of the assault eliminates recognition of the injustice of their victimization.

These community issues can also arise in situations involving the sexual harassment of women. Responding to Anita Hill's accusations of sexual harassment against Clarence Thomas, some black newspapers published strident, dishonoring accusations against her as a black woman.[12] In this case, Hill was dishonored (in the Herman sense) by allegations which labeled *her* as the one who had behaved dishonorably. Hill's complaints about verbal sexual intimidation by a black man became the basis for public attacks faulting her for dishonoring both black men and the black community as a whole. For instance, in a (somewhat slanderous) letter to the editor published in the New York City *Amsterdam News*, one reader said:

> I believe a "Black" woman, overly ambitious and self-centered, decided to lie, deliberately, to destroy a decent Blackman. As an African-American woman I am ashamed. . . . Clarence Thomas was lynched publicly and with blacks fashioning the noose. . . . Anita Hill was and is a liar.[13]

Without referring to any particular evidence, this community member asserted her complete certainty that Hill was a liar. Perhaps the unstated moral factor that renders a black woman "overly ambitious and self-centered," and identifies a black man colleague of hers as "decent" is the woman's pursuit of a high-status career. From this moral depiction, we are to assume that lying would come easily to such a woman, and that the specific "lie" that Hill "decided" upon brought her racial group identity into question. To be truly black and deserve no quotation marks around that adjective when it refers to you seems to require ignoring or hiding your complaints about sexual harassment by a black man.

In a similar vein, Sherman Miller, a columnist for Norfolk Virginia's *New Journal and Guide*, explained how these hearings signaled a new era with the black woman upstaging the white woman in the historic role of telling public dangerous lies about black men. Miller referred to the multiple historical examples of black males being lynched because white women falsely "cried rape." He called Anita Hill a "'Talented Tenth' soul sister who upstaged Miss Ann."[14] In his androcentric analysis of the Hill/Thomas case, black women and white women were equated as victimizers of the black male. The issues of sexual assault and harassment of women were portrayed as no more than female rhetorical tools used to harm black men.

The dishonoring lesson for black women found in these kinds of responses is not only that they will not be believed. In addition, their statements, deemed lies, even about verbal male sexual intimidation, may be construed as tantamount to causing the murder of black men. In this way, both the legitimacy of a woman's racial identity and her truthfulness are impugned. She is assigned the role of victimizer, and implicated in the commission of heinous brutality.

Black Women Are Often in Need of Black Male Beatings

Certain instances of explicit political legitimation of male assault which emerge from black leaders based within the black community, deserve special mention. The justification of male violence against women found within some expressions of the 1960s black nationalist movement epitomize this subcultural phenomenon. To be positioned at the receiving end of male violence was prescribed by some black nationalists as part of the proper display of deference by black women toward their men, within the so-called revolutionary context. It should be noted that the rape of white women was also advocated as a political act by some of these leaders.

Poet and playwright Amiri Baraka (aka Leroi Jones) had tremendous notoriety and influence in the cultural wing of the 1960s black nationalist movement. He wrote revolutionary plays and poetry which creatively expressed the movement's vision for social and political change. The dialogue in his 1966 play *Madheart (A Morality Play)*, presents the Black Woman and the Black Man working out their destiny. At one point, the Black Woman assertively tells the Black Man that in order to find his future, he'd better leave the white woman and return to her. In response to this insolent attitude, the Black Man hits her repeatedly across the face. He continues to slap her as she cries and pleads for him to stop. The Black Man tells her: "I want you, woman, as a woman. Go down. (*He slaps her again.*) Go down, submit, submit . . . to love . . . and to man, now, forever."[15] Finally, after he abuses her further, she announces her willingness to submit, they kiss, and she declares: "I am your woman, and you are the strongest of God. Fill me with your seed."[16] The misogyny in this purported revolutionary ideal of black gender relations is hardly subtle! Apparently, to authentically embody black womanhood a woman must literally be beaten into submission.

A similar attitude about the treatment of black women was expressed by those who focused on explicitly political strategies for the movement. Eldridge Cleaver, an officer of the Black Panther Party, was a key spokesperson in the movement who advocated revolutionary political change. His book *Soul on Ice*, written from his California State prison cell, became an important manifesto of the era. It documents his own political and spiritual odyssey, as well as his analysis of "the race problem" in the United States. At the beginning of this volume he admits to multiple rapes of women. At the time, he justified these by saying that the rape of a white woman was an insurrectionary act against the white man. However, he confessed that before graduating to white women, he practiced his "modus operandi" for rape on black ghetto girls. At the point in his life when this book was written, Cleaver, convicted and imprisoned for rape, asserted that he had now come to disapprove of rape. Instead of such assaultive behavior, he saw a need to bring the numerous issues that fueled the sickness between the black man and the white woman out into the open so that they may be resolved. What about black women? The political purpose of Cleaver's rapes perpetrated against black women was simply to "practice" antiwhite man tactics that would later be meted out in his assaults on white women. I suppose we are meant to conclude that attacks against black women are indirectly addressed by resolving the white woman-black man "sickness." The point is not clarified because Cleaver does not specifically analyze the issue or wrongness of his rapes of black women.

However, at the end of this volume, in a section on intraracial and interracial sexual/gender relations, Cleaver focuses upon the physical battering of black women. Although black men are allegorized as performing brutish acts against black women, the women are clearly implicated in their violence. The allegorical "Accused" black man and the "Infidel" may brag: "I wish I had a nickel for every b-tch whose -ss I've put my foot in!"[17] "I'd jump over ten nigger b-tches just to get to one white woman,"[18] or in a reference to a black woman "no, a b-tch:" "I had to knock her out every Saturday night."[19] However, black women are allegorized as deserving the violence because of their provocative behavior. Such behavior includes being silent allies with white men,[20] castigating and humiliating black men, especially with comparisons to white men,[21] starting physical "fights" with black men,[22] desiring to marry white men, and viewing such a union as the pinnacle achievement in life.[23] This allegorical section also asserts that a black woman will call out for Jesus in the midst of her sexual orgasm, thus hurting her black male partner's heart "like a knife" was thrust in it.[24] This woman's utterance of Jesus's name is then said to be just the same as her calling out the name of a "sneaky cat" (another man) who lives down the street. The volume closes with a depiction of a healing resolution to these "wars" between black men and women. This resolution involves the black man's repentantly saying to the black woman: "I will fail unless you reach out to me, tune me in with the antenna of your love."[25]

In this tract, Cleaver testifies to his former belief in rape as a political act, and more importantly, to the fact that he carried out numerous assaults against women based on this ideological construction. In addition, the battering of black women is paradoxically legitimated even as such male behavior is said to be "off the track" for black salvation. Black women, allegedly contemptuous of their men, especially in their reputed liaisons with white men, appear to be culpable for the violence committed against them. The salvation of black manhood, as well as the womanhood that is celebrated here (the kind that is undeserving of beatings?), requires a woman to dedicate herself to loving her man. The demands upon black women in this scenario are relentless. Responsibility for transforming the violence-ridden, heterosexual relationships Cleaver depicts rests upon the women's capacity for loving their men. Also, the significance of and redress for women's suffering due to the violence, is nowhere to be found in this male-centered vision of how to build a new restored black future.

Elaine Brown gives us some insight into the view from the other side of this politically legitimated violence—from one *woman's* vantage point. She provides a detailed account of her days within the inner leadership of the Black Panther Party in California during the 1960s. Brown describes a casual intimate relationship with a man named Steve who was also a member of the Panthers. Steve's segment of the Panther underground movement is described as functioning in an especially sophisticated manner. They wore fashionable clothes, lived in suburbia, and held ordinary jobs to avoid any appearance of affiliation with the party.[26] On one occasion, Steve accused Elaine of sleeping with another man and then proceeded to beat her throughout the night, sometimes taking a break to rest or to urinate, only to begin the beatings again "with increased rage."

Elaine Brown describes her emotional state during this torture, writing that: "In the corner of my mind that was holding on, I began to wonder exactly how many blows I would have to suffer before he stopped. I began to count them . . . beating me with so much force and vigor he was actually tiring, requiring rest more and more. I noted that, holding on."[27] She finally escaped in the morning. In order to achieve her getaway, she successfully mirrored the friendly, casual attitude that Steve displayed that morning.

She fled to Huey Newton, chairman of the party, whom she regarded as a trusted ally and mentor. In fact, as she describes the spiritual dimension of her reactions to her ordeal, Brown refers to Newton as one who "offered God-deliverance . . . like Jesus in the shadow of death. I had been in the shadow of death for three hours."[28] When she fled to Newton, she expected him to protect her and take steps to punish the batterer for his actions, particularly since she was now a member of the Panther Central Committee (the only woman member at that point). Instead, he shrugged it off and agreed with the men surrounding him when she told her story. They believed "it was about time" she "got her -ss kicked" since she was such an "arrogant b-tch."[29] It was at this point that she decided Newton was not a god and she experienced a strong emotional disengagement from the type of dedication to the movement she had previously had.

These examples demonstrate aspects of the black nationalist movement where ideas about the raping and beating of women were not only rhetorically celebrated and rationalized by depicting women's behavior toward their men as insolent. This political philosophy was put into practice at incalculable physical and psychospiritual cost to the women. These costs are made invisible by the constructed image of black women in this philosophy. The vision of gender relations and of liberation from white oppression offered by black nationalists such as Baraka and Cleaver effaced the human rights of women. The concerns of the women were superseded by the primary agenda of giving "all praises to the Black Man" (as Baraka subtitles his book collection of revolutionary plays containing *Madheart*).

Violating Women Is Sexy

A particularly enduring and potent aspect of the cultural mythology that negates the suffering of the victim-survivors of sexual assault is the perception of violence as romantic and erotic. This cultural assumption is reinforced by mass media images ranging from movie "classics" like Gone with the Wind to counterculture youth music like heavy metal and gangsta' rap. In *Gone with the Wind*, Rhett Butler forces himself sexually on a petulant, resistant Scarlett, who ultimately stops struggling and conveys her pleasure at being "taken" in this way. As Marie Fortune aptly concludes from the example of Rhett Butler and Scarlett O'Hara, "women learn that forced sexual activity is something to be accepted *and* enjoyed."[30] In contrast, suspense-thriller "classics" like Alfred Hitchcock's *Psycho* portray violence against women in an erotic way while depicting it as aberrant male behavior. In the infamous shower scene we know that a woman has just slowly stripped off her clothing offscreen. She steps into the shower and is sensually enjoying the water when she is stabbed to death by the main male character.[31] He is apparently confused by his sexual attraction to the woman and uses this method to express himself. Such images can help generate fear in women about their vulnerability, and fascination in men about the erotic possibilities of performing such acts.

Mass media advertising regularly utilizes images of the symbolic annihilation of women.[32] For instance, a 1997 television commercial for the Honda Prelude depicted the excitement that this automobile ostensibly generates in its owner by focusing on a small statuette of a Hawaiian native woman standing on the dashboard. Fast-paced rock n' roll music blares in the background as the car picks up speed and travels along winding mountainous roads. The statuette appears to come to life, with escalating signs of panic and terror conveyed by her facial expressions and the arrangement of her hair. The faster the ride, the more terrified she gets. Finally, at the climax of the fast ride, as well as of the commercial, the statuette (woman) explodes into several pieces. This is shown through slow-motion filming. The symbolic terrorizing and obliteration of this woman of color is supposed to exude thrilling excitement and an alluring sense of pleasure that will stimulate one (a man?) to buy the automobile. Advertising such as this, together with much of the mass media entertainment industry, make the connection between femicide and pleasure or eroticism an ordinary, legitimate aspect of our culture.

Gangsta' rap music has offered a generation of urban youth and young adults depictions of violence against women which equal those found in the more mainstream media. Yet there has been considerable protest and criticism of rap music for its violent, antiwoman messages, from sources ranging from high-profile politicians to popular national magazines.[33]

Unfortunately, the commonplace, steady diet of violent sexist images in cartoons, movies, and advertisements have not received the same degree of attention. Several gangsta' rap male artists do propagate misogynist images of women that portray violent acts against them as entertaining and sexy.

> N.W.A. [Niggaz With Attitude]:
> So if you at a show in the front row. I'm a call you a b-tch or a dirty -ss ho. You probably get mad like a b-tch is supposed to . . . So what about the b-tch who got shot? F-ck her. You think I give a d-mn about a b-tch.

> The Geto Boys:
> Her body's beautiful so I'm thinking rape, grabbed the b-tch by the mouth . . . opened her legs and commenced to f-ckin', she begged me not to kill her, I gave her a rose, then slit her throat and watched her shake 'til her eyes closed, had sex with her of course before I left her.

In addition, some of the references to "b-tches" in gangsta' rap illustrate how representations of women as vindictive or conniving help to justify coercive male sexual acts against them.[34]

> Snoop Doggy Dogg:
> Guess who's back in the motherf-ckin' house. With a big fat dick for your motherf-ckin' mouth. Hoes recognize it, niggas do too. Cause when b-tches get scandalous and pull the voodoo. What you gon' do?

The pejorative depictions of women in rap songs such as this one, as well as movie characters like Scarlett O'Hara, diminish the moral worth of women and hence rationalize the violence against them. Women's emotions are key to this perversion of moral worth. Women are portrayed as essentially unstable, unruly emotional creatures, governed by the desire to be manipulative and devious toward men. Men's violence against them is a justified reassertion of control over these out-of-control emotional creatures.

Catharine MacKinnon is one of the most adamant spokespersons to articulate the gender-related cultural meaning of sexualizing violence. She writes:

> Whatever it takes to make a penis shudder and stiffen with the experience of its potency is what sexuality means culturally. . . . Hierarchy, a constant creation of person/thing, top/bottom, dominance/subordination relations does [make it shudder and stiffen]. . . . what is called sexuality is the dynamic of control by which male dominance—in forms that range from

intimate to institutional, from a look to rape—eroticizes and thus defines man and woman, gender identity and sexual pleasure. It is also that which maintains and defines male supremacy as a political system.[35]

As mentioned in the earlier discussion of MacKinnon, heterosexuality, political domination, and violence are collapsed together in her theory. The social process of these overlapping categories infuses the notion of what is erotic. To MacKinnon, rape and sexual pleasure are indistinguishable in this culture because of the hierarchical construction of gender and the legitimation of violence as a means of controlling women. Since the domination of women is eroticized in our systems of social hierarchy, violence as an expression of male dominance informs what is likewise considered erotic. This formula for eroticizing male dominance applies to the battering of women as well as sexual assault. With regard to battering, the way that women are defined as sexual beings under the system of male supremacy gives meaning to the violence against them. MacKinnon argues that it is difficult to make a major distinction in this culture "in the level of sex involved between being assaulted by a penis and being assaulted by a fist, especially when the perpetrator is a man."[36]

Whether the assault consists of rape or battering, there is an inescapable sexual component to men violating women. The cultural definition of "woman" under the current system of male supremacy supplies this component. This formulation shows yet again how the quality of injustice is societally deleted from the male assault of women. The parts of women's identities that are unrelated to their morally tolerated function as objects to be assaulted are beyond the parameters of public concern.

In perhaps too extreme a fashion, however, MacKinnon creates cardboard women hopelessly trapped in a closed system of male dominance that sanctions their violation. In this system, sexual violence occurs even when women consider their coitus experience as sexual pleasure. Nevertheless, MacKinnon's insistence on examining the determining link (albeit a somewhat overly determined one in her theory) between the social construction of biological identity and male violence makes a crucial contribution. Appreciation of this linkage helps us understand how rape and battering are so thoroughly culturally embedded. Of course, the role played by the system of white supremacy must be added to this framework. Systems of gender/power dynamics are inseparable from those of race/power dynamics in shaping the social meanings of identity, which in turn help to determine the consequences of male violence for women.

A steady flow of media images helps us to accept this convergence of political domination, heterosexuality, and violence. The merger of social meanings that occurs in this convergence eroticizes the rape, battering, and even killing of women. As I have noted, this method of defining the erotic is metaphorically invoked in movies, on television, and in advertisements. Our reception of symbolic acts of violence against women as a pleasurable source of entertainment has become a commonplace ritual of daily life. This fact obviously nurtures public acceptance of male violence and builds up our immunity to recognizing real women's anguish. Also, the myriad violent images that bombard us exponentially expand the capacity of our erotic imaginations. Alarmingly, our erotic sensibilities are continuously schooled in the prolific variations on male brutalizing of women that saturate the culture. Male perpetrators are abetted and potential ones are cultivated.

Black Women's Faults Invite Violence

Another cultural image of black women that helps to foist blame for their victimization back upon them, labels them as innately flawed. Fault is found with their performance of key family and community roles, which then supposedly results in pathology in both those arenas. Contentions about black women as flawed and blameworthy are embodied in persistent stereotypes of them as lazy, emasculating heads of households, and promiscuous. These perceptions can have a highly destructive ideological influence on black women victim-survivors of male violence.

Stereotypes about laziness are pinned on poor black mothers in particular, and can help sanction male violence against them. Perceptions about poor black women as indolent single mothers who produce massive numbers of "illegitimate children," and who would prefer to live off public assistance rather than work are not limited to casual everyday conversation. These distorted images have been repeated by policy makers at the top levels of our government throughout the latter half of the twentieth century. When Congress debated welfare reform in the 1960s, some of the most demeaning images of black mothers were routinely invoked by lawmakers. For instance, in a 1967 debate Senator Robert Byrd (D-W.Va.) commented on statistics about women on welfare in Washington, D.C., a city where blacks made up the vast majority of the poor. He claimed to have found "a record of six women who have sixty illegitimate children, all on welfare. . . . There was another group of fourteen women with one hundred twenty-six illegitimate children, all on welfare. Another group of twenty women have one hundred sixty illegitimate children, all on welfare."[37] This atypical situation was presented as an accurate characterization of the typical family structure of poor black women. During the same debate, Senator Russell Long (D-LA) explained the need for legislation to correct the "sorry situation" of black ghetto mothers in Harlem that his colleague from New York (Senator Jacob Javits) had just referred to. Long declared that

> we do not want to have the mother sitting around and drinking wine all day. . . . We are so solicitous of people who never did a lick of work in their whole lifetime, and who do not propose to do so because they have a child of school age, that we are prepared to let them use that as an excuse to continue to draw welfare for their child from now on into eternity rather than help themselves.[38]

These insulting stereotypical judgments formed the basis of the enactment of national policy governing poor women's lives. Later, Senator Long was heard referring to African-American and Puerto Rican welfare rights protesters who disrupted these hearings as "Black Brood Mares, Inc."[39]

In congressional debates and hearings on welfare reform in the 1990s, leaders made statements that echoed this earlier period. The position of the 1990s political leaders, including President Bill Clinton, is summarily captured by the final outcome. The very title of the "Personal Responsibility and Work Opportunity Reconciliation Act" is revealing. The title of the 1996 law which decisively ended the entitlement of poor Americans to subsidies for food and basic survival needs, explicitly stigmatizes the population it regulates. Allegedly, subsidies were permanently withdrawn so that those with sufficient moral fiber and will to do so would have the "opportunity" to assume "responsibility" and go out and "work." The political leaders of this nation have made it abundantly clear in their speeches and actions that they must enact legislation to curb this population's innate proclivity toward laziness and general irresponsibility.

The fear of validating stereotypes such as these can exert pressure on women who are in situations of domestic violence. One victim-survivor interviewed by author Ann Jones commented on how she had tried to avoid falling into "the white folks stereotype" of a black family that consists of "mama on welfare and a bunch of delinquent fatherless children." So she "put up with violence all of those years trying *not* to be the welfare mother white folks hate, and then those same white folks had the nerve to turn around and tell me I should've left my husband and applied for welfare."[40] The woman cannot escape blame. On the one hand, there is something wrong with the black woman who leaves—she wants to be a lazy "welfare mother." On the other hand, there is something wrong with the woman who remains in an abusive situation. In either case, "her problems" are rooted in her own inadequacies.

The "white folks stereotype" that can influence victim-survivors such as this woman to remain in dangerous situations is hardly an idiosyncratic concern. Statements about black women's moral decrepitude like those quoted above generally undermine the innocence of women victimized by male violence. They particularly fuel a perception of women as willing participants in an immoral lifestyle bred within their subculture. Consequently, they find them at least partly responsible for immoral acts perpetrated in that subculture, including violent acts committed against them.

In the eyes of some, merely being a single mom can make black women responsible for the problems of black men and the black community. The 1965 Moynihan Report remains one of the most influential documents shaping discussions about the black poor from the mid-twentieth century onward. This federal government report, written by Daniel Patrick Moynihan, a political science professor then serving as Assistant Secretary of Labor (he later became U.S. Senator from New York), argued that black women's role in black families was responsible for disadvantaging the race. Under the chapter heading "The Tangle of Pathology," Moynihan reported that the "matriarchal structure" of the Negro family" seriously retards the progress of the group as a whole, and imposes a crushing burden on the Negro male and, in consequence, on a great many Negro women as well."[41] Because too many black families are headed by single moms they are "pathological" and spell doom for the progress of the race.

Moreover, as I have noted elsewhere, the 1995 Personal Responsibility Act, introduced as part of the Republican Contract with America, linked high crime rates to the proliferation of black single moms, thus targeting them for blame.[42] The legislation stated that "the likelihood that a young black man will engage in criminal activities doubles if he is raised without a father and triples if he lives in a neighborhood with a high concentration of single parent families."[43] Thus, according to Congress, when black single moms are present in high concentrations in a neighborhood, the cumulative effect of their innate attributes somehow causes crime to soar.

In recent expressions of concern about the black man as an "endangered species," black scholars sometimes accuse these same black mothers of concerted behavior that retards the progress of black males. Psychiatrist Frances Cress Welsing argues that

> as Black females are left to rear Black male children alone, the alienation, hate and disgust felt towards adult males are visited upon their sons subtly. ... She is much more inclined to say, "There you go looking and acting like that no good nigger father of yours." The black female teacher at school who may also be experiencing alienation from her black man . . . says it more subtly, says nothing, or simply acts out her hate, disgust and distrust of Black males, achieving the same result.[44]

In Welsing's view, black women, whether as mothers or as teachers, are self-centeredly destroying the psyches of young males because of prior emotional pain that adult males may have caused them. The behavior supposedly emerges when women are "left to rear Black male children alone." Therefore, some psychological and/or moral defect stemming from a prior personal experience with an adult male intimate partner, rears up and prompts them to emotionally abuse their own male children or students.

In black-woman-blaming constructions like these, the woman's relationship to black males in particular is characterized by her responsibility for causing them great damage. Even if inadvertently, she causes immense harm because of her place in the structure of the black family that "retards the progress" of the entire racial group. Not surprisingly, Beth Richie's study of battered black women's gender entrapment describes how black women were especially vulnerable to abuse because they were more likely than their battered white women counterparts to feel sorry for their male abusers, to internalize a sense of responsibility for their failed relationships, and to blame themselves for the abuse.[45] Voices ranging from the U.S. Congress to a variant of black community-based psychiatry, teach them that they are lazy, self-centered, pathology-inducing women, responsible for the dismal fate of the black family, community, and most importantly, the black male.

Perceptions of black women as inherently promiscuous can have a dampening influence on the recognition of sexual assault as a crime perpetrated against them. For over a century, social scientists have proclaimed the promiscuity of black women as fact, thereby giving formal academic validation to this vicious idea. Historian Patricia Morton usefully charts disparaging stereotypical images of black women in the "factual" literature of the social sciences from the 1870s to the 1970s. For instance, she cites scholarship of the early Jim Crow era that held the ex-slave woman's uncontrolled sexual "wantonness" accountable for the colored freedman's allegedly savage sexual pursuit of white women.[46] In academic treatments that began in the postbellum period and continued into the early twentieth century, it was understood that black women's sexual "depravity" stemmed from the legacy of slavery, when they developed a "permissive" response to white male overtures. A social psychology study by John Dollard, a white author in the 1930s, identified the "licentious" sexual behavior of black women as epitomizing the depravity of lower-class blacks. This behavior resulted from the "weak" family structure which allowed women too much independence from the control of husbands.[47] Pioneering black sociologists of this same period, such as E. Franklin Frazier, found the "loose sexual behavior" of black women key to the destruction of the Negro family and the general perpetuation of the "Negro Problem."[48]

As feminist scholars such as Morton have documented, a staggering historical legacy of social scientific "research" has been established that finds black women culpable for social problems in the black community. The assertion of shameful sexual proclivities as an intrinsic character defect, along with other distorting claims about black women's roles in the family and community, develop a cumulative avalanche of ideology. They inform the contemporary identity of black women, depicting them as women who "naturally" need to be reformed and controlled. Regulatory, even punitive, public responses to black women seem appropriate and all too reasonable. Male violence against them is given yet another "rational" basis. Communal numbness to the terrorizing effects of that violence evolves further. Meanwhile, women become well-rehearsed in the practice of self-blame.

Institutional Barriers and Perceptions of and by Women

Debasing ideological constructions of black womanhood are often concretely actualized through institutional responses to victim-survivors of male violence. The official agencies authorized by our society to respond to the needs of women, such as the police, courts, and hospitals can function in this capacity. Church practices and clergy responses to women sometimes reproduce the same effect as well. Sometimes these barriers are even found within organizations whose primary goal is to provide services that treat women in a countercultural fashion, such as battered women's shelters or rape crisis hot lines. Steeped in ideological presuppositions that stereotype black women or deny them their right to occupy a victim-status, the actions and silent disregard of state and private community groups exacerbates women's trauma.

Hidden Barriers That Silence Women's Needs before They Are Expressed

Institutional barriers linked to racism and poverty can sometimes join together to form hidden impediments for poor women victim-survivors. These combined elements can assail women through the state's powerful role in their lives. The state often fulfills a dual function related to their family needs and survival: first, as a source of support, and second, as an intrusive monitor. In one interview, a black woman victim-survivor of sexual assault described her fears about having her family broken up if she sought out her state-assigned counselor to discuss having been raped. She was interviewed immediately following her assault by psychology researcher Michelle Fine. Rejecting Fine's suggestion that she seek support from her social worker, the woman explained:

> She's the one who took away my kids. If they take my baby, I would kill myself. I ain't gonna get myself in trouble, all I got is my baby; and she already thinks I'm a bad mother. But I love my babies and I try hard to take care of them. I just don't understand why men have to rape. Why do they have to take, when they could just ask?[49]

Poor women who are dependent upon the state to meet their needs for counseling and therapy are also vulnerable to many forms of unrequested state intervention in their lives. In the interview cited above, the woman assumed that reporting her rape would get her "in trouble," and ultimately would result in her being blamed, in some way, for the rape. This illustrates how prevailing perceptions of poor black women as "guilty" for being poor and black, can infect their status with regard to being sexually assaulted. It shows how the poisonous notion of the innate "guilt" of poor black women can influence the self-perceptions of victim-survivors of male violence as well as their caregivers. Moreover, the interviewed woman's vulnerability to unwanted invasion by the state because of her poverty duplicates her experience with her rapist. The process of recovery for these women can be substantively thwarted by the fact that they are such routine targets of public blame (exemplified above in the discussion of welfare benefits). As a direct consequence of seeking help and support after being assaulted by male perpetrators, the women are vulnerable to revictimization by the sometimes arbitrarily wielded, punitive power of various bureaucracies.

Similarly, the state's history of racist intrusion renders its representatives untrustworthy for black women victims of male violence. Recall the incident Denise related when her family accompanied her father as he tried to carry out his duties as a bank security guard. The family was traveling in a wealthy white community known to be hostile to blacks when they were stopped by white police officers. Denise remembered that the officers immediately drew their guns without asking a single question and pointed them at her father's head as well as at the rest of the family sitting in the car. She was nine years old and terrified. Reflecting on this episode as an adult, Denise described how that moment taught her a definitive lesson about what it meant to be a black person in America. She had learned the indelible fact of her subjugated racial status and the role of the police in reinforcing that status. It was absurd for Denise to consider turning to the police for help when her father beat her mother or repeatedly violated her sexually during her childhood. The police represented yet another volatile source of terror and danger to herself and her family.[50]

Women sometimes make a conscious decision not to seek out the police because they have reliable information about the presence of perpetrators of intimate violence on the force.[51] One black woman who had been battered by her husband for twelve years, explained, "The cops are the worst people to get involved in a family problem, probably because they beat up on women too! I know it because my girlfriend's old man is a cop, and he is an abuser himself."[52] Quite obviously, the potential for simply inviting another perpetrator of male violence against women into the crisis a woman faces, erodes confidence in the police. Women's testimony about their distrust of the police or of state social workers based on specific experiences and "knowledge" demonstrates the hidden, informal barriers that leave them feeling stranded and trapped. Their subjugated knowledge belies the established, formal label of state institutions that are supposed to serve and protect the public interest.

Poor black female victim-survivors of male violence may regard state-operated services as a very unreliable option. As I have noted already, Prothrow-Stith's work on urban violence shows that public services to enhance life and assist with daily needs such as garbage collection and public transportation, or provide services to assist in life-threatening situations like fire fighters and ambulances, are notoriously unreliable in poor communities.[53] Under these conditions, why would a woman entrust to the emergency services a problem as emotionally complex and traumatic as intimate violence?[54] Reminders that the concerns and crises that effect women's daily lives are of minimal importance to society at large are evident to them on a routine basis. Wouldn't intimate violence be subject to the same standard of disregard? "Sarah" provides an account of a battering incident which dramatically illustrates this problem. She reports that "he [her husband] was hitting me and yelling 'I'll kill you b-tch!' 'I'll kill you!' while I was on the telephone with the police."[55] She continues to explain how her husband assaulted her with the knife that she had picked up to defend herself and then put a gun to her head, still declaring that he would kill her. At this point in her description, Sarah comments in a tone that carries no hint of surprise: "Needless to say, the police never came."

The Inability to Hear the Needs That Women Do Articulate

Churches represent a community resource that should offer women coping with the crisis of male violence a caring response. Unfortunately, church practices and leaders too often neglect or dismiss the needs of women who have been victimized. Such behavior reinforces social mores that assume that black women are, and ought to be, resilient, sacrificing, persevering martyrs in spite of such "trials." Sometimes the neglect is manifested in the tremendous demands that the "work ethic" of internal church culture places on its women members. This ethic is usually indifferent to the issues of male violence that women face and privately discuss with the pastor, in women's prayer groups, or informally with church friends. Of course, victim-survivors need to have confidential resources available to them, both informal and pastoral. Yet "secrets" about abusive husbands and fathers can become common knowledge within congregations, while failing to provoke any action to stop the violence. Meanwhile, endless cooking and serving for fundraisers, planning for revivals, arranging for bus trips, and organizing the church school remain the unaltered, energy-consuming agenda for church women.

No matter how many instances of male violence are confided to the pastoral staff or raised in the women's prayer group, the institutional priorities of the church seldom shift toward offering women a supportive and empowering response. At the same time, when Christian teachings that appear to sanction male violence in the home by advocating patriarchal authority over women and children remain unchallenged, the church environment functions as an incubator of abuse and a purveyor of the exploitative treatment of women.

In my interview with Dr. Baker, a therapist whose private practice focuses on individual and group work with black women, she described the church experience of a client. It underscores the costliness of this church "work ethic." The woman was struggling with recurring flashbacks of her sexual assault by an uncle which had taken place over a period of three years when she was about eight years old. Dr. Baker explained that though the woman never used the word faith in connection with it, she cared about her church very much. She also definitely relied on personal spirituality. But the woman described her church as "a place where she gets dumped on" and can't defend herself. It is "a demanding place" where she "does a lot of work," and that "takes a lot of time."[56]

Since she may not have shared her torment related to the childhood sexual assault with church members or the pastor, this example may better illustrate the church "work ethic" as a type of hidden barrier that prevents women from reaching out for help and support. Nevertheless, the church experience of Dr. Baker's client offers profound evidence of the way that church neglect of these concerns can replicate the experience of male abuse. Church as a place that "dumps on her," "demands," and "takes" from her may have an uncanny resemblance to her experience of her uncle's assaults. The church's neglect of issues of male violence, combined with its insistent demands for female labor and self-sacrifice, can exact an excruciating emotional and spiritual toll. What image of black women's innate capacity to withstand violence allows for this kind of church neglect of victim-survivors?

Other institutional practices also duplicate the abusive treatment a woman has already received from the male perpetrator. One woman reported being denied assistance by a religious-based program for battered women after she disclosed that she was sexually attracted to a woman, which was the excuse her boyfriend gave for beating her.[57] In this instance, the response of a religious-based program to the woman seemed to precisely mirror the reasoning of the male abuser in finding her deserving of violent assault. How is black women's human worth appraised that allows for this type of dismissal of victim-survivors by a religious institution?

Sometimes religious institutions demonstrate stronger cultural and political allegiances to the "needs" of black males than to those of women. Church responses toward black women too frequently contradict the principles of compassion and justice that Christian traditions espouse. Christian women who have been assaulted may expect these principles to be applied to them. An example of an appalling church response occurred when a Spellman College coed filed a report to the police about having been gang-raped by Morehouse College students. As the brother-sister college campuses reacted to the news of this rape charge, the dean of the Morehouse Chapel responded in an accusatory fashion toward the victim in a public forum.[58] During a worship service soon after the incident was made public, Reverend Lawrence Carter suggested that women who wear certain kinds of clothing and exhibit particular attitudes may provoke men to assaultive behavior.

In another case that received tremendous media attention, several prominent religious leaders also blatantly indicated their lack of concern for a black woman who was raped by a black man. When heavyweight boxer Mike Tyson was accused of rape by beauty pageant participant Desiree Washington, many religious leaders flocked to Tyson's side. Leaders of the Nation of Islam (including Louis Farrakan) gathered with Baptist leaders to decry the injustice they claimed was being done to Tyson before and after his conviction.

Baptist clergy circulated petitions, held prayer vigils for Tyson during his trial, and helped to organize a "welcome home" rally upon his release from prison. Reverend T. J. Jemison who, at the time of Tyson's trial was head of the nation's largest black Baptist denomination, the National Baptist Convention, was among the key supporters of Tyson. Jemison asserted that "the church has great respect for Black Womanhood. . . . However, I am concerned in general about the Black Male and his plight."[59] Reverend Al Sharpton, a political leader in New York City and fierce supporter of Tyson, defended a telephone call made by Jemison attempting to pressure Washington to rescind her story. Sharpton justified this action by Jemison by saying that the Baptist leader was concerned about the image of black people.[60] The actions and statements of these prominent clergy leaders made the unmistakable point that in the wake of a black woman's sexual assault by a black man, it is the black man who matters most to the church.

Jill Nelson has written about her efforts to stop a Harlem-based rally and street festival to confer "hero status on longtime black woman abuser and convicted rapist Mike Tyson" in Harlem.[61] Nelson is a victim-survivor of domestic violence by her husband who hit her so hard in the head that he punctured her ear drum. She reports the disappointing response of the religious community to invitations by antiviolence community activists to help counter the celebration of Tyson. With the exception of one prominent pastor,[62] Nelson describes a cold reception by area churches to their organizing efforts. Of those who joined in supporting the celebration of Tyson, she remarks, "What could those preachers be thinking every Sunday when they looked out on their overwhelmingly female congregants? Are they so complacent and corrupt that they too don't see black women even when we're the ones signing the checks?"[63] Regardless of their unfailing support of their churches, women victim-survivors of black male violence like Nelson are often notified that their churches will not support them. This abandonment is especially likely when the situation is exposed to the glare of the public spotlight. Church responses to black male violence against women appear to operate on the moral assumption that, first, black women are supposed to be self-sacrificing, and second, when such violence does occur women are the ones whose health and safety can and should be sacrificed by the community.

Even private community groups whose sole mission is to empathetically serve women victimized by intimate violence can keep black women from receiving needed assistance on account of devaluing assumptions about them. When I interviewed battered women's shelter worker Anna Carlson, she described attitudes by her white coworkers at the shelter that were sometimes more suspicious of statements by black women who called the crisis line expressing a need for shelter, than they were of white women making similar requests.[64] Carlson found that some shelter workers were more inclined to consider the possibility that black women who telephoned the shelter were not actually in crisis due to male violence. The white workers suspected that the black callers were "merely homeless women" or had been evicted from their housing because of a drug problem. In such instances, the sound of black women's pleas seems to carry a quality that differed from white women's pleas for help.

This example points out how poor black women's pleas can appear to some shelter workers to be encoded with clues indicating a particularly marginal social status. Such workers may have prejudices that associate black women callers with individuals popularly thought of as the unworthy or unredeemable poor, such as "urban crack addicts." Precisely labeling what cues about their social status are evident in black women's self-presentations that trigger this kind of rejection by hot-line workers is a complicated task. And sorting it out is less important than the fact that these cues can cause doubt about an imminent threat to the women. Indicators of race and class background can foster skepticism about the validity of a black victim-survivor's claims that her life is in danger because of male violence. In this way, joint stigmas related to race and poverty can obstruct recognition of black women's victimization and prevent them from gaining access to needed care and support.

In a few of my own discussions with staff and volunteers at battered women's shelters, I have found an alarming absence of concern about the way racist views can destructively impact their services to women of color. Too often, the area of antiracism is neglected among the criteria for employing and training staff. Even when the agency is led by an overwhelmingly white Board of Directors, staff, and volunteers, and offers its services to a population of predominantly black, hispanic, or immigrant racial/ethnic minority women, I have encountered staunch denial and resistance to confronting the presence of racism. Myopic cultural assumptions about white women are responsible for this fundamental institutional problem. An internally generated mythology that presumes the liberal white women staff to be incapable of racial prejudice in their treatment of battered women, sustains and hides the barriers erected by white racism. This kind of institutionalized neglect of the reality of white racism can assume numerous guises to injure battered black women who have articulated their need for help by contacting the shelter.

Racial stereotypes can impede access to support services for sexual assault victim-survivors as well. In their study of the consequences of rape, incest, and sexual harassment, Kathryn Quina and Nancy Carlson summarize troubling notions about black women that range from the charge of wanton promiscuity to the enduring label of tough superwomen. The researchers point out that these stereotypes have led to some of the following damaging and incorrect assumptions about black sexual abuse victims: that they are not as affected by trauma as whites, that they don't need counseling or emotional help, and that they are more difficult to help.[65] Such biases can certainly diminish the perception that black women need help, and that they are worthy of receiving it.

Prejudiced presuppositions about black women's emotional makeup represent a particularly troubling barrier. Anna Carlson also observed occasions when her white colleagues staffing the battered women's crisis hot line were unable to identify the extent of the terror experienced by black women victims of violence.[66] She explained that sometimes shelter workers do not believe that women of color are in danger because they "sound strong" on the telephone, and thus "don't really sound like they are in crisis." As a result, Carlson indicated that she devotes time to black women who use the services of the shelter, working with them on how to express their fears more vehemently so that they can receive help when they need it. Again, cultural assumptions delegitimized black women's anguish precisely as they were reaching out to express it. Racial/gender cultural labeling of black women as matriarchs, amazons, or otherwise invincible can shape the "sound" of their pleas for help when they are victimized by male violence. These cultural filters can modify the meaning of black women's pleas in a fashion that neutralizes their terror and mutes the immanent danger to their lives.

The expression of anger by black women can likewise be culturally interpreted in a way that invalidates the desperation of victim-survivors. Such interpretation is often institutionalized by courts when prosecuting victim-survivors of battering for defending themselves against their attackers. In Lenore Walker's discussion of women who kill their batterers, she notes a study she conducted where the ratio of black women to white women convicted for killing their abusers was nearly two to one.[67] Walker suggests that stereotypes about "the angry black woman" obstruct a victim-survivor's chances of acquittal.

> Most of the women I've seen convicted appeared to be angry. Many of those who appeared angry were also Black. Their palpable fear and terror were somehow obscured. Or perhaps, the mostly white juries that convicted these women were unable to see them as being vulnerable or terrified because the racism rampant in our society implicitly denies Black women the right to manifest a full range of emotions.[68]

Culturally circumscribed judgments about black women's emotions can be liabilities, whether victims seek conventional help from law enforcement and the courts or assistance from private services dedicated to combating violence against women.

Limiting cultural presuppositions about the emotional responses of black women can even influence the research of sympathetic investigators of the psychosocial consequences of male sexual assault and institutional community responses to it. In their early 1980s study of Anglo, Mexican-American, and black women rape victims, social scientists Joyce Williams and Karen Holmes simultaneously contest and lend credence to stereotypes about black women. They contend that black women "evidenced the lowest degree of crisis and the least withdrawn style of functioning,"[69] and then conclude that black women were, in a comparative sense, the most successful in coping with the impact of the rape experience. These researchers account for this finding with a variety of explanations. For example, they argue that black females are by necessity pragmatic and self-reliant in dealing with rape risks. Furthermore, they acknowledge that a broad spectrum of racial and gender exploitation encumbers black women victims. Thus, "while rape is by no means an inconsequential event to a Black woman, it may not, in fact, be the worst thing that has ever happened to her and because her identity is shaped more by color than by sex, it is not likely to destroy her."[70]

These conclusions may have been influenced by a stereotyped image of "the strong black woman." The judgment by Williams and Holmes that since black women are beleaguered by so many problems anyway, the effects of a rape experience are diluted, rests on a faulty assumption of a hierarchical ordering of the subjugating racial and gender dynamics that affect black women. It may also be tied to a "black superwoman mythology" that equates black women's multiple oppression with limitless sources of stamina.[71] Additionally, this formulation locks out consideration of black women's vulnerability to combined manifestations of racial and gender exploitation that could intensify the anguish of rape. The researchers' preconceptions about black women's resilience may have influenced them to deduce that the "low degree of crisis" evidenced by black women indicates their success in coping with rape, rather than the hidden depth of their woundedness. Of course, these dynamics need not be interpreted in an either/or fashion. Black women coping with rape may function well in some ways and bury their anguish in others. But this more complex manner of coping may be ruled out when they are viewed solely as indomitable figures.

Ironically, Williams and Holmes also point out that black women risk being viewed skeptically by those who respond to their assaults, ranging from police officers to rape crisis workers, since they do not appear to be sufficiently upset.[72] Below are examples of such skepticism by police officers, reported by two respondents to their study:

> She [the victim] felt that this detective never took the rape seriously and "he acted as if this was the kind of thing I should be used to." An even more blatant example of judgmental attitudes was described by a Black victim in her twenties who heard the patrol officer say to his partner: "This girl claims she was raped. I don't know how true that is."[73]

Here again, the meaning of a black woman's testimony is regarded with doubt, in one instance about the severity of the event and in the other about the veracity of the claim of sexual assault. A black woman's testimony about rape, when filtered through the invalidating cultural lens that her status invokes, can mean to police officers that either the rape didn't happen at all, or if it did happen, it was not a big deal for a black woman (i.e., it's not really a crime).[74]

Ideas that stigmatize, blame, and objectify women frequently take the form of precise ideological formulations that discount the trauma of African-American women victim-survivors. These women routinely negotiate barriers based on dismissive attitudes and cultural stereotypes about them when trying to gain access to critical rescue and support services. The practice of male violence is comfortably entrenched in these intricately articulated social sanctions and institutional barriers. Although it represents a formidable evil, it is one that can be resisted.

PART IV

Garnering Methods of Resistance

6

Identifying Resistance

The previous chapters have retraced some of the traumatic consequences of violence against women by amplifying their vantage point, and sorting through the social constructions that reproduce their trauma. However, this depiction of the relentless, crushing, and variegated pressures of domination on women would be highly inaccurate without attention to the quality of resistance that also occurs. In addition, such an omission would contradict my theo-ethical assumption of the presence of powerful divine resources available to us for resisting the forms of dehumanization leveled at black women.

Healing and resistance are key ingredients in the process of countering male violence against women. However, there are dramatic differences in their respective properties, how each may be accessed by victim-survivors, and how they are manifested in the broader society. Healing is a regenerative process that repairs the damage of violence. It takes place when the emotional costs to women and the spiritual bonds that have been ravaged by violence are restored and renewed. Healing implies liberation from social labels and structures of power that assure revictimization and repeated wounding of women. Healing within society would entail the elimination of all social instigators of intimate violence. Unfortunately, the extensive moral harm that the violence constitutes is seldom communally redressed in a manner that brings about authentic healing in society. Likewise, the women who survive intimate assault seldom achieve the fully restored and renewed state of well-being that healing promises. But women do engage in resistance.

Unlike healing, resistance involves any sign of dissent with the consuming effects of intimate and social violence. When a woman survives, she accomplishes resistance. It occurs when a community leader publicly contests through words and actions the male-centered notions of power, authority, and status that can appear to authorize violence against women. How is this resistance related to healing? Though hardly a guarantor of healing, acts of resistance can open up possibilities for a degree of healing to take place. These acts of resistance create the conditions for women to take steps toward their own renewed spiritual vitality, and for the local communities where the violence has taken place to begin to restore the trust that has been broken.

Yet, since the intimate and social violence against black women is comprised not only of particular incidents of assault but also of ongoing systemic violations, the rectifying work of healing is perpetually unfinished. Healing is a frustrating, unreachable goal under the present conditions of our white supremacist, male-centered society. Only acts of resistance can challenge the virulent strains of violence that are visited upon African-American women. And when communally carried out with a persistent and comprehensive approach that matches the violence, resistance bears the potential for igniting a broad-based transformation of cultural values and practices.

Challenging the varied combinations of oppressive realities that contribute to the trauma of black women victim-survivors of male violence involves a fierce struggle. Of course, this struggle is already being waged. To analyze it meaningfully we need to attend to both method and practice. In this chapter, consideration will be given to a method for conceptualizing the struggle to resist, as well as the concrete practices that have been and ought to be a part of it. While both broad-based communal and individual women's resistance are undeniably bound together in the struggle to stem the violence, this chapter will focus on the identification of individual women's resistance.

The Concept of Resistance

The first and most basic issue that requires attention when conceiving of a method of resistance to the trauma of intimate violence, is to define resistance behavior as being within the realm of possibility for victim-survivors. We need to break through ideological biases that impede us from considering even the potential for oppositional behavior by women. Certain racialized filters for interpreting behavior can obscure black women's acts of resistance. Similarly, conceiving of women as "victims" in an overly determining manner can hinder our appreciation of their help-seeking efforts.

Rejecting an Approach That Overstates
the Impact of Oppression

Overgeneralization about how societal oppression functions can sometimes create formidable barriers to recognizing and understanding resistance. Too unrelenting a focus on the destructive impact of race and gender subjugation upon black women victim-survivors helps build such a barrier. Alexander Thomas and Samuel Sillen, psychiatrists and scholars of the history of psychiatry, point out the dangerous implications of overstating the impact of racism upon blacks. They criticize psychiatric theories that conclude that racism creates an "essential" psychological deformity in blacks.[1] Generalizations about a uniform, devastating consequence of racism can lend credence to stereotyped claims about the innate pathology of blacks. Analyzing the impact of racial oppression with such a narrow degenerative focus actually supports a psychosocial theory of black inferiority. It impedes acknowledgment of the creative and healthy cultural resources and strategic responses that blacks draw upon and develop. Therefore, while it is important to describe the possible, potent destructive impact upon victim-survivors of heterosexist, sexist, and racist cultural norms, any such analysis needs to be nuanced with consideration of the range of tactics available to women for coping with and stymieing this impact.

Just as it is erroneous and crude to dub white supremacist dynamics a racial "malady" from which blacks suffer, so any single definition of black women's response to devaluing social norms is misleading. Any attempt to assign a single group response to the myriad subjugating cultural messages that intensify black women's experiences of male assault obfuscates analysis of their agency. Such oversimplification hinders appreciation of women's self-empowered oppositional activity.

In a general analysis of the psychosocial adjustment in black women, psychologist Beverly Greene cautions us about the balance that is needed. She explains the varieties of stress and psychic conflict that may be produced by demeaning racial and gender stereotypes and circumscriptions about skin color, body size, and shape. Greene urges therapists who are engaged in psychotherapeutic treatment of black women to be aware of these realities, yet also enjoins them to be cognizant of black women's individuality. She warns: "Although black persons share many group characteristics, an individual black woman will attempt to cope with racial life stressors with the same characterological and defensive structures used to respond to the other life stressors."[2] An understanding of resistance to the ways race and gender subjugation compound the trauma of male violence for black women needs not only to allow for human agency, but also to include an assumption of both the shared and individual elements of identity that nurture their agency.

To offer oversimplified and overgeneralized characterizations of black women's identities is to fall prey to the distorting terms set by the conditions in our white-dominated society. If lured into this trap, our conceptualization of resistance to the violence that they confront will miss its goal of capturing the intricate truths of women's responses.

Avoiding an Adversarial Approach of Oppression versus Individual "Victim" Behavior

How do we recognize women's resistance without ignoring the disabling realities of their trauma? Conversely, when these disabling realities are brought into view, how do we avoid overemphasizing them in a way that obscures women's acts of resistance? These tensions are usefully illuminated by the debate among feminist theorists of male violence about the relationship between the traumatic impact battering has upon women and the oppressive role of community support for woman-battering. Many of these tensions are generated by the thesis that women acquire the trait of "learned helplessness" as a result of having been battered by their male partners. Analyzing this controversy raises key points which need to be addressed in defining resistance to the violence against black women. I will offer an analysis that pulls our attention back and forth from one side of these feminist arguments to the other. My intention in using this approach is twofold. First, engaging the issues raised in this debate in this back and forth manner fosters an affective understanding of the difficult but necessary task of formulating resistance practices that will bridge these rival concerns. Second, it directs us toward a sense of appreciation for women's experience of coping with intimate violence in a world which imposes these bifurcated interpretations of their behavior upon them, and where the ground beneath them keeps shifting.

APPROPRIATELY DEFENDING WOMEN INVOLVES EITHER/OR

In the effort to correct misrepresentations of women's experiences of battering, the goals of the feminist advocate must be clarified. In our conception of resistance, a struggle must be waged against labeling women as innately pathological because they are in relationships with battering males. The manner in which women who endure male violence are dismissed as masochists has to be confronted and these claims about them refuted. Lenore Walker's initial theories of battered woman syndrome and much of her subsequent work on violence against women is dedicated to challenging a sexist ideology which presupposes that women who stay in abusive situations are pathological. On the other hand, defending against such labeling of battered women may misdirect feminist work. Rather than offering a corrective, it can reinforce a false interpretation of women's responses to male violence. It can also abet our society's tendency to relieve men from bearing primary responsibility for their recurrent violent acts. On these grounds, Walker has been strongly criticized for her focus on battered woman syndrome. Illustrating such critiques, Ann Jones writes,

> If researchers were not quite so intent upon assigning the pathological behavior to the women, they might see that the more telling question is not "Why do the women stay?" but "Why don't the men let them go?" But mired in reactionary anxiety, even feminists carry on valiantly, pointlessly, asking and answering the wrong question.[3]

Jones not only raises a general issue for all researchers on *which* questions need to be answered with regard to women's victimization by male violence, but also challenges feminist researchers on *whose* questions should consume their attention. She accuses feminists who ask why women stay in abusive relationships (among whom Walker is a prime example) of being "mired in reactionary anxiety." The implication in her argument is that feminist researchers engage in a worthless, "pointless" debate, merely adopting the agenda of sexist researchers who want to view women as pathological.[4]

Feminist goals would indisputably be derailed in the way that Jones asserts if women victim-survivors of violence were unaffected by depictions of their emotional responses to male violence as pathological. The kind of feminist challenge that theorists like Walker offer, in fact, serves the critically worthwhile cause of women victim-survivors of male violence. Recognition and comprehension of the psychosocial reasons why women remain in abusive relationships helps deter the revictimization of women by the sexist conventional attitudes of some professionals who respond to women in crisis.

WOMEN AS RESISTERS, NOT SIMPLY NEUROTIC
AND PSYCHOTIC INDIVIDUALS

Do all our efforts to oppose the knee-jerk identification of women as emotionally "sick" inevitably get us entangled in victim-blaming logic? The persistent question: "Why don't women just leave?" that is asked by many police officers, prosecutors, judges, hospital emergency room staff, as well as members of the news media, epitomizes their misplaced blame of women. This question creates a patently false impression that hides the reality of their repeated, resistant acts.

Allowing this woman-blaming question to remain the focus of attention permits societal responsibility for the violence as well as fundamental evidence of women's agency to be overlooked. One of the most strident and comprehensive critiques of the Lenore Walker approach that argues precisely along these lines, is offered by R. Emerson Dobash and Russell P. Dobash.[5] They accuse her of proposing a therapeutic solution to the problem of male violence when a broad, systemic one is required. To Dobash and Dobash, Walker neglects the patriarchal social, economic, and cultural factors that are responsible for the problem of violence against women, in favor of assigning the victim-survivor unique psychological traits that allow the abuse to continue. In their view, her approach is erroneously individualistic and locates the roots of battered women's victimization in their learned helplessness.

An individualistic approach places unacceptable limitations on our formulation of resistance because it legitimates a depoliticized social response to the violence. Such a response can easily mirror and perpetuate the white supremacist cultural fiction that assumes that every individual (woman) succeeds or fails solely on the basis of individual merit (responsiveness to her counselor/therapist). Even an organization such as a battered women's shelter might operate in accordance with this depoliticized therapeutic emphasis. It might interpret its goal (and many do) as simply the treatment of the problems of certain unfortunate women. A shelter with such a goal poses no real threat to the established arrangements of social power in its community. This approach fails to recognize that challenging the evils in the social order which maintain black women's subjugated status has to be part of our response to the violence they face. Hence, the Walker method seems to foster the exclusion of systemic methods of resistance that would challenge the forms of racism and economic exploitation that thrive in the community and help sustain male violence. Or at least her approach can be easily adapted to a vastly inadequate means of addressing the violence that black women confront.

Some of Walker's early work developing the theory of battered woman syndrome does indeed single out therapeutic responses to battering.[6] She is "guilty" of placing primary emphasis on the individual psychological dynamics between a couple based on the vantage point of the woman being battered. Arguments by Walker about sex role socialization may allow for an interpretation that blames the victim-survivor of violence. Some of her assertions about women's learned helplessness exemplify this problem. For instance, based on her theory of learned helplessness, she argues for women's "susceptibility to remaining a victim." This susceptibility, she contends, "is exacerbated by traditional sex role stereotyping which encourages women to respond with passivity and acquiescence to aggression and dominance by males."[7] This kind of open-ended statement about women's susceptibility to remain victims can leave the impression that women are willing participants in their own abuse. In her later writings, Walker seems to be more careful about consistently nuancing her theories by emphatically stating that violence against women is a social problem caused by men's need for power and status in our society.[8]

WOMEN AS VICTIMS OF BOTH SEXISM AND MALE ASSAULT

Any critique that accuses Walker of assigning blame to the woman victimized by violence is overstated. Even in her early work Walker did not contend that women caused the violence by their abusers or that they could stop it.[9] Her theory does in fact hold society accountable for the anguish women endure as a result of male violence. Her claims about sex role socialization demonstrate her belief that women have internalized disempowering, devaluing social norms that reinforce the violence of their batterers. Recognition of the life-threatening nature of the partnership between these norms and the violence in women's lives helps to counter the tendency to blame the victim-survivor, that is, to view her as psychologically flawed. Pointing out its lethal consequences, Walker's theories indict the sexist social construction of gender. Our ability to see the role that culture plays within the psyche of women victimized by violence is enhanced by this approach.

Underlying some of these clashes about "learned helplessness" is a dispute over the urgent need to recognize women's anguish as a societal problem that must be addressed. The anguish that arises from male vio-

lence can be too easily neglected by antiviolence feminist advocates because they regard it as a derivative issue that will disappear after the larger
problem of male violence has been eliminated. In their view, the anguish
can be most effectively eradicated by deterring and changing actual and
potential male perpetrators of violence, or ferreting out the broader systemic sanctions for violence against women. But meanwhile, what about
the desperation, the emotional and spiritual injury that women experience daily as they try to cope with male violence? Sometimes the psychological terror of the abuser, abetted and reinforced in a myriad ways by
the culture, does succeed in teaching women to feel helpless.

WOMEN AS ANGUISHED SURVIVORS

Admittedly, emphasizing women's psychic damage and highlighting
women's resistance may seem to be two disparate, competing goals. Furthermore, defeating the cultural tendency to erase women's acts of resistance certainly seems like the harder task. The prevalence of social impediments to women's resistance is not as readily established in common
perception as the assumption that woman-battering in intimate relationships is prolonged by the "helpless" behavior of women.

In a study that focused on women who used the services of battered
women's shelters, Edward Gondolf documented the profoundly false nature of learned-helplessness theories of women in long-term battering relationships.[10] Based on this research, Gondolf maintains that women
coping with male violence do not display the "victim" characteristics usually ascribed to those who are battered; instead they act assertively and
logically as "survivors."[11] He argues that the greater the danger to themselves and to their children from male partners, the more women's help-
seeking behavior increases. He contends that the depiction of women as
paralyzed by the trauma of male violence is a gross misrepresentation.
The effort by battered women

> to survive transcends even fearsome danger, depression or guilt, and eco-
> nomic constraints. It supersedes the "giving up and giving in" which occurs
> according to learned helplessness. In this effort to survive, battered women
> are, in fact, heroically assertive and persistent.[12]

This analysis does not suggest that emotional turmoil, including traumatic shock, bouts of depression, or self-doubt are absent from battered
women's experience of abuse. Rather, these should be seen as healthy reactions which have been inaccurately assessed as helpless and hence inap-

propriate victim behavior. Gondolf insists that the mere questioning of the healthiness of these responses reflects our male-dominated society which overvalues "cool" detachment as the most useful approach to difficult and threatening situations. Moreover, self-doubt and anxiety are all the more appropriate, given the community's unresponsiveness to women's help-seeking behavior.[13] Gondolf asserts that helplessness and other "deficiencies" attributed to battered women should more appropriately be credited to the inadequate community resources to which women appeal.

The appreciation of women's moral agency is dramatically increased when the psychosocial issues that prolong and perpetuate long-term cycles of abuse are reframed as community deficiencies, rather than as flaws embedded in the psyches or moral characters of the women who are abused. Nevertheless, Gondolf and his associates may too rigidly polarize the choice between wrongly identifying "victim" behavior or rightly pointing to institutionalized sanctions of violence as the key to recognizing women's resistant "survivor" behavior.

It is entirely consistent with the innate nature of political subordination in western societies that women's resistant behavior is expunged from the "official transcripts" of history. Political scientist James Scott contrasts the term "official transcripts" with the "hidden transcripts" of those who are socially subordinated. Scott's theory of resistance to social domination delineates the features of each of these types of transcripts. It is part of the very essence of domination to maintain the invisibility of resistance to the dominant culture. Scott explains that "on those occasions when subordinate groups do put in an appearance [in the official transcripts], their presence, motives and behavior are mediated by the interpretation of the dominant elites."[14] In the case of male violence against women, often neither the violence that women have endured nor their resistance to it are recorded as a significant part of world history. Particularly when women utilize "private" resources seeking help from friends or family members, it "doesn't count." There is no record of the multiplicity of tactics that women use in "private" settings to survive the varied forms and circumstances of male violence. The police and courts, who so often fail to take women's complaints about violence seriously, provide the official transcripts which shape public perceptions of women's help-seeking behavior. Not surprisingly, these official transcripts most frequently attribute the errors in judgment or procedure that help perpetuate domestic violence to women rather than to state authorities. The erasure of black women's resistance behavior is an endemic feature of their subordinate political status.

However, an exclusive focus on women's courageous survivor responses helps to negate their actual victimization and obscure an important truth about male violence. Black women certainly are "victims" of male violence and often feel quite helpless during or after an attack. It is essential to recognize this if we are to dispel cultural myths which maintain that women desire to be violated by men and/or ask for it in some way. Validation of women's victimization need not be synonymous with woman-blaming. Acknowledgment of women's experience of "helplessness" in response to male attacks must incorporate an admission of the cultural propensity to blame them for being victims and to overlook the ways that they seek help to stop the abuse. Additionally, this acknowledgment must direct concern toward the routinized, inept response by the community. A concept of resistance that fails to appreciate the linked personal and political nature of women's experience of male assault by allowing for a systemic response directly supportive of individual women's efforts, will be fundamentally ineffectual in opposing the violence. Resistance must encompass a broad-based movement for social change that pays particular attention to the intense anguish generated by the violence.

Embracing an Integrated Approach

Most importantly, overstated assertions and competing sets of claims classifying women as either victims or survivors misrepresent the conditions of women's lives. They tear away partial truths to support one of two categories of analysis. A feminist assessment relevant to black women victim-survivors of male violence requires a multifaceted concept of resistance. The web of subordinating social dynamics that ensnare women discourages a dichotomous notion of victimization and agency. As feminist legal theorist Martha Mahoney notes, the use of such a dichotomy rests upon the separation of the act of physical violence from its context of broader patterns of social power, and from other issues related to the complexity of needs and struggles in a woman's life.[15] Pitting notions of victimization against those of agency nurtures the false assumption that a woman can isolate the male violence in her life and then choose to respond to it in one of two ways depending upon the strength of her character or her psychological health.

These unrealistic conditions for understanding "authentic" resistance are created by the way the terms are commonly defined. As Mahoney points out,

> In our society, agency and victimization are each known by the absence of the other: you are an agent if you are not a victim, and you are a victim if you are in no way an agent. In this concept, agency does not mean acting for oneself under the conditions of oppression; it means *being without oppression*, either having ended oppression or never having experienced it at all.[16]

Within this logic, black women's agency is clearly imperceptible for the resistance of black women victim-survivors always involves "acting for oneself under the conditions of oppression." Under the existing conditions of white supremacy and male dominance some degree of victim status is constant for African-American women. When this rigid victim-agency duality is accepted, victim status is conflated with powerlessness, which, of course, effaces acts of resistance. Likewise, victimization usually encourages shame in women when it is understood as the absence of agency. To counter this process of erasure and shaming, and to more adequately capture the intricate fabric of women's realities, a resistance paradigm for African-American victim-survivors must include the roles of both victim and agent. These roles should be configured in a resistance framework that allows them to exist as alternating and overlapping dynamics.

This conceptual adjustment precludes any facile prescription about what constitutes proper resistance behavior. Even among advocates and caregivers, there is sometimes serious danger of fueling more prejudice against women when resistance behavior is defined in terms of static categories which denote certain responses as correct. As Mahoney points out, sometimes "economic oppression becomes an issue that is raised defensively, to 'explain' why a woman 'failed' to leave, instead of being understood as always part of the matrix of her choices and decisions."[17] Racism is sometimes invoked in a similar fashion to "explain" why black women "fail" to report their male abusers to the police. Racism should be understood as thoroughly interwoven into all their life-choices, not as an isolated phenomenon that rears its head when the victim-survivor is trying to decide whether or not to call the police. It is also critical to define resistance in a manner that does not stigmatize victim-survivors by setting up certain women as failures and others as heroic.

The need to relinquish judgments that divide women into competing categories also applies to the survival and liberation goals that are primary for acts of resistance. Obviously, different types of resistance behavior serve different functions. Some methods of coping and surviving may even have self-destructive dimensions. Carey explained that she and her siblings "played" her childhood sexual abuser for their "very own sucker" by frequently getting him to take them out for ice cream. (Recall that he abused Carey's sister too.) She also pointed out that "selling her body on the street" at the age of twelve ended the sexual abuse by this man who was her mother's boyfriend. Carey developed these strategies to help her cope and survive in response to male assault. This example illustrates the varying degrees of emphasis on survival and liberation that may underlie different resistance strategies.

Liberation goals of resistance that seek to ensure freedom from brutality and exploitation for women and girls would be least applicable to strategies like street prostitution at the age of twelve. Certain resistance strategies have healthier effects than others, but they are all integral to making even the possibility of healing viable. Our view of resistance must ensure that all its manifestations count. In the "space" created by resistance, one is able to assert a degree of self-control over one's circumstances. Of course, survival and liberation goals are best realized through both individual and community actions against the annihilating agenda of the violence confronting black women.

To conceive of this resistance we must employ our feelings. As Audre Lorde explains in her essay, "Poetry Is Not a Luxury,"

> When we view living in the European mode only as a problem to be solved, we rely solely on ideas to set us free. . . . The white fathers told us: I think, therefore I am. The black mother within each of us—the poet—whispers in our dreams: I feel therefore I can be free.[18]

The intensity and scope of violence against black women represents a problem that we cannot simply think our way out of. Emotional and spiritual resources are a crucial component in perceiving and prescribing methods of resistance to violence. The "knowledge" located in these resources may be easily overlooked, largely because of the Eurocentric cultural biases that Lorde mentions. But a developed cognizance of women's psychic vulnerability that may result from studying the impact of violence might also lead us to devalue the "knowledge" located there. Based on this heightened awareness we may retreat from the attempt to productively utilize the psychospiritual dimensions of experience. After gauging the severity of the injury to the emotional and spiritual resources of victim-survivors, we may consider them tainted with "weakness" or instability and therefore unusable. To constructively employ the emotional and spiritual content of our senses, we must overcome the persuasive cultural influences that deny and obscure their worth as authoritative resources. The collective assault that has been detailed in earlier chapters can most effectively be resisted by engaging these psychospiritual resources, for both comprehending the violence and taking specific steps to stem it.

Recognizing a polymorphous structure for resistance enables us to aggressively and thoroughly challenge the varied and closely knit dimensions of social and intimate violence. The psychosocial and spiritual consequences of male violence merge to formulate a personal and political assault on African-American women victim-survivors, which requires a similarly variegated resistance response. Examination of some of the precise strategies that comprise resistance work will clarify the content of this response.

The Work of Resistance

Naming some of the precise strategies for resisting violence against black women heightens our recognition of women's defiant acts, serves as a deterrent against being overwhelmed by the resilience and pervasiveness of the problem, and challenges community complacency that is too often premised upon the sense of being overwhelmed. Women's stories serve as instructive examples for identifying exactly what the work of resistance involves and guide us toward appreciating other related patterns that should be taken into account.

"Trying to sing it whatever way he wanted"

In her autobiography, popular entertainer Tina Turner described her resistance responses to the unpredictable attacks by her abusive husband, Ike Turner. When he would suddenly lash out at her, verbally abusing her, she explained that she would "try to be sweet." She recounts: "I'd be sitting there wondering if he was going to hit me, and when. Waiting for it. . . . And finally—*bam*! *Bam*! and then *whomp*!"[19] At other times, to forestall his assaults, she would make an effort to appease him by trying to meet his eclectic demands. Ike would wake her up in the middle of the night with a telephone call ordering her to come to the recording studio and rehearse. She would go and do her best to follow his directions on how to sing his lyrics. Tina writes about how especially difficult this was when his directions were unintelligible because he was so deeply under the influence of drugs or alcohol. He would tell her: "'You b-tch, you're not into this, you're not tryin' to learn it.'" In response to him, Tina explains: "I would be standing there *crying*, trying to sing it whatever way he wanted, but it was never right. I was always singing out of fear."[20]

As she silently tried "to be sweet" in one instance, or stood in that studio trying to sing "whatever way he wanted," Tina Turner was engaging in survival resistance work. This work includes accessing whatever coping techniques are needed to survive not only the eruption of brutality, but also daily life under the constant threat of it. Survival resistance may include acquiescent behavior toward the abuser, as well as emotional dissociation or psychic splitting by the victim-survivor. These responses might be counted among what womanist theologian Delores Williams terms the "subtle and silent" strategies of women. Williams is one of the most insistent spokespersons for the appreciation of black women's survival ethic. She asserts that "almost from the day when they first arrived as slaves in America in 1619, African American women have rebelled against their plight. They have used a variety of resistance strategies, some subtle and silent, others more dramatic."[21] This tradition of rebellion against multiple forms of subjugation for the purpose of survival, constitutes a potent social ethic. The women refuse to believe the devaluating assumptions about their human worth that would deny their right to exercise any control over their fate. These assumptions are defied by their deliberate acts to cope and survive. In this process, they reconstruct their worth and facilitate the preservation of black women's lives.

Victim-survivors may utilize this method of attempting to block out the destructive potential of intimate and social violence in multiple ways. Carey's coping behavior illustrates this tactic when she kept the "wall up" against the harassing "men cops" during her "humiliating" experience of being in prison, performed sexual acts as a prostitute by imitating the way that she "numbed out" as a child during her sexual abuse, and when she "just [couldn't] watch" television programs like *Roots* which displayed the ways that whites have historically degraded and oppressed African-Americans. Each of these situations possessed some of the same unpitying, colluding ingredients of dehumanization which Carey sought to elude. She

did what she could to prevent the violation from infecting her consciousness. Though we have seen the multiple ways that silence is imposed
upon women by intimate and social violence, we must now recognize
that women may also choose silence as a mode of resistance. A woman's
choice to silently keep "the wall up" can signal her refusal to accept the
debasing terms of the violence as well as an effort to exercise the only re-
course available to her by exerting her own will.

Women may even utilize the debilitating experience of shame in order
to survive male violence. In the midst of the estrangement from other
people that shame generates, an intensified, nurturing awareness of and
bond with a divine or spiritual presence may emerge for some women.
Here shame may serve an adaptive function of guardianship in the psyche.[22] During a crisis, it can offer a defensive and protective psychic shield
against a hostile environment. A magnified view of how this reaction occurs might incorporate the following steps. A defensive mode emerges in
response to communal attitudes and active rejection, indifference, or
blame of a woman in the aftermath of intimate assault. Shame, then,
forces an internal retreat. At this point women may seek out God or any
other spiritual resource that they find meaningful, and develop a strong
bond with this source of spiritual power. It sustains and nourishes them
in their isolation. Under the conditions of hostile attack, spirituality can
take root and grow in the intimate space carved out by shame. Thus,
women may engage in spirit-nurturing defiance even while thoroughly
ensnared in the web of psychic assault woven by male violence.

"I bit him so hard"

Employing less subtle and less silent tactics, women sometimes engage
in survival resistance with physical combat. Recall how Aisha used every
ounce of her strength to battle her rapist. Carey physically fought off her
abusing male partner's attempt to throw her out of the window. Hence,
even when completely outmatched in physical strength and thus faced
with a lethal threat, women may contest male assault by summoning up
their own physical forces. Robin Quivers, co-host of the popular New
York City radio talk show *The Howard Stern Show*, describes such an act
at the age of eleven. She challenged her father who had been sexually
abusing her. Quivers writes: "He was much bigger than I was and incredibly strong. There was no way that I was a match for him physically, but I
decided that he'd have to beat me to death before I'd ever let him force

himself on me again."[23] She then bit her father "so hard" that he threw her across the room. It was the last time that he attempted to abuse her.

One evening when she was home suffering from a bad cold, Fredrica Gray, executive director of the state of Connecticut's Permanent Commission on the Status of Women, tried to fight off the stranger who entered her home to rape her.[24] As he placed his knee on her chest along with the rest of his weight, he started to pull off her pajama bottoms. She struggled against him to no avail, trying to free herself. Then she used her keen, quick mind to try to prevent the assault or at least trap him into making a mistake that would get him caught later. She told her attacker that she had AIDS and pointed to her medicine that had actually been prescribed by her doctor for her cold. He proceeded to rape her anyway. However, she succeeded in fueling his fears about getting AIDS, arranged for him to call her, and then later had him return to her home for the "AIDS medicine." Gray was able to trap her rapist and make it possible for the police to arrest him.

Obviously, these examples should not be measured in terms of their success in eliminating the violence that befalls women. Most women's efforts are futile in terms of that goal. Moreover, women who physically battle their male abusers incur high physical costs. Though researcher Janice Joseph found that black women were more likely than white women to physically fight back against their batterers, in correlation with that finding she also points out that they were more likely than white women to be hospitalized with abuse-related injuries.[25] These tactics certainly do not insure greater safety for women.

In addition, combative strategies should not be evaluated in terms of their sufficiency as psychically healing remedies for women. For Quivers, the assaults by her father did indeed end after she fought back physically. Yet she acknowledges the indelible costs that resulted from the childhood abuse, such as the loss of her father as a beloved parent and her inability to ever trust people again.[26] Gray's psychological offensive succeeded in getting her rapist arrested and imprisoned, but certainly could not ward off how "it hurt so much." She explained: "I had no idea how deep emotional pain could be. It rivals the worst physical pain."[27] Just as some of the silent, numbing strategies may have as much emotionally destructive potential as they do the ability to alleviate psychological harm, these combative responses do not allow women to escape such injury either. Nonetheless, each of these strategies must be valued for the valiant acts of resistance they represent. That value rests upon the survival and some justice, in the case of Gray, that the women accomplished.

"If the Lord had not been with me, he could have killed me"

One black woman I interviewed regarding her attempted rape spoke of how God's intervention saved her life. Referring to the rapist, she commented repeatedly: "He could have killed me! If the Lord had not been with me, he could have killed me!"[28] This woman was very badly beaten by her attacker and suffered several disfiguring blows to the face. Based on the strict teachings of her particular Christian church tradition, she also felt some guilt about admitting the terror that seized her during the incident. Apologetically, she said: "I felt so scared. I know that fear is not of God, but I felt so scared."[29] She may have questioned her worthiness to receive God's protection because of her fears, but she was unequivocal about the potent salvific content of that protection. It had effected her survival of the assault.

Altamese Thomas, a gang rape victim-survivor, offered a slightly different type of testimony to God's power in her experience of male violence. She commented: "Where I live, nobody's gonna testify. Not to the Police. Anyway, I'm a Baptist and I know God is punishing him right now. He done bad enough and he's suffering."[30] Thomas was referring to the sociopolitical marginality of her community and the consequences of that fact for her as a victim-survivor of male assault. In her community, the state as represented by the police was not recognized and trusted as a source of protection. The absence of such an authority left her without official means to bring her perpetrator to justice. Yet, where the concrete social realities that conspired to support male violence seemed to prevail, Thomas was certain that God's just punishment of the perpetrator would triumph.

The combination of both accounts provides texture and detail for a theology that acknowledges God's active presence during and after male sexual assault. Women recognize divine power as definitively located on their side. God intercedes on their behalf. In one instance God ensures survival, in the other God can be depended upon to bring justice. As theologian Delores Williams contends, "God becomes the element of necessity in the emergence of black women's survival and quality of life strategies."[31] These women's stories illustrate how this "element of necessity" can form a crucial support system for victim-survivors. Faith in God can bring certainty under the conditions of everyday instability and physical assault, restoring to a woman her sense of worth denied by the attacker and often absent within the social realities that govern her community life.

"Salvific prayers came from friends and ancestors"

In her written account, Andrea Benton Rushing poignantly depicts the sustaining spirituality that she experienced when she was being raped.

> My body responds to his vicious parody of intimacy while my brain whirls to read his mind so I can save my life by satisfying him. The sustaining, salvific prayers came from friends and ancestors on the other side of the membrane that separates the living from the dead. While I moan and whimper, some choir is singing, "I don't know where, but I know that you do. I can't see how, but I know you'll get through. God please touch somebody right now, right now."[32]

She received the powerful spiritual gift of intercessory prayer sung by the ancestors "on the other side of the membrane." The spiritual presence of friends and family nurtured and comforted Rushing, providing a "salvific" ingredient for her to endure the horror of sexual assault. This spiritual presence also brought her a connection to God.

For some women, the spiritual presence of family members permits a vital connection to self. A source of strength and support for resisting violence, the spiritual presence of family members can aid in women's survival from the damaging consequences of intimate assault. Denise spoke of the spirit of her deceased grandmothers as "nudging me to continue on" while she coped with the trauma of reviving her memories of childhood sexual abuse. When Denise attempted suicide during this period, the presence of her grandmothers created a spiritual connection that enabled her to survive.

There are also some distinctively Afrocentric depictions of the spiritual resources that are useful in resistance work aimed at the psychospiritual consequences of intimate violence. Nursing professor Mary Alice Saunders describes the intervention of the Ancestors as a form of African spirituality that aided in the healing process of her client "Sarah."[33] This client had experienced severe sexual abuse in her childhood and battering in her marriage. The description by Saunders of this ritual process is based upon the therapeutic journal writing of Sarah. She explains that the Ancestors were sent to Sarah by God. The Ancestors

> told Sarah that she could call them whenever she was in need. She did, and the instant she called they came to her. They stood protecting her soul from the onslaught of evil! The Ancestors want her to know that she was chosen to be of African descent.[34] The Ancestors encircle her, protecting her with their awesome power. They have sustained "her will to live during the dark days of the abuse."[35]

Utilizing these principles within a very different framework, Oya Odumidun Olufumni outlines strategies of resistance rooted in the Yoruba religion of West Africa.[36] One element of this tradition that can be invoked in response to domestic violence is the power of the "Great Mothers." Olufumni explains that the term "Great Mothers" refers to "the collective voices of the gods and revered ancestors."[37] Rituals that call upon this spiritual power establish the authority of communal justice meted out by female ancestors. These rituals emphasize the need to protect the victim and to exact justice on her behalf. This particular idea of an ancestral bridge can root women in a protective "home base" that helps transport them out of isolation and restore self-worth.

It is imperative to remember that resistance work does not belong solely to victim-survivors. This strategy of recognizing ancestral and family connections can also stimulate community resistance to the violence against black women. Activist and musician Bernice Johnson Reagan provides a blueprint for this approach when she narrates her own conscientization and survival-oriented resistance in relation to the case of Joan (pronounced Joanne) Little. When Johnson Reagan was moved to publicly embrace Joan Little as a family member, she created a model of solidarity for community resistance work. The case received notoriety in the 1970s when Little was sexually assaulted by a guard while she was in jail on a burglary charge. Little defended herself by killing her attacker and escaping from jail.

In a reflective process that was at first unrelated to this incident, Bernice Johnson Reagan relates how she began letting "those women in my history and in my contemporary experience [into her psyche] who carried heavy scars in their spirits from the full force of abuse this society unleashes on women."[38] This quest coincided with the publicity surrounding the Little case. Johnson Reagan relates an incident in a local barber shop when she angrily reacted to derisive comments that mislabeled the violence against Little as a sexual act, as "a known experience that they could connect with—the man's climax!"[39] In response to such attitudes Johnson Reagan created a public defense of this black woman victim-survivor. In her music and activism she recognized and claimed Little as sister, mama, lover, and family member. For Johnson Reagan, it became as if "anything anybody said about [Little], they also said about me."[40] Opening herself up to Little's struggle and to women present in her daily life who were abused by their husbands became a life-preserving strategy for Johnson Reagan. She noted: "It might have saved my life, this letting broken women into my world."[41]

Staking out our familial connection to women victim-survivors can disturb us, motivate us, and offer us salvific power to counter the toxicity of the violence in our midst. The concept of familial ancestral ties can link both the women and the community to the vital power needed to express their defiance and attain a long-awaited freedom. Countering male violence spiritually is an essential part of resistance work whether it entails knowing God as Rescuer or Avenger, relies upon the spiritual presence of ancestors propelling a woman toward survival, or involves some other formulation reflective of the religious belief system of a victim-survivor. Spiritual power may be embodied in the presence of family members and ancestors, or divine power may be made accessible by their presence. But in any case, the resistance work involves unleashing a woman-preserving spiritual force. Into the face of so many negating and shaming consequences of violence is launched a spiritual power that insists upon justice and compassion for women and establishes their kinship to woman-centered spiritual authority.

"I claimed my anger"

Linda Hollies describes anger as a key resource when she engaged in recovery work from childhood sexual abuse by her father.[42] Unfortunately, as she points out, anger is a resource often suppressed in Christian spirituality. For much of her life, Hollies believed that her inability to forgive her father and forget what he had done to her stood in the way of her relationship with God. Once she tried asking her father to forgive her for hating him. But partly because of his inadequate response to her, she was still unable to forgive and forget, and to move "the Mountain" (her euphemism for the stultifying emotional effects of the abuse). Once she even confessed this "fault/blame" that she says "had to be mine" to a pastor. Later in her life, when Hollies became a seminary student, she continued to work on moving "the Mountain." She was in a group session of Clinical Pastoral Education (CPE), a training program in crisis counseling for seminarians. As her anger surfaced it became a very valuable resource in her recovery process. Hollies explains:

> Finally I was able to place blame where it belonged—on my father, not on myself. I was also able to experience anger freely for the first time. Because our family equated anger with sin, there was never a way for my siblings or me to have an open or positive expression of anger.[43]

In this breakthrough moment, the experience of anger prompted and encouraged the truth about who was responsible for the violence to emerge. In the face of shaming, blaming lies about women that are constructed by abusers and in the dominant culture, anger is a critical resource that enables women's truthtelling to occur.

At another CPE group session that was pivotal for Linda Hollies, she found herself deeply disturbed by a Bible verse that was presented. She became so upset that she had to run from the room. As she barricaded herself in a stall in the women's bathroom, the CPE supervisor came to help her sort through the emotional and spiritual turmoil she was experiencing. At one point during their exchange, the pastoral counseling supervisor asked if she was angry. At first, she denied it. Hollies recounts: "I could not conceive of anyone who would want to admit to being angry with God. . . . I realized authentic anger that day. I claimed my anger. I chipped at the mountain. The mountain moved."[44] It was anger that definitively loosened the oppressive psychospiritual hold of the abuse that Hollies had been trying so hard to deal with throughout her life. In particular, claiming her anger at God was freeing for her.

For women like Hollies whose lives are rooted in their Christian faith, the struggle to utilize anger as a resource for resistance often begins by negotiating with Christian notions of forgiveness. Anger and forgiveness are frequently opposed in the Christian tradition, as in "Let all bitterness and wrath and anger and clamor and slander be put away from you, with all malice, and be kind to one another, tender hearted, forgiving one another as God in Christ forgave you." *Ephesians* 4:31–32 (RSV)

First, a universalizing interpretation of forgiveness that equates the power and position of the perpetrator with that of the victim-survivor, calling upon them both to "forgive one another," has to be jettisoned. This "neutral" framework for interpreting forgiveness merely perpetuates the injustice against women, silently aiding and abetting in women's victimization. Since victim and attacker obviously do not share the same role in the crime, they do not have the same moral responsibilities in its wake. The crime is his. It is the male perpetrator who needs to repent and to be held accountable by society. Women's productive anger can help circumvent the ways that this truth about male violence can be twisted.

Second, for women to benefit from the use of anger to resist male violence, an oppositional relationship between forgiveness and anger must be rejected. Rather than embracing this rigid polarity, anger should be seen in this context as a form of forgiveness. A woman claiming her anger expresses her subjectivity. For the expression of anger requires self-assertion. It is a revolt against the objectifying and muting force of violence. Claiming her subjectivity represents a vulnerable, courageous act for a woman. Her engagement of God in this way, honors God and forgives God. Her self-assertive act of truthtelling evoked by the anger is a gift that she "gives for" the sake of a relationship with the Divine. This act is premised upon the woman's fundamental worth and dignity. If women do not claim their anger, the subjugating lies about them may remain intact, and thus continue to hamper an authentic, liberating relationship with God, that God wants and needs.

Accessing one's anger might also help identify God's righteous anger. As in the case of Altamese Thomas cited above, recognizing God as Avenger can lend spiritual support to some women. Far from being defined as mere human sinfulness, anger may be seen as a respected prerogative of God. In this view, God's anger can be an indication of God's identification with women and condemnation of the violence. A woman's anger can prompt the realization of God's powerful advocacy on her behalf.

Anger as a key resource for opposing male violence also involves a vision for a broad-based shift in social realities. Feminist ethicist Beverly Harrison explains that anger is a necessary part of social transformation.

> Anger is—and it always is—a sign of some resistance in ourselves to the moral quality of the social relations in which we are immersed. Extreme and intense anger signals a deep reaction to the action upon us or toward others to whom we are related. . . . We must never lose touch with the fact that all serious human activity, especially action for social change, takes its bearings from the rising power of human anger. Such anger is a signal that change is called for, that transformation in relation is required.[45]

In accord with Harrison's argument, anger is an appropriate response to the moral wrong suffered by African-American women brutally assaulted by the combined web of intimate and social violence. But anger does more than benignly recognize such violation—it signals resistance. It helps transform the pernicious forms of social sanction for violence against women.

Denise exemplified this kind of transformative anger in her response to belligerent public reminders of her subjugated social status. On her college campus, she answered the homophobic threats and violence toward her with bold, defiant anger that asserted her subjectivity. She reported that the series of incidents against her made her "sooo angry" that she wanted "to tear that campus apart." Denise expressed her anger by confronting her tormenters. She attended dances where she was unwanted because she was a lesbian and courageously faced the threatening behavior she encountered. By conspicuously dancing with a woman partner, she protested the animosity and prejudice surrounding her that treated her like she "was a blotch on their community." She also walked around her campus wearing a "queer nation" T-shirt, and with an attitude that would "defy anybody to say something." Denise declared that it was liberating not to be silent. Her anger fueled protest and struggle for the recognition of her dignity and full personhood. Countering the collaborative effects of intimate and social violence in her life involved daily public acts of dissent. She illustrates how anger can serve a creative function, helping to develop constructive shifts in social relations.

It can also clarify what is morally wrong about subjugation. This recognition can mobilize all of us toward deliberate acts of opposition. Together with victim-survivors such as Linda and Denise, collective communal indignation is required to transform social norms that devalue and objectify African-American women. Anger expressed in and by the community can create a hostile environment for social and intimate violence, and reduce the trauma reproduced by that violence.

Using anger for social transformation requires a fierce commitment. bell hooks reminds us that "to perpetuate and maintain white supremacy, white folks have colonized black Americans, and part of that colonizing process has been teaching us to repress our rage."[46] For black Americans, gaining access to anger as a resistance strategy means unlearning this repression, or struggling against the colonizing process which teaches us forms of self-hatred and implicates us in the exploitation of others. Often

bolstered by appeals to Christian notions of forgiveness and reconciliation, anger is precisely one of the behaviors that this colonizing process
requires blacks to surrender.[47]

The label of the "angry black b-tch" can be called up as a means of cen-
sure. Once applied to a woman she will most assuredly be penalized for
any display of anger. Therefore, let us not naively or superficially acknowledge anger as a resistance strategy. A tenacious struggle may be demanded of women to elicit and utilize their anger, and even then, their
success at doing so will likely be quite costly to them. This resistance work
is probably best sustained when a support network is available to encourage it.

"I've been in so many groups and so many different kinds of therapy"

Finding a context to foster many of the emotional and spiritual forms
of resistance that we have been reviewing represents another critical element in this pursuit. Therapeutic groups can be a vital resource for
women. In addressing the topic of spirituality and sexual abuse, pastoral
theologian Nancy Ramsay asserts: "to thrive, people need a sense of connectedness with the human community" because it is life-giving and provides a larger meaning and purpose to their lives beyond their own efforts.[48] Women are often able to find this sense of connectedness in
groups made up of other victim-survivors.

The healing capacity of therapeutic groups is widely celebrated by
therapists who work with victim-survivors. Judith Herman, another ar-
dent advocate of interpersonal groups, contends that a well-organized
group provides the antidote for many of the toxic effects of intimate violence. She explains: "Trauma isolates; the group recreates a sense of belonging. Trauma shames and stigmatizes; the group bears witness and affirms. Trauma degrades the victim; the group exalts her. Trauma dehu-
manizes the victim; the group restores her humanity."[49] The group can
have an invaluable, regenerative, therapeutic effect on women. It can
counteract the damage wrought by violence and replenish the painful
emotional crevices left in its wake.

As I have emphasized, however, the benefits of interpersonal groups
for victim-survivors need to be viewed within the context of the social
conditions of women's lives. I have argued that social forms of violence
such as those rooted in racial and/or class barriers relentlessly distort and

attenuate the sense of "connectedness" to community, and prevent complete fulfillment of the restorative goals set forth by Herman. Explicit issues of power regarding racial\gender identity require attention because they too influence the dynamics of any group process and shape its healing efficacy. For example, Denise hardly felt affirmed, exalted, and restored to humanity when surrounded by white women blithely using metaphors about blackness that, for her, had disparaging racial connotations. In this instance, the whites in her group exercised their culturally conferred privilege of denying the relevance of race to their discussion of incest survival. Denise's insight in connecting the personal and political spheres of experience was refused in this therapeutic group setting. "[It's] because I've been in so many groups and so many different kinds of therapy and feminist therapy sessions," Denise explained, as she insisted that healing is only possible in a group context that takes race into account.

Dr. Anderson concisely and bluntly summarized these problematic issues of group therapy with the statement: "If I send a black woman to a support group on domestic violence and she's the only black woman, I have negated that treatment for her."[50] She maintained that there is a desperate need for support groups focused on rape, domestic violence, and incest where African-American women can surround and help one another. Such a setting minimizes the chances of racially based affronts by other participants in the therapy group which can compound the psychic damage the women have already endured. Echoing this view, Denise concluded that "healing has to be done in the company of sisters." Denise acknowledged that when surrounded by white women in a group therapy setting, she suspected that their perceptions of her were laden with racial stereotypes. She felt "that these women have no idea who I am." Of course, validation of one's identity and life struggles is needed on multiple levels. But the affirmation and sense of belonging necessary for resistance work against multivalent forms of oppression must go beyond the personal aspects of violation recognized by most therapists. The social factors that also contribute shaming and stigmatizing elements to the trauma of African-American women victim-survivors must be addressed in this group process.

Finding space for "I'm sad and I need to cry"

The cultivation of "space" to be vulnerable is another key ingredient to be attended to. Serious resistance work has to make it possible for women to elude the consigned cultural roles that forbid displays of weakness in response to violence. Acknowledgment of this need for space reflects the unified conceptualization of "helpless" victim behavior and women's agency for survival that is an essential basis for resistance work. As Denise said, African-American women victim-survivors need "a space to heal and time and place" to break down. Anna Carlson, whose comments are based on her observations of women in the groups she facilitates at the battered women's shelter, also made a strong plea for black women victim-survivors' need for space to feel vulnerable. She commented: "We're so used to being strong. . . . There's just no room for 'I'm sad and I need to cry.'"[51] It seems there is no cultural space for a sad, weak, crying black woman.

Of course, finding "space" requires that the victim-survivor deal with a vast array of cultural constraints, like being interminably cast in the role of the invincible and unceasingly "strong" woman. The barriers to self-awareness leveled by the male assault itself must be sorted through by women seeking emotional and spiritual "space." Pressures from the unrelenting demands of family, work, and community commitments such as church work must also be mediated in this quest. Even locating physical space conducive to in-depth individual reflection may present a serious challenge for women living in cramped family quarters.

Moreover, it should not be assumed that "the space" to be vulnerable is instantly attained by surrounding oneself with other black women victim-survivors. Nancy Boyd-Franklin, a psychologist and researcher, enthusiastically recommends black women's therapy groups. Yet, based on her experience in facilitating such groups, she sees several sociopolitical issues related to race that remain, even within a racially homogeneous setting.[52] Her black women clients in group therapy still felt vulnerable about being labeled "dysfunctional" or "pathological," and were distrustful about discussing their "family business." This sense of vulnerability is fed by the potent cultural messages that demean and stereotype blacks. Boyd-Franklin's clients did succeed in surmounting their fears and apprehensions about disclosure, and eventually some women were able to reveal painful childhood incidents, including sexual abuse. To achieve the degree of trust necessary for this deeper level of sharing, she argues that therapy groups must encourage "African American women to look at the strengths in their families as well as dysfunctional patterns."[53] The tenacious grasp of social ideologies that devalue black women is never totally absent from the room. Regardless of the racial/ethnic makeup of the group, these cultural cues can inhibit and even prevent women from finding the space to be vulnerable. Such barriers must be sorted through and steps taken to counter them in order to create the space that women crave and deserve.

Apart from concern about group members' reactions to "family business," there are often inescapable realities related to social identity and power that psychically weigh upon women and thus also need to be addressed. Even when the therapeutic group is racially homogeneous, effective resistance work must consider a range of social vulnerabilities manifested as daily threats to the survival and dignity of black women. One woman I interviewed talked at length about the inadequacy of the sexual abuse survivor groups that she had attended. She was adamant that "healing" includes more than just sitting in a circle and talking about what happened to you as a child.[54] This victim-survivor pointed out that the healing process will be perpetually unsatisfactory and insufficient if recurrent obstacles such as job and housing discrimination that demoralize and thwart black women are not addressed in these settings.[55] Furthermore, the efficacy of the therapeutic process will be hampered by attempts to create or respect false boundaries between the private and public realms of women's lives. Intimate violence resistance work with "healing" goals must incorporate black women's empowerment in arenas such as housing and employment.

The need for space that is "safe," a related concept described by some therapists as a necessary part of the recovery process, is another issue which has political implications. In her extensive study of the traumatic impact of violence, Herman emphasizes victim-survivors' critical need to rebuild and reestablish a sense of safety. Given the nature of these intimate violations, survivors often come to feel unsafe in their bodies and in relation to other people.[56] Psychotherapy is often recommended as a useful method for building a trusting relationship to address these safety concerns. Herman contends that the process begins by "focusing on control of the body and gradually moves outward toward control of the environment."[57]

However, the realities of sexual harassment on the job or of street crimes against women can make safety and the control of one's environment a perpetual problem.[58] This may be especially true for poor women who reside in certain urban settings with a high rate of assaults and robberies by strangers. The very act of leaving home at night, even for the purpose of attending a women's support group, often means subjecting ones self to further danger. Likewise, at work that ranges from restaurant staffing to corporate professional, a woman may be subjected to an array of harassing or assaultive behaviors by her male customers, clients, or colleagues. Control of one's body and environment are in many respects elusive goals for women in our cultural climate where violations of women are so routine. While the psychotherapeutic relationship can obviously assist in addressing specific emotional consequences of intimate violence, the lack of control over bodily safety that is an inherent feature of our society for women is probably not overcome or restored by therapy.

Therefore, the issue of safety needs to be recognized and addressed in a way that takes our broader social context into account. The term "safety" is perhaps unhelpful in depicting which conditions can and cannot be made available to black women in this culture. It may be more useful to envision the need to create "respite space." "Respite space" should be conceived of as a place to pause, however briefly, right in the midst of the unrelenting threat of intimate and sociopolitical violation. Since the total freedom of a space safe from the onslaught of demeaning and invalidating cultural cues is unattainable, the creation of respite space with a maximum degree of identity validation is needed to foster women's psychic survival. Seizing some respite space can be an achievable aim, allowing women to defy the effects of male violence. However, the truthful naming of and struggle against the ongoing threats they face must also be accepted within that process.

"I felt it was time to finally bring it out in the open"

Breaking the silence surrounding intimate and social violence constitutes substantial liberation resistance work. When researching and writing her book on incest, Melba Wilson had to speak with several members of her family who had previously not known about the occurrence of incest in their family. In urging other women to speak out about their experiences of abuse, she describes her own act of informing her adult nephew. She had heard that he was wondering why she "had to bring it all up now."[59] She told him that she "felt it was time to finally bring it out in the open . . . that I no longer wanted to cover it up anymore."[60] She hoped that her witness would stimulate in him and others who heard it, principled action to prevent or stop abuse of little black girls. Whether addressing her own family members or the public audience of her book, her speaking out constitutes social change on behalf of black females. In so doing Wilson demonstrates one of the most important resistance strategies, one that should not be overlooked because it is so basic; nor should the courage it requires be minimized.

We must continually work against the ways in which recognition of the multiple acts of silence-breaking resistance may be subverted. Indeed, the very assertion of silence about violence against women, necessary to understand the concept of "silence-breaking," is already biased in favor of what James Scott has called the "official transcript." The victim-survivors of male violence have never truly been silent about their treatment. Additionally, there have also frequently been supporters and advocates of women's rightful human dignity. Throughout the extensive history of deprecating ideologies about black women in the United States, these racial/gender claims have hardly been met with silent assent. For instance, important 1920s leaders like Lucy Laney and Mary Church Terrell publicly challenged the stereotyping of black women as sexually immoral by refuting the notion of an "inherent moral defect" in black women.[61] These leaders insistently challenged white and black male public figures about the degrading claims against the character of black women that trivialized the harm of male assaults against them.

Past and present public sphere opposition by authors and activists that challenges violence against women and the ideas that can justify it, reflects only one aspect of silence-breaking resistance. Outward expressions of truth about the violence may also signify a liberating internal achievement by victim-survivors. When Carey disclosed her story of sexual abuse during a group therapy session, she engaged in a silence-breaking act. At first, she angrily told the counselor facilitating the group: "I'm not tellin' you nothin'! Nothin' about me! Nothin'! Didn't nothin' happen to me!" She then started to cry and the details of her childhood sexual abuse "began to pour out." She described how, during that moment: "my gut seemed like there was a chip off of it now." The depths of her trauma and sense of agency were exposed in this cathartic but wrenching event. Her public declaration to the group was both self-affirming and self-assertive. It was a self-freeing act.

Finally, another means of silence breaking that validates some of the realities that victim-survivors experience might be called "intercessory witnessing." Andrea Benton Rushing exemplifies this form of resistance in the act of writing about her rape experience. Her essay describes her futile search for personal accounts of sexual violence by other black women victim-survivors. Partly because this unsuccessful quest exacerbated her sense of isolation in the aftermath of rape, Rushing offered her testimony:

> Some raped woman needs my witness. Not emotions recollected in ele-gant tranquility when I am *finally* out of the tunnel it takes all my faith to believe even exists. She needs to taste my terror, hear my gasps for life, watch me inch through brambles of despair, reaching for life and sanity with bleeding stigmata all over me.[62]

Just as the ancestors "on the other side of the membrane" reached out to Rushing and ensured her survival, she extended a lifeline to other victim-survivors.

We are mindful that this self-giving, silence-breaking act of Rushing's, as well as other examples cited here, are part of a much wider legacy of struggle. Although such acts are often buried in "hidden transcripts," their significance extends beyond the category of silence breaking. They constitute freedom-making speech: the creation of language customs that undermine the potent impact of the violence.

No matter how severely women are brutalized and demoralized there is still evidence of their resistance. Once we train ourselves to perceive the means that individual victim-survivors utilize for their survival and lib-eration, our ability to envision broader possibilities for woman-empow-ering change increases.

7

Maintaining the Momentum, Sustaining an Ethic of Resistance

As women initiate resistance on behalf of themselves and in so doing advance the interests of a civil society, it is incumbent upon their communities to continue that momentum. We who are committed to countering the social and intimate violence against black women must overcome our reluctance to join them. We need to participate in specifying a direction for constructive communal change. Of course, the effort to sustain a deliberate commitment to address violence in women's lives represents a formidable challenge. Some base points for the kind of ethical analysis and practice that can nurture this ongoing work are needed. How do we maintain an ethical vision of human wholeness and well-being that is directly responsive to the converging forms of violence confronted by women?

The ethic that we embrace must not only envision inclusive, truthtelling, moral communities which resist assaults on women; it must also help to build a social movement that brings such communities into existence. These goals have specific implications for the crafting of Christian social ethics. Those implications will be considered here alongside further elaborations on what the decision to construct this ethic of violence resistance requires. Concrete strategies for community action will be enumerated as well. They will emphasize ways in which a local church might become involved in this effort.

Structuring the Ethic

Committing Ourselves to Pay Attention to Women

In the continuing work of developing Christian social ethics, activating a commitment to taking violence against African-American women seriously dramatically affects our methodology. This commitment amends and molds the terms of the starting point. It realigns the focus and assumptions about the moral center and norms of our culture. Pursuing this commitment not only means adjusting the lens of our critical thinking, but also involves wrestling with some of our own anxieties that may be evoked in making that adjustment.

In our endeavor to identify and comprehend the moral costs of violence, we must start from the vantage point of a concrete understanding of women's lives. Bringing a feminist approach to Christian social ethics, I eschew objectivist moral claims that are based on an anonymous, rational agent. As Virginia Held explains, feminist moral inquiry attends to the actual experience of suffering domestic violence or of being conceptualized in terms of one's sexual availability. It "suggests that women must be listened to as we express our actual experience and our efforts to act morally and to arrive at morally sound judgments in our actual, not hypothetical, lives."[1] Since the act of listening to women must be the starting point for our method, African-American women's voices are a nonnegotiable source for developing an ethical assessment of, and response to, violence. This type of listening will not involve a passive or merely pitying reaction. Rather, it requires politically engaged, active expressions of empathy.

It is one thing to understand the need for such a basic starting point, but quite another to do it. Listening to women's stories of violence is uncomfortable and deeply disturbing. There is an enormous temptation to tune them out, partly because we fear that we will be swallowed up by their anguish. Perhaps we are afraid that the destructive power of the violence will seize and overwhelm us if we open our sensibilities up too widely in empathy with them. We need to remember that listening is an act of solidarity. It means tarrying awhile in that place of isolation and degradation created by the violence our sister has endured. No one wants to be there, not even as an observer and supporter. Awakening our senses from their dulled state of apathy or hiding demands courage as well as a compassionate commitment to resist violence.

Women who reach out to one another in this act of listening will have to give up any romantic notions they may harbor about solidarity among women. These listeners will need to let go of any expectation that such solidarity is implicitly comforting or comfortable. A woman listener has to fashion a quality of empathy that does not subsume the victim-survivor in the listener's own need to also be heard. Perhaps out of an intense desire to heal their own woundedness, some women listeners will want to jump quickly to conclusions about the painful experiences of women being "*basically* all the same." That assertion of sameness can produce a soothing reassurance that some may crave, but it is only a superficial one. Our anxieties about our differences, and fears about the conflicts that can arise between us when we face up to those differences, can completely close us off to genuine engagement. They will have to be confronted and bridled if we are to offer the intent listening that each victim-survivor deserves.

There are also racialized anxieties that may have to be braved in the act of listening to women. To name black women's torment at the hands of black men is to take the risk of stoking white supremacist assumptions about black humanity. For African-American listeners, to let the spotlight remain for very long on women's stories of depraved black male behavior also means increasing one's own susceptibility to falling into the deep well of racial shame that white supremacy creates. White "recovering racists"[2] may hesitate to listen to such stories because of their fears about stirring up and fueling their own residual racial biases that they would prefer to keep in check. These sympathetic whites may also be reluctant to engage in such listening because they wonder if they are already too deeply implicated in the racism that engulfs the realities of black males to participate in a critique of men's behavior. We cannot allow our apprehensions over the psychic risks that we may take by listening to women paralyze us or lead us to turn away.

To truly listen is to give attention, significance, and verification to the reality of women's anguish. It is to develop a countercultural valuation that is especially needed in a world of denial. In our society, dispassionate detachment is valorized as the most "professional" stance for engaging the problems of others. And because the social construction of black women's worth too often rests upon the assertion of their indomitable, unceasing strength, the need for empathetic, affirming listening can appear even less obvious. It may even seem like a betrayal of the women to undermine this "positive" cultural image of "the strong black woman" (albeit one of mythic proportions) and instead acknowledge their vulnerabilities. But no excuse can stand in the way of naming the emotional and spiritual turmoil and scarring that violence inflicts upon women. The act of personally engaged listening to which we are called, serves as an insis-

tent declaration that women's anguish genuinely matters; that it constitutes significant moral harm which must be accounted for, addressed,
and challenged.

Recognizing Women as Occupying the Moral Center

To sustain an ethic of resistance, black women must be understood as
prototypical of the way agency is conceived in moral discourse. As such
they cannot be relegated to a special class or peripheral status that treats
them as moral outsiders and exceptions. Situating them at the very focal
point of moral discourse is based on their innate equality with every
other human being. Clearly, black women's social plight is conditioned by
a particular nexus of dynamics that cannot be ignored in analysis relevant
to that configuration of social forces. But the peculiarities of oppression
that delineate women's unique social plight do not ground their moral
claim to human personhood. Their social victimization should not be
conceived of as subsuming their moral standing.

For, on the face of it, the logic of black women's social subjugation de-
fies existing practices for constituting the subject of Christian ethical
construction. After all, how does one qualify to occupy the center and
norm of moral discourse? Stated differently, what are the criteria for
being considered *the* paradigmatic case for such discourse? Does the population size of one's social "identity group" (such as white males or white
females) within the broader society or in the academy secure one's place?
Does the severity of social injury that can be established, such as demonstrating double, triple, or more layers of oppression enhance a group's
claims for attention in moral discourse? In light of certain realities of social marginalization, why does the burden of proof seem to fall on analysis such as feminist, womanist, or mujerista theories for legitimating the
status of women as significant moral agents?

It should be noted that black women certainly have been represented
as the "object" of more popular moral critiques related to contemporary
social problems, but usually in instances when the topic is something like
welfare policy or sexual promiscuity. Being singled out on such issues
means that black women are easily straitjacketed within categories of
moral deviance or degeneracy and relegated to the margins. In traditional
ethical analyses, those who are imaged as moral norm, whose family and
social achievement patterns are seen as more characteristic of standard

moral behavior, are invariably the socially, politically, and economically advantaged members of society. They are also usually Euro-Americans.

Constructing Christian social ethics from a stance of resistance involves rejecting the notion that some form of special permission is needed to embrace the value of black women's humanity. No competition over intellectual, material, or status qualifications should have to be won for black women's unjust treatment and neglected needs to be the focal point in assessing the moral health and practices of this society. We must measure Christian ethics by the extent to which its rhetoric on violence is applicable to the circumstances of women's lives. This is the proper test of the viability and adequacy of its moral prescriptions.

Renouncing Cultural Falsehoods about Women

Throughout preceding chapters of this book, I have reviewed numerous myths and cultivated falsehoods which mute women's experience of violation. We observed many of the ways that this cultural mythology is institutionalized in virtually every sphere of life that women depend upon for survival. Women's social inequality is legitimated through an elaborately woven web of prescribed roles and projected personal attributes. These prescriptions and projections justify limited access to the conditions and rights of human personhood. As I have argued, an ethic of resistance must include the unequivocal declaration that the assault and traumatizing of black women constitutes a most heinous moral obscenity. When this truth is promoted, the hegemonic lies that justify violence against women are unmasked. Dehumanizing ideologies and practices are revealed for what they are. Through truthtelling comes the development of alternative social norms that adjust our practices as a society and allow for the total participation of black women in shaping the evolution of society. Simultaneously, by changing our violent practices toward women and more effectively responding to those who are victim-survivors, the social constructions of black womanhood will become more life-affirming.

To take these steps will mean waking ourselves up to cultural customs of deception that we often find too terrifying to confront. A commitment to engage in acts of truthtelling about women involves risking the security to which many of us cling in our concerted blindness to daily deceptions by government, corporate and industry leaders. Catastrophic hazards are denied or misleadingly "packaged" in public statements and policy decisions by "officials." These public and private sector leaders routinely manufacture deceptions about critical matters such as the dumping of toxic and other hazardous wastes that pollute our air and water.[3] Similar deceptions are perpetrated about health and safety risks that endanger us in our workplaces.[4]

At the same time, it takes very little effort to become mired in a general attitude of malaise (sometimes masked as cynicism) toward inaccurate representations of international crises. We have grown accustomed to announcements by political authorities concerning "international terrorists" or "national security interests" that are well-crafted falsehoods or indicate a calculated bias in the inconsistent manner that these terms are applied. In this moral fog of denial where too many of us choose to remain, the consequences of deceptive practices can start to seem benign or inevitable. In the eyes of many of its citizens, the use of such manipulation to justify U.S. military incursions into small, less powerful countries merely represents a sad and unfortunate occurrence. In recent memory, United States political justifications for its military assaults on Grenada, Nicaragua, Libya, Panama, and Iraq are examples of such manipulation.[5]

As Adrienne Rich writes, "We assume that politicians are without honor. . . . We are accustomed to the contempt inherent in the political lie."[6] We usually bow to such contempt with resignation, or participate in the charade with our silence. It seems reasonable to avoid honest confrontation and comprehension of assaultive, life-threatening practices. We become well-practiced in ignoring how they impact us locally or how lethal they are to poor people in other parts of the world. For some, it can even seem as if these realities carry the potential to psychically overwhelm us if we were to openly engage the magnitude of their destructive consequences. Of course, others are either indifferent or celebrate that destructive power with a mixture of fascination and national pride. Moreover, the deceit and greed that these practices are usually predicated upon come to seem "natural." The ability of the United States and its western European allies to determine what is good and right and to dominate over others becomes a hidden entitlement. The projection of the socioeconomically advantaged, Euro-American individual as the model of meritocratic achievement is steadily ingested in our culture. The resulting rationalization of an array of inequalities and injustices in the political economy come to be seen as plain, common sense.

We have to break through this deliberately constructed moral lethargy. To insist upon a communal ethic that challenges the multiple layers of racial and gender-based falsehoods which legitimate violence against women, requires us to invest our own political energy. It makes little difference whether that energy is invested in being "loyal (read uncritical) Americans" or resigned to "informed observations of American corruption." The nature of our overall stance toward life-threatening, cultural fictions generated on a daily basis by official sources is critical to our success in constructing this ethic of resistance. A compartmentalized gesture in the direction of women's freedom will not be adequate for maintaining this ethic. The rhythms of our engagement with political culture will need to be completely altered, so that we become wholly out of step with its pervasive reliance upon lies that cover up its dehumanizing practices.

Building a Social Movement

Communal opposition to the violence must be conceived of and structured as a social movement to infuse communities with an alternative moral consciousness, and to foster a heightened moral sensibility. This heightened sensibility stimulates a particular transformative vision of social change. It injects the moral life of communities with the will to turn back the tide of violence assailing women. As Audre Lorde has reminded us, where women are concerned, poetry, "the revelatory distillation of experience," is not a luxury.[7] Maintaining this transformative vision constitutes the "poetic work" instrumental in accomplishing change. It involves an expansive process of inciting dreams, passions, images, and contemplation about women's well-being and dignity. As I have previously noted, intuitive resources must be utilized in constructing a vision for the movement in combination with critical, analytical investigations of male dominance. Our "poetic" movement work also includes the creation of language and ideas that generate possibilities for survival by contemporary victims of male violence and complete freedom from it for future generations of girls and women. Finally, it requires the invention of strategies to safeguard that freedom.

This envisioning process must be sustained, in part, by connecting useful components of politics and spirituality. Both politics and spirituality make up the active dynamics embedded in the everyday interactions of our communal lives. Most importantly, they contain revitalizing and constructive properties that can fuel the ongoing struggle to generate and hold onto the alternative values that comprise this ethic of violence resistance. Mining these beneficial aspects of politics and spirituality allows the social movement (a concrete expression of the ethic) to be guided in a liberative direction.

In utilizing the term politics, I do not refer to the election of officials. Nor, most assuredly, do I limit its definition to the forms of discourse that take place in our contemporary public spheres. The relegation of violence against women to the private personal realm where public political concerns are excluded has already served quite effectively to perpetuate that violence. Politics exist within any conflict or consensus, particularly when it can be shown that existing social narratives that confer freedom or subjugation on those who are involved, inform the outcome. Accordingly, politics abound in the personal interactions between intimates as well as in public arenas like the mass media or a county domestic court system. Focusing on the politics of our social relations can become a means for marshalling the social power that sanctions women's freedom.

This liberative capacity within political dynamics can then be connected with similar possibilities offered by spiritual dynamics that are also present in our social relations. The liberative spirituality mentioned here might be based on an awareness of God's presence, inspiration from nature or one's ancestors, or some other form of spirituality with the capacity to affirm the innate human dignity and worth of women. An insistent, unified assertion of women's political entitlement and spiritual affirmation can counter the barrage of subjugating influences that are a part of so many of the prevailing communal responses to intimate violence.

Strategically linking politics and spirituality not only gives the movement direction and stamina, but also provides it with a moral basis that permeates both the private and public spheres of societal interactions. In short, it offers access to critical resources for advocating the liberation of black women within every realm of experience that manifests or buttresses the violence against them. Of course, making this linkage also demands that we persistently challenge the institutions that embody oppressive expressions of politics and spirituality, such as government agencies and churches.

This social movement is most fundamentally about establishing these types of strategic connections. To name a few examples, this movement presses for the following objectives: recognition of women's spiritual needs while they reside in battered women's shelters; attention to racism in feminist legal remedies; injecting feminist political voices into black church responses to black male violence against black women; and debunking public myths about the sexual promiscuity of "welfare mothers" in rape awareness education on college campuses. Moreover, in its commitment to bringing about communal social change this movement makes wide-ranging societal claims, thus assuming a need for broad-based coalitions. The claims on society by black women victim-survivors cut across federal, state, county, neighborhood, racial, and ethnic boundaries. In order to achieve any approximation of justice, the call for communal accountability and redress for black women must not be mistakenly identified as the exclusive domain of "their own" black communities.[8] We must avoid the racist parochialism that labels it a "shameful lack of independence" when black Americans make claims on "their own" American society for improving their conditions. The collective efforts of all of us who are willing to engage each other and the multiple communities we live in are needed to challenge the powerful collaborative forces that assault women.

Undoubtedly, some will find my suggestion of societal transformation based on the participation of ordinary individuals naive. Significant influence is wielded in the culture by sophisticated, deeply entrenched methods of manipulating information such as the use of propaganda by corporations and industry to control public opinion.[9] Their networks of control involve think tanks organized by representatives of business to influence policy makers and to set the terms of policy debates. Furthermore, this means of exerting power includes corporate-owned media whose reporting of the news responds primarily to their corporate sponsors and the profit motives of their organizations.[10] To a large extent, the media constructs political reality with its power to control who speaks, for how long they speak, how credibly they are introduced, and what they can speak about.[11] In this way, they often control how an issue such as "violence in our communities" is framed in the public mind. For instance, predominantly white suburban and rural communities are usually portrayed as low-crime areas. This portrayal is possible, in part, because the domestic violence that occurs in these areas is hidden from public scrutiny and therefore does not "count" as crime. This constructed political "reality" is verified by parallel information on "other" communities, like frequent depictions of predominantly black urban communities as high-crime areas. Though also minimally reported in the press, intimate assaults on women in black communities do "count" as evidence for locating the preponderance of criminality there. But because of the way this framework for understanding community violence is encoded with racist and sexist denial of white criminality, black women's victimization is most often interpreted as yet another aspect of black racial group pathology. It only helps to "prove" black people's proclivities toward criminal behavior.

The struggle to make its truth claims visible in the media could completely consume a movement focused on marginalized groups such as black women victim-survivors.[12] However, concentrating on the power of the media as an arbiter of moral claims must not be allowed to envelop our vocabulary and objectives for change. Any attempt to penetrate the corporate media in order to gain control of information provided to mass audiences and policy makers would contradict basic elements of the movement. It would mean trying to assimilate the existing terms for navigating the public arena that are created by the corporate media. Instead, we must focus on the development of new public spaces where dialogue between ordinary people about social values can occur. In such spaces, alternatives to dominant, subordinating values can be constructed.[13] This focus is crucial for maintaining a social movement that nurtures resistance ethics.

To engender this intense degree of activity among members of our communities requires a shift in consciousness from the stagnant consumer/client notion of citizenship that is so prevalent now, to a commitment to a more participatory citizenship.[14] One result of the tremendous power wielded by commercial interests in the structuring of our society is the commodification of everything. Ideas, values, racial identity, community, and history are treated as products to be marketed and sold to people. This is illustrated by the marketing of products ranging from self-help books with keys to finding happiness to the Hollywood version of historical events like mutinies on slave ships in the United States. Within this communal ethos our individual contribution to society is principally as consumers of these ideas, values, and the like.[15]

Simultaneously, the presence of the state is too often experienced by individuals as a set of bureaucratic agencies that we have to please. We cooperate so that we may gain needed services like highways, social security benefits, regulations on sewage pipelines, or traffic lights on the streets for ourselves and our families. We also cooperate to avoid the state's punitive interference in our lives, like fines for tax evasion or criminal prosecution for failing to educate our children. Our relationship to the state reduces the meaning of citizenship to functioning as a client of the state. The movement to resist violence against women can only be advanced by contesting the passive role of the consumer/client who uncritically imbibes mass media definitions of political reality. Listening to women means assuming an active, direct, communal role that includes decision making, creativity, and confrontation with one another over the running of society.

Thus, another important ingredient for upholding this social movement is to avoid being swallowed up in bureaucratic logic or systems. In other words, the primary structure required to sustain an ethic of resistance to violence against women is a social movement, not a bureaucracy. The chief goal of the movement should not be infiltrating the media, judiciary, law enforcement establishments, or the clergy with those who will initiate, support, and put into practice antiracist, feminist reforms to stem violence. I hasten to add that reforms in these areas would be significant ethical advances and absolutely essential to the movement. Yet, as feminist political theorist Kathy Ferguson points out, voices of opposition are always engulfed and diffused in bureaucracies.[16] The very nature of bureaucracies mystifies the politics inherent in their policies in order to insure the smooth functioning of their operations. Conflict is immediately absorbed and neutralized in administrative language or procedures, such as the task force on racism, the mandatory diversity workshop, or the annual women's day worship service. Hence the necessary infiltration of agencies whose social power impinges upon violence against women must never be regarded as a sufficient end. The requisite transformation of attitudes and behaviors cannot be achieved through bureaucratic reform.[17] Again, repeated, direct confrontations between individuals and groups from diverse sectors of our communities are necessary for sweeping attitudinal shifts to occur.

Avoiding the dangers of bureaucratic thinking also means that the primary goal of the movement is not to establish our own feminist, antiracist organizations to eliminate violence against women. Once more, an immediate qualification is in order. Aside from a significant increase in activist networks, many more feminist antiracist organizations are needed to offer comprehensive support services to women victim-survivors and educate the community members they seek out for help. Such organizations should be regarded as imperative. They are indispensable and principal tools that help bring about change, but they should never be understood as the culminating purpose of the movement.

Endemic to the organizational world that all institutions create is a central drive toward self-maintenance and self-perpetuation. Defining the movement as centered wholly on multiplying women's organizations, especially those that provide services to victim-survivors, can undermine the radical social transformation it seeks to bring about. This exclusive focus can result in advancing the reactionary cause of perpetuating a new industry of experts and clients in the field of violence against women. In most instances, the nonprofit agencies that presently deliver these services preserve class inequalities (and usually racial ones as well) between the women/clients and the well-connected board members—those with elite socioeconomic status who raise and manage the funding. This class hierarchy is also often institutionalized in the everyday relationship between an "expert" agency counselor who must have advanced higher education degrees and the woman/client who need "only" bring her experiences. These agencies can become merely social service providers that are considered feminist because of their commitment to serving women who have been victimized by male violence. Yet they simply mirror the wider society where certain "experts" on domestic violence are relied upon to testify in the courtroom[18] or to give quotes to the press on this topic. Victim-survivors can become infantalized by this authority structure and their own articulation of their anguish and resourcefulness submerged within the bureaucratic process.

The social movement has to develop an identity distinct from the organizational arenas that may tangibly represent it in local communities. We must launch and cultivate widespread, effectively maintained organizations that offer responses like comprehensive rape crisis services to women and girls. Yet the social movement that calls for such organizations and is largely comprised of participants in these organizations, must not become synonymous with them. If it does, the purpose of our work will be confined to providing services in reaction to the crises generated by the violence. Activist energy will be concentrated on finding the funding to maintain the agencies and the experts to staff them, making the rules to govern them, and so forth. As organizers and organizations do this necessary work they need to continually devise ways to retain an identity that links them to a social movement and contributes to it. And the primary goal of this movement has to remain focused upon arresting the practice of violence itself and transforming the false assumptions about women which justify the violence against them.

To overcome any sense of defeat or cynicism about being outmatched by proliferating political lies, media conglomerates, or diverting bureaucratic logic, we pay attention to the women. The examples of black women victim-survivors demonstrate the capacity of ordinary individuals to resist colluding, monstrous foes that assault them on a societal level as well as in the most intimate ways possible.

Ideas for Maintaining Communal Resistance

With the preceding guidelines in mind, what might an ethic of resisting violence against women actually look like in local communities? What kind of tangible, ethical practice might exhibit this communal resistance? This is always raised in my discussions with groups comprised of those who are not solely oriented toward academic endeavors. When I talk about the combination of issues that may be of concern in black women's experiences of male violence, someone invariably asks: "What can we do about all of this?" In response to the need for concrete suggestions, I offer the following eclectic, "brainstormed" sampling of ideas.

Vision Quests

The arts provide one avenue for sharpening our ability to conceptualize possibilities for stemming social and intimate violence. The performing arts, in particular, can enable us to sing, dramatize, and visualize alternative ethical realities in unique ways that deepen our sensitivity and embolden our spirits. For instance, community theater and dance efforts with a combined focus on racism, sexism, and women's experiences of intimate violence can creatively guide and construct an intermingling of politics and spirituality in communal life. This would allow the participants to literally rehearse alternative ways of being in relation to one another.

Moreover, we need to collect and then celebrate examples from all over the nation and the world that reveal imaginative and effective efforts to resist male violence.[19] We should create group projects to solicit, compile, and publicize this information on a routine basis through schools, media, or religious organizations. Most importantly, groups should put together "critical" celebrations of these examples. Questions that engage underlying assumptions about issues such as race/ethnicity, gender, class, and sexual orientation must be incorporated in the information given. It would then be possible for us to learn, for example, how to recognize and analyze assertions of white supremacy within specific community practices, at the same time as we are exposed to the range of antiviolence strategies that they have created.

Multiple methods should be utilized to place deliberate, public emphasis on questioning attitudes and actions that foster the varied expressions of white supremacy, male dominance, and intimate violence. Local civic groups, neighborhood boys' athletic teams, or ethnic group organizations could develop ceremonies or other regularly practiced traditions that encourage such questioning. In addition, sets of questions could be crafted that are written in a pithy and insightful manner, and invoke alternatives to conventional attitudes about the treatment of women. Perhaps by using a framework that asks: "What if we. . . ?" these public questions and slogans could offer concrete illustrations of the manner in which community priorities can be restructured and resources re-allocated to heighten community resistance to violence against women. These questions might be posted in corporate elevators, on the sides of buses, or banners across the narthex of a local church.

For all these projects, an interactive, shared group process of decision making, reflection, and evaluation must be non-negotiable components.

Encouraging Female Defiance

Another means of fostering communal resistance is the encouragement of unruly behavior in girls and women that fuels a defiant spirit in them. Women need to be able to decode the subjugating myths about themselves and perceive the truth of their moral worth. In particular, we must teach and reward audacious and insubordinate qualities in black girls and women in ways that confirm a propensity to disobey the social dictates of male dominance and white supremacy. The development of an attitude of resistance should be a quintessential principle of child rearing for girls. The categories of "good girl" and "nice girl" behavior have to be eliminated or fundamentally altered so that they no longer extol acquiescence and pliability toward authority. Instead, we need to implement specific ways of openly commending behavior by girls and women that is questioning of, uppity, and rebellious toward any individual, institution, or set of values that would constrain them based on their social identities.

Woman-Empowering Antiviolence Training

Woman-empowering education has to be one of our community responses, in order to counter the particular social burdens of male violence for women. Existing "training" programs that are supposed to help women avoid and fend off male assault can sometimes be heavily laden with messages that can add to women's shame and self-blame if they are assaulted. For instance, when women receive training about sexual assault prevention, there is too often an exclusive concern with how women should avoid "risky" behaviors and/or learn to be more assertive.[20] These lessons on "risky" behavior may communicate the erroneous message that women's actions cause sexual assault. It is important that women not be misled into believing that assertiveness can control the behavior of perpetrators.

While warnings about situations where women are likely to incur danger and the encouragement of self-assertion are extremely valuable for women, the social norms that set up their choices in those situations need to be analyzed within the same educational forums where the warnings are presented. The emphasis on what changes women can make to protect themselves has to be matched with discussions about the ways that male dominance is valued in the culture and generates woman-blaming messages. Therefore, woman-empowering training about male violence should address societal accountability and stress the need for a wide range of cultural penalties for this behavior. Issues such as the objectification of women's sexuality, victim-blaming practices of the media, and dismissive attitudes about the emotional costs to women need at least to be named. Affirmations of women that contradict these ideological obfuscations should be offered in these training courses about countering and preventing violence. In short, we need a design that acknowledges women's victimization and supports their personal and political agency.

For black audiences, introducing black cultural education may be a vehicle for developing women's resources for resistance. As we saw, for Denise watching television segments when she was a young child that featured Fannie Lou Hamer, Angela Davis, and Malcolm X helped to radicalize her consciousness about possibilities for social change. Likewise for

Aisha, the experience of listening to Malcolm X in Harlem instilled a new sense of pride that was emotionally and spiritually stimulating for her.

Now many Afrocentric activists and scholars make similar recommendations, but usually for a different purpose than the one I am suggesting here. Indeed, some of them specifically promote black cultural education as an intimate violence prevention measure for black youth.[21] It is thought that advancing positive black cultural images with the purpose of developing healthier male-female relationships and unity in the black community can help prevent intimate violence. Healthier male-female relationships and black unity may well be one result of intensified black cultural education for youth and even contribute to deterring violence. But, as with Denise, black cultural education that focuses upon risk-taking liberation activists can radicalize women toward bolder opposition to social and intimate violence within the black community. Women's radicalization may lead to increased black male-female discord. *I* am suggesting that black cultural images be incorporated to empower women to resist the racially mediated patterns of male dominance that support male violence, even when "black unity" appears to be sacrificed.

Building Woman-Empowering Networks

There is a need for community-wide organizational networks that jointly express community intolerance of male violence. As Ann Jones suggests, there should be coordinated and integrated community measures that stress consideration of the material conditions of women's lives. This network should include "agencies and institutions that may think they have no role to play in helping battered women: the housing authority, for example, the vocational school, the credit union. They must build in to their design specific ways to monitor one another's work . . . provide mutual support, and overcome institutionalized sexism, racism and homophobia."[22] Separate networks that focus on rape and incest could also be established, and for each of these areas a slightly different set of agencies may be involved. When these networks are activated, their goals and practices must focus on community change and treat victim-survivors as resourceful peers in that process rather than as the "client/problem."

Similarly, a network of organizations who have traditionally concentrated their efforts on national black community goals should come together to devise practical strategies on this issue for local communities.

They might devise a response to the question: What concrete means of support and advocacy are needed if black women's right to lives free of male assault is treated as a primary moral concern for "the black community"? This strategy summit could include representatives from organizations such as the NAACP, 100 Black Women, the National Bar Association, the Urban League, historically black religious organizations, and Sorority and Fraternity groups. In addition to the joint responsibility of monitoring and evaluating their efforts in local areas, they would need to make specific plans about how to keep this commitment on the "front burner" internally within each national group.

Justice Making for Women

An aggressive communal response is a critical weapon for thwarting the evil of social and intimate violence. When we insist upon an approach that emphasizes the standpoint of the victim-survivor, the need for justice-making action arises as a key component of communal resistance. Speaking the truth about the reality of violence is a starting point. Yet, as Marie Fortune helps to spell out, a justice-making process in response to violence is also imperative.[23] Among other steps, she calls for the offender to be held accountable, for some restitution to the victim, and for some form of vindication for the victim. The community has to be instrumental in enforcing the offender's accountability. In addition, it must attend to the severed or damaged relationship between itself and the victim-survivor. At the heart of this understanding of justice making is the presumption of the community's responsibility in perpetuating violence against women and an assertion of its corresponding compensatory duty. However, because of the potent relationship between social and intimate violence this formula must not rely upon an individualistic understanding that isolates "incidents" of sexual or physical assault for redress.[24] Justice-making action calls for a continuous struggle with the manifold cultural assaults that reproduce the conditions of male violence. As noted earlier, it demands much more than a "healing" response to a particular interpersonal ordeal. Those who benefit from and perpetuate the ongoing social subjugation of African-American women must be held accountable in the justice-making process for women. Pursuing this accountability might include convening a local tribunal that resembles an international tribunal for war crimes. It would place on trial those public and private sector leaders (perhaps some of them in absentia) who have made pivotal political and economic decisions that help to foster the violence and to marginalize those women who survive it. The tribunal could be organized by local advocates and activists already working on this issue, together with other sympathetic community leaders. Selected representatives from nongovernmental, human rights, and women's rights organizations might be brought in to serve as judges. Testimony would be offered about the harm endured by women and some form of restitution decided upon. The role that myths and stereotypes based upon race and gender play in perpetuating violence against women of color would be made explicit in the formulation of the charges and in the way that testimony is elicited.

Case Study in Community Action: Local Church Involvement

In order to suggest even more specific responses, I will focus on the local church as a community organization with the capacity to embody this ethic.

Rationale for Christian Involvement

A primary task of Christian faith communities is to provide leadership in the midst of desperate and urgent problems such as this one.[25] The requisite Christian engagement in definite practices that uphold women's genuine moral worth can be called "truth-work." Truth-work exemplifies an important tenet of the Christian faith that commends the appropriation of Jesus Christ as truth. This appropriation does not consist of an intellectual assent, rather it demands a specific praxis.[26] Knowing and doing are thoroughly interlocked in this christological understanding. In the Christian faith, to know Jesus is to participate in the ways of Jesus. This kind of "knowing and doing" involves an interactive process of becoming empowered. It involves reaching outside oneself to stretch and grow toward the embodiment of justice, and reaching within oneself to tap rich inner resources of courage and passion. To recognize what is truly just, Christians rely upon their ability to access power from God, their communities of accountability, and resources within themselves. They can live out this realization of truth by working to create conditions in the world that reflect it. This process of participating in the incarnation of justice requires literal engagement with distorting human realities such as violence, white supremacy, and male dominance. It means doing the work that enables the truth of human wholeness, worth, and dignity to be fulfilled.

Churches can play a critical role in organizing, sponsoring, and engaging in this truth-work. If they choose to exercize it, they possess an independence from corporate and state control that enables them to play a unique advocacy role in community life. Churches can function as effective and vital organs of the Christian faith by offering victim-survivors needed confirmation of the death-dealing realities that threaten their lives, and by opposing those realities. They have the chance to act compassionately by paying direct supportive attention to those caught in the anguishing circumstances and consequences of intimate violence.

When Aisha founded a church made up primarily of urban black women, she included a ministry to respond to the neglected concerns of women victimized by violence as a fundamental component of the church's mission. She was convinced that women need reinforcement of the fact that God does not require them to suffer abuse. She explained: "That's why it was important to me to have a different type of ministry than what I see being performed in traditional churches, because of my own pain and the pain of so many women around me that was going un-addressed."

Church Resistance Strategies

SELF-CRITIQUE

Churches must be engaged in a continual self-critique that focuses on eliminating acts of violence among its members and ferreting out messages that reinforce the acceptability of violence against women within its traditions and practices. Churches need to account for all the ways that their scriptures, liturgies, icons, polities, and teachings uphold the subjugation of women. To identify what their precise participation might be in nurturing these destructive messages, local churches should conduct a regular audit of their practices within their existing committee and organizational structures. For example, the worship committee could audit liturgy, and the trustees could audit icons in stained glass windows and paintings on display. In addition, churches have to distill and reject all theological tenets and organizational strictures that deny women authority and autonomy. This includes explicit affirmations of the integrity and worth of women's bodies and sexuality. Christian traditions that even imply a denial of God's concern for women victim-survivors must be openly challenged and reinterpreted.

Moreover, violence and abuse that occurs at the center of church life, perpetrated by clergy and/or laity against their own family members or other members of the faith community, has to be confronted. When the formal and official practices of the church ignore the extent of abuse against women and children that people in the faith community are well aware of in their own families or in those of their friends and acquaintances, a blatant lie is maintained. The message advocating the cultivation of loving, trusting, right relationships with one another that churches preach on a weekly basis is deeply betrayed.[27] If they fail to activate direct methods of resistance, churches will continue to be thoroughly complicit in male violence, functioning as simply another cultural conveyer of indifference to women's torment.

RESISTANCE RITUALS

Churches can integrate rituals to resist violence into their internal practices as well as their community outreach efforts. For instance, in a discussion of the need to thwart existing forms of social bias and exploitation, theologian Delores Williams suggests that black faith communities create resistance rituals based on doctrine that reflects African-American people's experiences and cultural sources. She explains that the doctrine would be "'decoded' of *all* androcentric, gender, homophobic, class and color bias."[28] It should be enacted "as regularly in the African-American denominational churches as the eucharist," so that it is firmly implanted in the community's minds and memory.[29] Though not specifically mentioned by Williams, this proposal could also incorporate opposition to male violence. By naming it and ritually denouncing it on a frequent basis, a recognition of the cultural sanctioning of male violence could be cultivated among church members. Ceremonial affirmations that offer alternatives to debasing and trivializing means of valuing black women's sexuality and emotional needs might also be woven into these rituals.[30]

Moreover, churches should gather together across racial and neighborhood boundaries for public rituals that give witness to their insistence on women's freedom from male violence. Their witness should emphasize the unique spiritual orientation that faith communities contribute to communal work on this problem.[31] The rituals could include prayer vigils outside police stations, courthouses, town halls, or state legislature buildings. The group would need to offer specific prayers for judges, prosecutors, legislators, and bureaucratic officials who make daily decisions that affect women's safety. They would need to collaborate on the kinds of prayers needed for each, and on how issues related to race and gender would be named within the ritual. New songs could be created in the tradition of 1960s black civil rights movement music, that called out the names of these key officials. Churches in predominantly white suburban communities should also conduct these rituals along the streets of their "secluded" neighborhoods. They would thereby ritually express their opposition to the "privileges" of white supremacy that help to keep the intimate violence occurring in their neighborhoods hidden from public view, and reinforce racialized myths about violence against black women.

TRAINING FOR RELINQUISHING MALE DOMINANCE

Nothing is more important for churches and the wider community than challenging men to interrogate the relationship between a desire for dominance over others and cultural definitions of manhood, especially those related to male sexual prowess. Of course, this interrogation of male dominance would be inadequate without attending to intersecting issues of social power like race and sexual orientation that appropriately address the particular composition of the group. This training process must involve repeated or continuing opportunities for men to become conscienticized about what constitutes controlling and abusive behavior toward women. Models for the kind of conscientization needed can be found in Latin American Christian base communities.[32] It is especially appropriate for churches to sponsor this sort of investigation of maleness in Sunday school classes, confirmation classes, or youth group programs, when ideals about what it means to lead a Christian life are initially taught to youth. Adult education forums and men's group meetings should additionally be utilized as venues for male reeducation about violence resistance. Men could be trained as peer counselor-educators to help one another learn behavior toward women based upon equality and respect. Special emphasis has to be given to the topic of sexually appropriate behavior toward children. The scope of this emphasis on sexuality should range from their treatment of female youth within the church to the parenting of their own girl children at home. In addition to fostering concern about routine attitudes and behavior, these male peer educators and other church leaders must directly confront sexually harassing and abusive acts that occur. Again, ongoing opportunities for men to engage in discussions about how to prevent and stop this behavior are critical.

For example, male training sessions could utilize exercises that promote an understanding of the parallels between a male abuser's self-justification of his acts and popular legitimations of white supremacy. Paul Kivel, an activist and writer on antiracism and men against domestic violence, offers categories like denial and blame that are ideal for grasping this concept.[33] For instance, just as abusers refuse to accept responsibility for their actions by blaming the women for "having asked for it" or instigated it by their "henpecking" behavior, whites try to avoid responsibility for racism by blaming blacks with accusations like "if they weren't so lazy" or "if they didn't spend so much time complaining about racism." In creative exercises based on these types of blaming statements, participants would gain a systemic understanding of the way power interests are defended and sustained. Male training needs to help white men enhance and develop an ability to make connections between the perpetration of male violence and the maintenance of their white privilege. Similarly, it should help black men deepen their comprehension of the link between male violence and the social nurturance of their internalized racism.

INCREASED RELIANCE UPON COMMUNAL AND PEER RESOURCES IN DEVELOPMENT OF CHURCH RESPONSES

In every way possible, church education and advocacy efforts need to involve a peer approach. The overreliance on "expert" professionals to present the perspective of women victim-survivors must be actively discouraged. It is essential to invite women to represent themselves, including them as strategists and colleagues when church resistance efforts are developed. Victim-survivors must not be the mere objects of mission projects to be pitied and "helped" in a paternalistic fashion. The insights that they bring with regard to the experience of violation need to be highly valued.

An acute consciousness of what organizational models churches emulate is imperative as they reach out to women in crisis situations. In what ways is the treatment of a victim-survivor at the church-sponsored program like the process and assumptions she finds at the "welfare" office or the hospital emergency room? How should it be different? Church crisis intervention efforts must consciously attempt to reflect their solidarity with victim-survivors. This commitment requires churches to maintain their independence from state and corporate control. When these interests fund and regulate church programs it is especially difficult (if not impossible) to create a countercultural structure and climate.

TEACHING COMMUNAL ETHICS

The teaching of ethics must be done from frameworks that illumine the reality of structural power such as male dominance and white supremacy. The systemic character of moral wrong fashioned against specific communities, cultures, and groups of people needs to be taught from a very young age. Therefore, learning how to analyze power relationships and make moral judgments about those relationships should be a crucial component of Christian ethical education. These tools of discernment need to be offered in Sunday school curriculums, weekly preaching, parenting education, and other adult educational opportunities offered to the congregation. Teaching Christian ethical behavior in local churches must intentionally embrace justice education that takes account of past and present acts of corporate sinfulness. This includes the ways that groups of people are marginalized and dehumanized.

Conjointly, the design of basic moral education has to accentuate the recognition of how a communal Christian response can be a sustaining resource in the midst of individual struggles for wholeness that church members face. For instance, teaching about the process of healing in a congregational setting should help people to appreciate the corporate (rather than merely the individualistic) and participatory (rather than simply the passive) elements that can be tapped in that process. This approach to healing facilitates the faith community's acceptance of its indispensable role in violence resistance. To equip people to speak the truth to violence, a sense of moral accountability derived from an awareness of collective responsibility must be encouraged. Furthermore, in a congregation that retains this enhanced awareness of such corporate evils as racism and sexism, women victim-survivors may be assisted in shaking off some of the shame they experience. It can perhaps guide them away from self-blame, and toward correctly identifying the potent imprint of those evils in the messages that shape their self-perceptions.

DOCUMENTATION

Churches need to assist in the documentation of women's stories of abuse and resistance. The distortions contained in the "official transcripts" of women's violation and help-seeking behavior should be countered with subversive record keeping. Documentation is not only a tool of validation for women, but also serves as an inhibitor and sanction against perpetrators.

Churches could devise a means for logging women's depictions of the violence they encounter in their daily lives. It should take every site of community contact into consideration, including interactions within their congregations. For instance, a women's group might sponsor a session for writing prayers of petition about various assaults the women have endured, with an accompanying opportunity to write prayers of thanksgiving that name their concomitant modes of defiance. Another approach might enjoin the appropriate administrative body of the congregation to design a process for receiving written testimony about abusive behavior that may have taken place in the home, church, or community. The design would incorporate guidelines for the content, and when appropriate a mechanism for response to women's testimony. This process would have to be structured so that it is easily accessed by the women of the congregation. These written statements would be a constant source of accountability to the faith community.

MONITORING

Congregations should engage in monitoring the public and private neighborhood and community agencies that immediately respond to the crisis of violence against women. There are numerous areas to be evaluated, such as: How promptly do the police respond to women's calls? In their general region, does the police response time differ according to the racial and ethnic makeup of the community or neighborhood? How are women's spiritual and emotional needs attended to by the nearest battered women's shelter? What kind of antiracism training are hospital emergency room personnel provided with? Since church staff must often make referrals in situations of violence to local social service agencies, the quality of those services must be routinely assessed.

One means of doing this is to make personal inquiries of representatives from the community agencies that are the most crucial in providing services to women. Hospital administrators, doctors, police officers, prosecutors, and judges should be invited into the churches and questioned about their practices with regard to violence against women. The results of this monitoring should be publicized through every available means, ranging from the church newsletter to the local news media. Battered women's shelters, rape crisis intervention programs, and even private therapists should also be contacted and their work evaluated in terms of their treatment of black women victim-survivors. Community service providers have to be held accountable for adequately serving African-American women.

ADVOCACY

Solidarity with victim-survivors must literally be embodied by advocates who serve in these women's interests. Certain women and men of the congregation could be trained as advocate-friends working against violence and abuse toward women. These individuals would ensure that issues related to this abuse are consistently aired in the congregation and integrated into its mission and structures. Also, in the event that a sexual harassment complaint surfaces against the pastor, this group would provide an advocate to support the woman who brings the complaint.

This group could help generate ideas for political action in the community such as prayer vigils at the local police precinct or posters that voice community concern about violence against women (both mentioned above). Advocacy could also include support for progressive national and local legislative initiatives relevant to ending the violence. In its internal monitoring duties, the congregation's violence-resistance advocates would ensure that these legislative concerns were included on the agenda of the appropriate church social concerns committee. Churches should also advocate for connections between violence against women, white supremacy, and patriarchy to be spelled out and incorporated into the law school education and law enforcement training of prosecutors, judges, and police personnel. At the initiative of churches, methods could be devised for monitoring and evaluating the extent to which officials in their communities have received this kind of education. Congregations might also join together to create ecumenical and interfaith coalitions that work with local activists to write local ordinances that contribute to this struggle.

In these advocacy efforts, churches must insistently make the traumatizing consequences of violence a public priority. Churches should track administrative policies and laws that are directly responsive to the anguish visited upon women victim-survivors. They should explore the question of what legislative changes could be made to send a clear signal of community intolerance for this behavior. For instance, what if, in the prosecution of perpetrators of male violence, the traumatizing of a woman was considered one of the crimes that was committed? Testimony about the emotional and spiritual agony involved in incidents of violence could be solicited from neighbors, friends, and relatives and considered pertinent evidence of such a crime.

We need more communities with crisis support teams that are available to be part of the response women receive when they request emergency assistance from the police. These persons can hold the victim-survivor's hand, cry with her, be silent with her, or be supportive in whatever way she wishes. Furthermore, church advocates could press for the cost of a wide range of support services for women victim-survivors of male violence to be established as part of all health care insurance policies, including government-funded health services for poor women. The many details related to these advocacy ideas that need further discussion and debate could be developed by church advocates working in coalition with others in the community committed to this work.

Organizing Strategic Conversations

Churches should initiate consultations to strategize about specific racial and gender issues that reinforce violence against black women. They could bring together small groups of victim-survivors, service providers, activists, scholars, and community leaders who are already actively working on this issue. These consultations might explore some of the ethical problems that arise in devising community responses that are both feminist and antiracist. One subject for such a consultation should be a candid discussion about how to address the dual realities of white supremacist assaults against black men and black male violence against black women. The session should seek appropriate responses to the competing agendas that these realities create. They could discuss questions like: When launching a public campaign to mobilize community concern, how do you oppose the silencing of violence against black women without contributing to the degradation of black men? How should the issue of black men's violence against black women be raised with black audiences? With white or racially mixed audiences? Should whites be spokespersons on this issue? If so, how can they do so in an antiracist manner? Should black women's photographs be featured in advertising campaigns to raise public consciousness about domestic violence? If so, what are the possible sociopolitical implications of doing this? It is important that such strategic conversations not follow an academic model of one "expert" person delivering a monologue to an audience. Instead, churches should use a consultation model that facilitates dialogue and encourages the joint development of concrete suggestions.

As we face these challenges we can find hope in the reality that society evolves continuously and that shared moral commitment and communal effort can help shape the direction of these changes. We can move toward becoming a less violent environment for African-American women if we seize and hold fast to a radical vision for freedom from the violations that besiege women. This liberation can take place if we commit ourselves to participate in an ethic of resistance that will not give up the struggle. As Denise describes it, this involves a conscious decision.

> And the times that I decided to live and what I wanted to do—you know, like trying to resist, being in the spaces of resistance, were the most empowering. . . . I made a commitment to live and to resist this world's oppression. That is the only place [in which] I could live. I mean, that's the only space of actually living. It is in resistance, or else I give up and that's— it's too terrifying there.

Notes

NOTES TO THE INTRODUCTION

1. Beverly Wildung Harrison, *Making the Connections: Essays in Feminist Social Ethics* ed. Carol S. Robb (Boston: Beacon Press, 1985), 18.

2. This term is used to incorporate women from the wide range of American ethnic groups gathered in the United States with significant ancestral ties to Africa, such as those whose cultural heritage may include several generations of South Carolina Gullah islanders, third-generation Caribbean Americans, second-generation Liberian Americans, Canadian immigrants with US slave ancestry, and so forth.

3. Since male violence is the only form of intimate violence that I discuss, the terms intimate violence and male violence are used interchangeably in this book.

4. Zillah Eisenstein, *Feminism and Sexual Equality* (New York Monthly Review Press, 1984), 90.

5. Out of one hundred black females 4.5 are victims of intimate assault each year. This includes rape, sexual assault, robberies, and aggravated and simple assaults. Ronet Bachman and Linda Saltzman, "Violence against Women: Estimates from the Redesigned Survey," *Bureau of Justice Statistics, National Crime Victimization Survey* (August 1995). One out of every 2.5 African-American women has experienced some form of sexual abuse involving bodily contact before the age of eighteen. Gail E. Wyatt, "The Sexual Abuse of Afro-American and White American Women in Childhood," *Child Abuse and Neglect: The International Journal* 9, (1985): 507–19. In the United States during 1985 more than 603,000 black women were victims of husband-to-wife violence and more than 244,000 black women were victims of extreme husband-to-wife violence. Robert L. Hampton and Richard Gelles, "Violence toward Black Women in a Nationally Representative Sample of Black Families," *Journal of Comparative Family Studies* 25, no. 1 (spring 1994): 105–19.

NOTES TO CHAPTER 1

1. Aisha [pseud.], interview by the author, tape recording, New York City, N.Y., 12 April 1993.

2. Orlando Patterson, *Slavery and Social Death* (Cambridge: Harvard University Press, 1982).

3. Jacqueline Jones, *Labor of Love, Labor of Sorrow: Black Women, Work and the Family, from Slavery to the Present* (New York: Vintage Books, 1986), 20.

4. For her discussion of domestic violence and rape among slaves, see Deborah Gray White, *Ar'nt I a Woman* (New York: W. W. Norton, 1985), 151–53.

5. The autobiography by Gussie White, which is excerpted in this collection of women's voices, was also dictated to a white interviewer.

6. There were black and white interviewers for the narratives collected during the 1930s by the Works Progress Administration workers. I have excerpted several of the narratives collected in the George P. Rawick series. For a discussion of racial dynamics and other issues pertinent to the relationship between the content of the slave narratives and the way the slave narratives were collected, see John Blassingame, "Using the Testimony of Ex-Slaves: Approaches and Problems," *Journal of Southern History* 41, no. 4 (November 1975): 473–92. For thoughtful treatment of race and gender dynamics on this subject, see Melvina Johnson Young, "Exploring the WPA Narratives: Finding Voices of Black Women and Men," in *Theorizing Black Feminisms*, eds. Stanlie James and Abena Busia (New York: Routledge, 1993), 55–74. Also see George P. Rawick, "General Introduction," *The American Slave*, supplement series 1, volume 1 (Westport, Conn.: Greenwood Press, 1977), xvi–xlii; and Paul D. Escott, "The Art and Science of Reading WPA Slave Narratives," in *The Slave's Narrative*, eds. Charles T. Davis and Henry Louis Gates, Jr. (New York: Oxford University Press, 1985), 40–47.

7. Olaudah Equiano, *The Life of Olaudah Equiano, or Gustavus Vassa, the African* (Boston, 1837), as quoted in Thomas Howard, ed., *Black Voyage: Eyewitness Accounts of the Atlantic Slave Trade* (Boston: Little, Brown, 1971), 30.

8. George P. Rawick, ed., *The American Slave: A Composite Autobiography* (Westport, Conn.: Greenwood Press, 1972), Series 1, *Alabama Narratives*, volume 6, 66.

9. Rawick, Series 1, *Mississippi Narratives*, volume 7, 171.

10. James Mellon, ed., *Bullwhip Days: The Slaves Remember* (New York: Weidenfeld and Nicolson, 1988), 297.

11. Rawick, Series 1, *Oklahoma Narratives*, volume 7, part I, 362.

12. Alabama Former Slaves Interviewed, 1910, by Mary White Ovington, in *Slave Testimony, Two Centuries of Letters, Speeches, Interviews, and Autobiographies*, ed. John W. Blassingame (Baton Rouge: Louisiana State University Press, 1977), 540–41.

13. Herbert G. Gutman, *The Black Family in Slavery and Freedom: 1750–1925* (New York: Pantheon, 1976), 84–85.

14. Rawick, Series 1, *Arkansas Narratives*, volume 10, part VI, 195.

15. Elizabeth Keckley, *Behind the Scenes: Or Thirty Years a Slave, and Four*

Years in the White House (1868; reprint, New York: Oxford University Press, 1988), 39.

16. Anonymous, Rawick, Series 1, *Georgia Narratives*, volume 13, part IV, 293–94.

17. Linda Brent, *Incidents in the Life of a Slave Girl*, ed. by L. Maria Child, New introduction and notes by Walter Teller (New York: Harcourt Brace Jovanovich, 1973), 26–28, 54–55.

18. Sara Rice, *He Included Me: The Autobiography of Sara Rice*, ed. Louise Westling, (Athens: University of Georgia Press, 1989), 45, 63, 86, 88, 92, 105, 121.

19. The Oral History of Maggie L. Comer as told to James P. Comer, in James P. Comer, *Maggie's American Dream: The Life and Times of a Black Family* (New York: New American Library, 1988), 23, 25–26.

20. Sara Brooks, *You May Plow Here: The Narrative of Sara Brooks*, ed. Thordis Simonsen (New York: W. W. Norton, 1986), 162, 165, 167.

21. Billie Holiday's biographer, Robert O'Meally, comments on this event in *Lady Day: The Many Faces of Billie Holiday* (New York: Little, Brown, 1991). On p. 79, he writes:

As easy as it is to believe that Eleanora [Billie Holiday] was raped and blamed for it—and that she and her mother were powerless to obtain justice—the documents pertaining to that first arrest tell a different tale. Court records show that the fourth-grader was on the hook from school so often that a probation officer named M. Dawson took her to juvenile court, where, in January 1925, Magistrate Williams declared her guilty of being "a minor without proper care and guardianship" and ordered her to spend a year in Baltimore's Catholic-run House of the Good Shepherd for Colored Girls.

The fact that the court records do not mention the sexual assault does not refute Holiday's account of being raped since she indicates that neither the police nor the court seemed to believe that she had been victimized.

22. Billie Holiday, with William Dufty, *Lady Sings the Blues* (New York: Doubleday, 1956; reprint, New York: Penguin Books, 1992), 15–17, 103–4.

23. Ossie Guffy, as told by Caryl Ledner, in *Ossie: The Autobiography of a Black Woman* (New York: W. W. Norton, 1971), 124–25, 145–47.

NOTES TO CHAPTER 2

1. The accounts in this chapter are based on personal interviews that I conducted. Respondents were chosen on the basis of word-of-mouth contacts. The content of the interviews focused upon the evolution of the women's gender and racial consciousness, their definitions of spirituality, and incidents of intimate violence that had occurred in their lives. The women's stories are reported pseudonymously to protect their confidentiality.

2. Aisha [pseud.], interview by the author, tape recording, New York, 12 April 1993.

3. Denise [pseud.], interview by the author, tape recording, Albany, N.Y., 26 May 1993.

4. Carey [pseud.], interview by the author, tape recording, Boston, Mass., 22 April 1994.

NOTES TO CHAPTER 3

1. Judith Lewis Herman, *Trauma and Recovery* (New York: Basic Books, 1992), 30.

2. See Diana Scully, *Understanding Sexual Violence: A Study of Convicted Rapists* (Boston: Unwin Hyman, 1990); R. E. Dobash and R. Dobash, *Violence against Wives* (New York: Free Press, 1979).

3. Herman, *Trauma and Recovery*, 52.

4. Ibid., 74.

5. David Theo Goldberg, *Racial Subjects: Writing on Race in America* (New York: Routledge, 1997), 80.

6. Ibid., 107–8. The elaborate tactics and casual brutality in the FBI response to 1960s black nationalists or the bombing of the MOVE community in Philadelphia serve as examples of this aspect of black visibility.

7. Marie Fortune, *Sexual Violence: The Unmentionable Sin* (New York: Pilgrim Press, 1983), 202.

8. For a detailed analysis of children's dependency on adults for their needs, and the destructive impact of sexual abuse in relation to the natural drive of children to do anything to get the care and attention of adult caregivers, see Alice Miller, *Thou Shalt Not Be Aware: Society's Betrayal of the Child*, translated by Hildegarde and Hunter Hannum (New York: Meridian, 1984), especially 119.

9. Joann M. Garna, "A Cry of Anguish: The Battered Woman," in *Women in Travail and Transition*, eds. Maxine Glaz and Jeanne Stevenson Moessner (Minneapolis: Fortress Press, 1991), 133.

10. Marie Fortune and Judith Hertze, "A Commentary on Religious Issues in Family Violence," in *Sexual Assault and Abuse: A Handbook for Clergy and Religious Professionals*, eds. Mary D. Pellauer, Barbara Chester, and Jane Boyajian (San Francisco: HarperCollins, 1987), 76. See also Joy M. K. Bussert, *Battered Women: From a Theology of Suffering to an Ethic of Empowerment* (New York: Kutztown Publishing Co., 1986), especially chapter 4; Carole R. Bohn, "Dominion to Rule: The Roots and Consequences of a Theology of Ownership," in *Christianity, Patriarchy, and Abuse: A Feminist Critique*, eds. Joanne Carlson Brown and Carole R. Bohn (New York: Pilgrim Press, 1989).

11. bell hooks, *Talking Back: Thinking Feminist, Thinking Black* (Boston: South End Press, 1989), 6.

12. For assistance in developing this idea, I am indebted to the comments of womanist ethicist Joan Martin at the 1995 Feminist Ethics Consultation, Cambridge, Mass.

13. Sapphire, "Reflections of Breaking Glass," in *Life-Notes: Personal Writings by Contemporary Black Women*, ed. Patricia Bell-Scott, (New York: W. W. Norton, 1994) 243.

14. Lenore Walker, "Post-Traumatic Stress Disorder in Women: Diagnosis and Treatment of Battered Woman Syndrome," *Psychotherapy* 28, no. 1 (spring 1991): 26. See also Herman, *Trauma and Recovery*, 42–47.

15. Walker, "Post-Traumatic Stress Disorder in Women," 21; Lenore Walker, *Terrifying Love: Why Battered Women Kill and How Society Responds* (New York: Harper and Row, 1989), 180.

16. T., "Manner of 'De Light'—a New Kind of Talk," unpublished paper, 1994.

17. Lenore Walker and Angela Browne, "Gender and Victimization by Intimates," *Journal of Personality* 53, no. 2 (June 1985): 180.

18. James N. Poling describes a correlation between the psychoanalytic constructs of the self and the patriarchal expectations of men and women. He argues that women are less able to protect themselves from abuse because under the conditions of patriarchy, they are expected to be submissive and adaptive at the cost of essential elements of the self. See James N. Poling, *The Abuse of Power* (Nashville: Abingdon Press, 1991), 105.

19. For further discussion of the impact of heterosexism in the black community on black lesbians see Vickie M. Mays, Susan D. Cochran, and Sylvia Rhue, "Impact of Perceived Discrimination on the Intimate Relationships of Black Lesbians," *Journal of Homosexuality* 25, no. 4 (1993): 1–14; Darryl K. Loicano, "Gay Identity Issues among Black Americans: Racism, Homophobia and the Need for Validation," *Journal of Counseling and Development* 68 (1989): 21–25.

20. See Mary D. Pellauer, with Susan Brooks Thistlethwaite, "Conversation on Grace and Healing: Perspectives from the Movement to End Violence against Women," in *Lift Every Voice: Constructing Christian Theologies from the Underside*, eds. Susan Brooks Thistlethwaite and Mary Potter Engel (San Francisco: HarperCollins, 1990), 178.

21. Margaret T. Gordon and Stephanie Riger, *The Female Fear* (New York: Free Press, 1989), 8, 9.

22. Aisha [pseud.], interview.

23. Mary D. Pellauer, "A Theological Perspective on Sexual Assault," in *Sexual Assault and Abuse: A Handbook for Clergy and Religious Professionals*, eds. Mary D. Pellauer, Barbara Chester, and Jane Boyajian (San Francisco: HarperCollins, 1987), 89. Also see the work of anthropologist Mary Douglas referred to by Pellauer for an intricate theory describing the cultural functions of dirt. Mary Douglas, *Purity and Danger: An Analysis of Concepts of Pollution and Taboo* (New York: Routledge, 1991).

24. Pellauer, "A Theological Perspective," 89.

25. Kathryn Quina and Nancy Carlson, *Rape, Incest and Sexual Harassment: A Guide for Helping Survivors* (New York: Greenwood Press, 1989), 30.

26. Pellauer, "A Theological Perspective," 90.

27. This discussion of the internalization of racial inferiority is based on the theories of Frantz Fanon, especially *Black Skin, White Masks* (New York: Grove Press, 1967).

28. For a discussion of the psychology of shame and gay and lesbian identity, see Gershen Kaufman and Lev Raphael, *Coming Out of Shame: Transforming Gay and Lesbian Lives* (New York: Doubleday, 1996).

29. Sarah [pseud.], "Reflection Paper on *Next Time, She'll Be Dead*" Unpublished 10 April, 1997, 2.

30. *Ibid.*

31. Fortune, *Sexual Violence*, 200; see also A. Imbens and I. Jonker, *Christianity and Incest*, translated by Patricia McVay (Minneapolis: Fortress Press, 1992).

32. Marie Fortune, "Forgiveness: The Last Step," in *Violence against Women and Children: A Christian Theological Sourcebook*, eds. Carol J. Adams and Marie Fortune (New York: Continuum, 1995), 201; Also see Pamela Cooper-White, *The Cry of Tamar: Violence against Women and the Church's Response* (Minneapolis: Augsburg Fortress, 1995), 253–62.

33. Jennifer Manlowe, *Faith Born of Seduction: Sexual Trauma, Body Image, and Religion* (New York: New York University Press, 1995), 68.

34. Several of the comments by practitioners that are cited in this section are taken from interviews that I conducted. I interviewed Afro-American women therapists (in private practice and public hospital settings), psychology researchers, and battered women's shelter workers. The background of some of these professionals encompassed more than one of these categories. I randomly selected respondents who not only had interests and qualified experience in treating black women victimized by intimate violence, but who also had antiracist and feminist/womanist commitments. To protect the confidentiality of their clients, the insights of these practitioners are reported pseudonymously.

35. Dr. Anderson [pseud.], interview by the author, tape recording, New York, 6 April 1994. On black women victim/survivors internalizing stereotypes about needing to be strong as an obstacle to seeking help, see also Jo-Ellen Asbury, "African-American Women in Violent Relationships: An Exploration of Cultural Differences," in *Violence in the Black Family: Correlates and Consequences*, ed. Robert L. Hampton (Lexington, Mass.: Lexington Books, 1987), especially 100ff.

36. Nancy A. Matthews, "Surmounting a Legacy: The Expansion of Racial Diversity in a Local Anti-Rape Movement," *Gender and Society* 3, no. 4 (December 1989).

37. *Ibid.*, 525–26.

38. *Ibid.*, 527.

39. A black woman rape victim, 1985, quoted in Julia Boyd, "Ethnic and Cultural Diversity: Keys to Power," in *Diversity and Complexity in Feminist Therapy*, eds. Laura S. Brown and Maria P. P. Root (New York: Harrington Press, 1990), 156.

40. Gail Wyatt, "The Aftermath of Child Sexual Abuse of African American and White Women: The Victim's Experience," *Journal of Family Violence* 5, no. 1 (March 1990), 66–81.

41. *Ibid*, 71.

42. T., "Manner of 'De Light,'" 4.

43. Reverend Frame [pseud.], telephone interview conducted by the author, April 1994.

44. Kesho Yvonne Scott, *The Habit of Surviving* (New York: Ballantine Books, 1991), 62–63.

45. *Ibid*.

46. Anna Carlson [pseud.], interview by the author, Boston, Mass., 22 April 1994.

47. Ibid.

48. This term has sexist connotations because it is commonly used to refer to single-parent homes, implying that two-parent homes constitute male-headed households.

49. See Barbara Omolade, *It's a Family Affair: Real Lives of Black Single Mothers* (Latham, N.Y.: Kitchen Table Press, 1986).

50. Dr. Denson [pseud.], interview by the author, tape recording, New York, 11 May 1994.

51. Evelyn White, *Chain, Chain, Change: For Black Women Dealing with Physical and Emotional Abuse* (Seattle: Seal Press, 1985), 12.

52. Jean Anton and Marie Fortune, producers, *Broken Vows: Religious Perspectives on Domestic Violence—Parts I and II*, Center for the Prevention of Sexual Violence, Michi Pictures, 1994, videocassette.

53. Denson [pseud.], interview.

54. Carlson [pseud.], interview.

55. Andrea Benton Rushing, "Surviving Rape: A Morning/Mourning Ritual," in *Theorizing Black Feminisms: The Visionary Black Pragmatism of Black Women*, eds. Stanlie M. James and Abena P. A. Busia (New York: Routledge, 1993), 132.

56. Ibid.

57. Lottie L. Joiner, "Healing the Scars," *Emerge* 8, no. 7 (May 1997): 38.

58. For a discussion by practioners from a women's shelter in Boston on the women's struggles with racial guilt when reporting black perpetrators to white authorities, see Hyatt Imam and Spring Redd, "The Elizabeth Stone House: A Residential Mental Health Program for Women," *Sage* 2, no. 2 (fall 1985): especially 66.

59. Melba Wilson, *Crossing the Boundary: Black Women Survive Incest* (Seat-

tle: Seal Press, 1994), 87, 89. For a brief discussion of racialized stigmas that impact black women incest survivors, see Janet Liebman Jacobs, *Victimized Daughters: Incest and the Development of the Female Self* (New York: Routledge, 1994), 47.

60. The assault of white racism in "the public domain" may increase the need to rigidly demarcate the home as a private sphere. Feminist legal theorist Kimberlé Crenshaw argues that privacy needs may be an impeding element which affects decisions by women of color to seek intervention. She explains:

> There is also a more generalized community ethic against public intervention, the product of a desire to create a private world free from the diverse assaults on the public lives of racially subordinated people. In this sense home is not simply a man's castle in patriarchal terms, but is also a safe haven from the indignities of life in a racist society. In many cases, the desire to protect the home as a safe haven against assaults may make it more difficult for women of color to seek protection against assaults from within the home. "Mapping the Margins: Intersectionality, Identity Politics, and Violence against Women of Color," in *The Public Nature of Private Violence: The Discovery of Domestic Abuse*, eds. Martha A. Fineman and Roxanne Mykitiuk (New York: Routledge, 1994), 103.

In this same volume, for a discussion of the affirmative role that privacy can play for battered women, see Elizabeth M. Schneider, "The Violence of Privacy." On how issues related to sexual violence against black women are linked to the needs of black male-female couples for private intimate space free from white domination, see Barbara Omolade, "Hearts of Darkness," in *Powers of Desire: The Politics of Sexuality*, eds. Ann Snitow, Christine Stansell, and Sharon Thompson (New York: Monthly Review Press, 1983), especially 363.

61. Sebina, quoted in Beth E. Richie, *Compelled to Crime: The Gender Entrapment of Battered Black Women* (New York: Routledge, 1996), 87.

62. *Ibid.*

63. Sarah [pseud.], "Reflection Paper," 3.

NOTES TO CHAPTER 4

1. Susan Griffin, "Rape: The All-American Crime," in *Forcible Rape*, eds. Duncan Chappell et al. (New York: Columbia University Press, 1977), 59. Reprinted from *Ramparts* (September 1971).

2. Lynn A. Curtis, *Violence, Race, and Culture* (Lexington, Mass.: Lexington Books, 1975), 83.

3. Joyce Williams and Karen Holmes, *The Second Assault: Rape and Public Attitudes* (Westport, Conn.: Greenwood Press, 1981), 27.

4. Susan Brownmiller, *Against Our Will: Men, Women and Rape* (New York: Simon and Schuster, 1975). For examples, see 356, 362–63, 367.

5. bell hooks critiques Brownmiller's minimal consideration of the sexist dynamics in the analysis of sexual violence against black women during slavery and postbellum times. Because Brownmiller neglects the issue of sexism in favor of a primarily race-based analysis, hooks accuses her of contributing to the devaluation of black womanhood. See bell hooks, *Ain't I a Woman* (Boston: South End Press, 1981), especially 51ff.

6. Brownmiller, *Against Our Will*, 247.

7. Ibid., 233.

8. For Angela Davis's extensive criticism of Brownmiller for providing a racist interpretation of the Emmett Till case, see *Women, Race and Class* (New York: Random House, 1981), 178ff, 196ff.

9. Brownmiller, *Against Our Will*, 248.

10. For a discussion of the anti-rape movement that mentions some of the tensions between black women and white women, and where definitions of "feminism" play a role in those tensions, see Nancy A. Matthews, *Managing Rape: The Feminist Anti-Rape Movement and the State* (New York: Routledge, 1994).

11. Davis, *Women, Race and Class*, 179.

12. Calvin Hernton, *Sex and Racism in America* (New York: Grove Press, 1965).

13. Calvin Hernton, *Coming Together: Black Power, White Hatred, and Sexual Hang-Ups* (New York: Random House, 1971).

14. Hernton, *Sex and Racism in America*, 129.

15. Hernton, *Coming Together*, 59. Emphasis in original.

16. *Ibid.*, 17.

17. See also Angela Davis's critique of Hernton's sexist depiction of black women in *Women, Race and Class*, 182–83.

18. Robert Staples, *The Black Woman in America* (Chicago: Nelson Hall, 1973).

19. *Ibid*, 49.

20. *Ibid*, 65.

21. Joyce A. Ladner, *Tomorrow's Tomorrow* (New York: Doubleday, 1971).

22. *Ibid.*, 52.

23. She is specifically writing in response to depictions of poor black women in the work of E. Franklin Frazier, *The Negro Family in the United States* (Chicago: University of Chicago Press, 1939); and Daniel Patrick Moynihan, *The Negro Family: The Case for National Action* (Washington, D.C.: Government Printing Office, March 1965).

24. See Ladner, *Tomorrow's Tomorrow*, 145–46.

25. Also see Robert Hampton, "Institutional Decimation, Marital Exchange, and Disruption in Black Families," *Western Journal of Black Studies* 4, no. 2 (summer 1980): 132–39; R. J. Sampson, "Urban Black Violence: The Effect of Male Joblessness and Family Disruption," *American Journal of Sociology* 93, no. 2

(1987): 348–82; Robert Staples, "The Political Economy of Black Family Life," *Black Scholar* 17 (1986): 2–11.

26. Hampton and Gelles, "Violence toward Black Women."

27. Results were collected from the Second National Family Violence Survey, reported in Richard Gelles and Murray Straus, *Intimate Violence* (New York: Simon and Schuster, 1988).

28. Hampton and Gelles, "Violence toward Black Women," 115.

29. Also see Odell Uzzell and Wilma Peebles-Wilkins, "Black Spousal Abuse: A Focus on Relational Factors and Intervention Strategies," *Western Journal of Black Studies* 13, no. 1 (1989): 10–16. They survey the literature on black spousal abuse. In their conclusions, they argue in favor of the idea that increasing community networks on the macro and micro levels is a crucial prevention strategy. They recommend approaches such as community-wide networks addressing issues such as unemployment at the macro level, and reinforcing extended family bonds at the micro level of the family.

30. William Oliver, "Sexual Conquest and Patterns of Black-on-Black Violence: A Structural-Cultural Perspective," *Violence and Victims* 4, no. 4 (1989): 257–73.

31. Oliver, "Sexual Conquest," 257.

32. Some even argue that black patriarchy is needed to bring stability to black families. In *Empower the People: Social Ethics for the African-American Church*, (Maryknoll, N.Y.: Orbis Books, 1991), 82, Theodore Walker explains the need for a reestablished patriarchy since "the socio-economic resources available to black males have been decreasing faster than for black women, and it is becoming less and less possible for black men to fulfill the positive roles expected of them." He cites sociologists Nathan and Julia Hare extensively to support this claim. For Walker, the white feminist and gay liberation movements are to blame for the gender confusion and male-female conflicts among African-Americans.

33. Oliver, "Sexual Conquest," 265.

34. Gelles and Straus, *Intimate Violence*.

35. They reported a 47 percent decrease in family violence over the ten-year period from 1975 to 1985! See ibid., 108–15, for a defense of their findings amidst wide skepticism from other scholars and practitioners who address the problem of family violence.

36. *Ibid.*, 59.

37. Ibid., 25.

38. Deborah Prothrow-Stith, *Deadly Consequences* (New York: HarperCollins, 1991), 76.

39. For a catalog of the dire, impoverished conditions perpetuated by social neglect, particularly as they affect urban youth and children, see Children's Defense Fund, *Report on the Costs of Child Poverty: Wasting America's Future* (Boston: Beacon Press, 1994).

40. Prothrow-Stith, *Deadly Consequences*, 76.

41. Feminist theories are not exclusively articulated by women, but are distinguished by their incorporation of gender and power analysis as central to their discussion of violence against women. Emilio Viano, a male author, is included among the theorists discussed in this section.

42. This feminist argument is not to be confused with similar assertions in family violence literature that refer to men's physical superiority. Gelles and Straus argue that men assault women "because they can," just as parents beat their children when they are young and discontinue the practice when their children get to be teenagers because as teenagers they usually become larger and stronger than their parents. In this view, family members can perpetrate assault against other family members because of superior physical size and strength. In contrast, the feminist argument discussed in this section sees male violence as a male sociopolitical right.

43. Elizabeth A. Stanko, *Intimate Intrusions: Women's Experience of Male Violence* (London: Routledge and Kegan Paul, 1985), 71. Emphasis in original.

44. For a brief introduction to the field of victimology, citing its origins in the 1970s women's movement, see Emilio C. Viano, "Introduction," in *Critical Issues in Victimology: International Perspectives*, ed. Emilio C. Viano (New York: Springer, 1992), 1–13.

45. Emilio C. Viano, "Violence among Intimates: Major Issues and Approaches," in *Intimate Violence: Interdisciplinary Perspectives*, ed. Emilio C. Viano (Washington, D.C.: Hemisphere Publishing, 1992), 4.

46. Ibid., 6.

47. Catharine A. MacKinnon, *Toward a Feminist Theory of the State* (Cambridge: Harvard University Press, 1989), 127.

48. *Ibid.*, 178.

49. Camille Paglia, a "pro-sex feminist," and rabid critic of MacKinnon, vehemently opposes any notion of the structural sex/gender disempowerment of women, arguing that "woman rules the sexual and emotional sphere, and there she has no rival. Victim ideology, a caricature of social history, blocks women from recognition of their dominance in the deepest, most important realm." *Vamps and Tramps* (New York: Vintage Books, 1994), 31.

50. For a detailed critique of Catherine MacKinnon's racial essentialism in her theory of male dominance, see Angela P. Harris, "Race and Essentialism in Feminist Legal Theory," *Stanford Law Review* 42, no. 3 (February 1990): 581–616.

51. For an example of such a critique that is primarily leveled at Walker, though it includes Herman, see Donald Alexander Downs, *More than Victims: Battered Women, Syndrome Society, and the Law* (Chicago: University of Chicago Press, 1996).

52. Lenore E. Walker, "Psychology and Violence against Women," *American Psychologist* 44, no. 4 (April 1989): 696.

53. For further discussion of expressions of white racism in white feminist theorizing, see Robyn Wiegman, *American Anatomies: Theorizing Race and Gender* (Durham, N.C.: Duke University Press, 1995), especially chapter 6; Michelle Fine et al., eds., *Off White: Readings on Race, Power, and Society* (New York: Routledge, 1997); and Ruth Frankenberg, *The Social Construction of Whiteness: White Women, Race Matters* (Minneapolis: University of Minnesota Press, 1993).

54. Judith Herman, with Lisa Hirshman, *Father-Daughter Incest* (Cambridge: Harvard University Press, 1981), 67.

55. For a discussion white survivors of incest that analyzes race and ethnicity, see Marian Schmidt, "Anglo Americans and Sexual Child Abuse," in *Sexual Abuse in Nine North American Cultures,* ed. Lisa Aronson Fontes (Thousand Oaks, Calif.: Sage, 1995).

56. Lenore E. Walker, *The Battered Woman* (New York: Harper and Row, 1979), 22.

57. See Bussert, *Battered Women*, where issues related to race are interjected into her "Sociological Overview" with a description of several of the ways that racist attitudes in the community impede women of color from seeking help. She pointedly dispels stereotypes about violence being less of a problem for whites. Also see Poling, *The Abuse of Power*, for a detailed discussion of the African-American family and acknowledgment of the dual bind of racism and sexism that African-American women face. However, his study painstakingly explains how the psychoanalytic process surrounding abuse is thoroughly gender-defined. Black women are discussed in the context of his critique of culture, where he points out patterns of societal devaluation of "women and persons of color." Factors related to race are absent and assumed to be irrelevant to the gender-based, psychoanalytic explanation of the impact of abuse.

58. Ann Jones, *Next Time, She'll Be Dead* (Boston: Beacon Press, 1994), 96. Many feminists such as Jones now prefer to use the term "woman battering" rather than "battered woman" because, by implication, the latter locates the problem in the identity of the woman, while the former emphasizes an act perpetrated against a woman. Ibid., 84. Also see hooks, "Violence in Intimate Relationships: A Feminist Perspective," in *Talking Back*, 84–91. hooks critiques the term "battered woman" because it obscures less severe cases of male violence and often connotes a separate and unique category of womanhood.

59. Jones, *Next Time, She'll Be Dead*, 83.

60. Jane Caputi, *The Age of the Sex Crime* (Bowling Green, Ohio: Bowling Green State University Popular Press, 1987), 10, as quoted in Mark Baker, *Nam: The Viet Nam War in the Words of the Men and Women Who Fought There* (New York: Morrow and Company, 1982), 182.

61. Jones, *Next Time, She'll Be Dead*, 145.

62. Susan Schecter, *Women and Male Violence* (Boston: South End Press, 1982), 238.

63. *Ibid.*, 236.

64. Ibid., 237.

65. Cheryl Townsend Gilkes, "The 'Loves' and 'Troubles' of African-American Women's Bodies: The Womanist Challenge to Cultural Humiliation and Community Ambivalence," in *A Troubling in My Soul: Womanist Perspectives on Evil and Suffering*, ed. Emile M. Townes (Maryknoll, N.Y.: Orbis Books, 1993), 240.

66. *Ibid.*, 235.

67. Toinette M. Eugene, "'Swing Low, Sweet Chariot!': A Womanist Response to Sexual Violence and Abuse," in *Violence against Women and Children: A Christian Theological Sourcebook* eds. Carol J. Adams and Marie M. Fortune (New York: Continuum, 1995), 189.

68. *Ibid.*, 187.

69. Delores S. Williams, "African-American Women in Three Contexts of Domestic Violence," in *Violence against Women, Concilium*, eds. Elisabeth Schüssler Fiorenza and M. Shawn Copeland (Maryknoll, N.Y.: Orbis Books, 1994), 34.

70. Eugene, "'Swing Low, Sweet Chariot!'" 195.

71. Frances E. Wood, "'Take My Yoke upon You': The Role of the Church in the Oppression of African-American Women," in Townes, *A Troubling in My Soul*, 40.

72. Ibid.

73. *Ibid.*

NOTES TO CHAPTER 5

1. Martha R. Burt, "Cultural Myth, Violence against Women, and the Law," *Drew Gateway* 58 (fall 1988): 28.

2. Katie Roiphe, "Date Rape Hysteria," *New York Times* (Op Ed), 20 November 1991.

3. See Louise Armstrong, *What Happened When Women Said Incest: Rocking the Cradle of Sexual Politics* (Reading, Mass.: Addison Wesley, 1994).

4. Lynne B. Rosewater, "Diversifying Feminist Theory and Practice: Broadening the Concept of Victimization," in *Diversity and Complexity in Feminist Therapy*, eds. Laura Brown and Maria Root (New York: Harrington Park Press, 1990), 301.

5. Burt, "Cultural Myth," 35.

6. Scully, *Understanding Sexual Violence*, 40–45. See also John Forrester, "Rape, Seduction and Psychoanalysis," in *Rape: An Historical and Social Inquiry*, eds. Sylvana Tomaselli and Roy Porter (New York: Basil Blackwell, 1986), 57–83.

7. Scully, *Understanding Sexual Violence*, 45.

8. Lauretta Bender, "Offended and Offender Children," in *Sexual Behavior and the Law*, ed. Ralph Slovenko (Springfield, Ill.: Charles C. Thomas, 1965), 688.

9. Alexandra Symonds, "Violence against Women and the Myth of Masochism," *American Journal of Psychotherapy* 33 (1979): 161–73.

10. Walker, *Terrifying Love*, 180.

11. Herman, *Trauma and Recovery*, 67.

12. I use the term "black newspaper" to describe newspapers whose central objective is to report news about and relevant to African-Americans and to present views by African-Americans on any subject that the newspaper deems to be of concern to African-Americans.

13. Claire Lacneau, "Why Didn't Our Black Leaders Defend Thomas," *Amsterdam News*, 26 October 1991, 12.

14. Sherman Miller, "It Scares American Males," *New Journal and Guide*, 22 October 1991, 2.

15. LeRoi Jones, *Four Black Revolutionary Plays* (New York: Bobbs-Merrill, 1969), 81.

16. *Ibid.*, 83.

17. Eldrige Cleaver, *Soul on Ice* (New York: Dell Publishing, 1968), 158.

18. *Ibid.*, 159.

19. Ibid., 167.

20. Ibid., 162.

21. Ibid., 159.

22. Ibid., 168.

23. Ibid., 169.

24. Ibid., 170.

25. Ibid., 206.

26. Elaine Brown, *A Taste of Power: A Black Woman's Story* (New York: Pantheon Books, 1992), 307.

27. Ibid., 309.

28. Ibid., 310.

29. Ibid., 313.

30. Fortune, *Sexual Violence*, 24.

31. Jane Caputi, "Advertising Femicide: Lethal Violence against Women in Pornography and Gorenography," in *Femicide: The Politics of Woman Killing*, eds. Jill Radford and Diana E. H. Russell (New York: Twayne, 1992), 213.

32. Caputi, *The Age of the Sex Crime*, 161. See also Jean Kilbourne, writer, and Margaret Lazarus, producer and director, *Still Killing Us Softly* (Cambridge: Cambridge Documentary Films, 1987).

33. Nation, "Bad Rap," *Time*, 1 September 1986, 20; Editorial, "Momma Dearest; Ice T's 'Cop Killer' Song Deserves Criticism," *New Republic* 202, no. 7 (10 August 1992): 7; Jerry Adler, "The Rap Attitude," *Newsweek*, 19 March 1990, 56; Richard Lacayo, "The Rap against a Rap Group," *Time*, 25 June 1990, 18; Judith Dobrzynski, "Up against Rap: C. Delores Tucker, a Crusader against Rap Music,"

Good Housekeeping 221, no. 4 (October 1995): 30; Esther Iverem, "Decrying Rap's Influence," *Washington Post,* 7 November 1997, G02; David Klinghoffer, "See No Evil: Failure of Media to Deal with Crime and Violence committed by Rap Singers," *National Review* 46 (24 January 1994): 73; Paul Delaney, "Gangsta Rappers vs. Mainstream Black Community," *USA Today Magazine* 123, no. 2596 (January 1995): 68; Kevin Merida, "Pop Culture Takes the Rap as Congress Battles Violence, Lawmakers Cite Concern for 'Moral Decline'," *Washington Post,* 10 May 1994, A1.

34. Just as all "classical" movies of popular culture do not glamorize violence against women, so every rap artist does not include mysogynist depictions of women. For instance, the self-sacrificing, ideal mother figure, Maria of *The Sound of Music,* who is the antithesis of the Scarlett O'Hara character, has her counterpart in rap music. In "Sister, Sister" or "Black Coffee" by Heavy D, and "Momma's Always on Stage" by Arrested Development, women are portrayed as self-sacrificing, strong, and dignified maternal figures. For a strong defense of gangsta rap that makes an attempt to be sensitive to issues of sexism against black women, see Michael Eric Dyson, *Between God and Gangsta Rap* (New York: Oxford University Press, 1996), especially chapters 24 to 27.

35. MacKinnon, *Toward a Feminist Theory of the State,* 137. Camille Paglia offers a "pro-sex feminist" viewpoint on rape completely antithetical to MacKinnon's. She rails against "feminist overstress on power differentials" and argues instead for an understanding of rape as an enactment of natural aggression. See Paglia, "Sex Crime: Rape," in *Vamps and Tramps.*

36. Catharine A. MacKinnon, *Feminism Unmodified* (Cambridge: Harvard University Press, 1987), 92.

37. Congress, Senate, Senator Byrd of West Virginia, 90th Congress, 1st session, *Congressional Record* 113, pt. 25 (14 December 1967): 36768.

38. Congress, Senate, Senator Long of Louisiana, 90th Congress, 1st session, *Congressional Record* 113, pt. 24 (21 November 1967): 33543.

39. As quoted in Lucy A. Williams, "Race, Rat Bites and Unfit Mothers: How Media Discourse Informs Welfare Legislation Debate," *Fordham Urban Law Journal* 22, no. 4 (summer 1995): 1184.

40. Jones, *Next Time, She'll Be Dead,* 127.

41. Daniel Patrick Moynihan, *The Negro Family: The Case for National Action* (Washington, D.C.: Government Printing Office, March 1965), 29.

42. Traci C. West "Agenda for the Churches: Uprooting a National Policy of Morally Stigmatizing Poor Black Single Moms," in *Troubling the Welfare Waters,* eds. Elizabeth Bounds, Pamela K. Brubaker, and Mary Hobgood (Cleveland, Ohio: Pilgrim Press, 1999).

43. *Personal Responsibility Act of 1995,* 104th Congress, 1st session, H.R. 4, title I, sec. 100, para. 3 (O).

44. Frances Cress Welsing, *The Isis Papers: The Keys to the Colors* (Chicago: Third World Press, 1991), 88.

45. Richie, *Compelled to Crime*, 72, 76, 88.

46. Patricia Morton, *Disfigured Images: The Historical Assault on Afro-American Women* (Westport, Conn.: Praeger, 1991), 28. For an insightful and thorough analysis of the history of issues of race and rape laws that gives specific attention to the delegitimation of black women as victims of sexual violence, see Jennifer Wriggins, "Rape, Racism, and the Law," *Harvard Women's Law Journal* 6 (1983): 103–41. For other summaries of the history of derogatory stereotyping of black women, see Patricia Hill Collins, *Black Feminist Thought: Knowledge, Consciousness and the Politics of Empowerment* (Boston: Unwin Hyman, 1990), especially 67–90; and hooks, *Ain't I a Woman*, especially 51–86. Bonnie Thornton Dill focuses on images in social science literature in "The Dialectics of Black Womanhood," in *Black Women in America*, eds. Micheline R. Malson, Elisabeth Mudimbe-Boyi, Jean F. Barr, and Mary Wyer (Chicago: University of Chicago Press, 1988): 65–77.

47. Morton, *Disfigured Images*, 73–74. See also John Dollard, *Caste and Color in a Southern Town* (New York: Doubleday Anchor Books, 1957; orig. pub. 1937).

48. Morton, *Disfigured Images*, 74–83; see especially E. Franklin Frazier, *The Negro American Family* (Chicago: University of Chicago Press, 1947; orig. pub. 1939).

49. Michelle Fine, "The Politics of Research Activism: Violence against Women," *Gender and Society* 3, no. 4 (December 1989): 550.

50. Angela Davis underscores the reasonableness of black women's distrust of state authorities to responsibly respond to rape. She supports this contention with examples of police as perpetrators of rape against black women in their custody during the civil rights movement. See Angela Davis, *Violence against Women and the Ongoing Challenge to Racism* (Latham, N.Y.: Kitchen Table Press, 1985), 10. Also see Gail Elizabeth Wyatt et al., *Sexual Abuse and Consensual Sex: Women's Developmental Patterns and Outcomes* (Newbury Park, Calif.: Sage, 1993), 93. I would add to this point, an example out of my own experience of sexual harassment by police. I remember walking down the street in a black neighborhood of Harlem (NYC) when I was thirteen years old. I was with my sister and we were dressed up in new Sunday outfits and feeling quite good about ourselves. Two white police officers approached us. Even at that young age, I knew enough to be slightly apprehensive about my safety when I saw them. One of the officers grabbed my buttocks and they both laughed loudly and continued walking past us. I remember feeling humiliated and frightened. The experience of sexual harassment or intimidation by police prevents many black women from seeing them as a helpful resource.

51. For discussion of police protecting "their own," even when they are guilty of domestic violence offenses, see Lawrence W. Sherman, with Janell D. Schmidt

and Denis P. Rogan, *Policing Domestic Violence: Experiments and Dilemmas* (New York: Free Press, 1992), 33ff.

52. Richie, *Compelled to Crime*, 95.

53. Prothrow-Stith, *Deadly Consequences*, 75–76.

54. See Natalie Pardo, "Black Rape Victims Lack Refuge," *Chicago Reporter* 26, no. 6 (October 1997): 3–5.

55. Sarah [pseud.], unpublished paper, 2.

56. Dr. Baker [pseud.], interview with author, New York City, N.Y., 14 April 1994.

57. Richie, *Compelled to Crime*, 94. For illustrations of rejection that lesbian sexual abuse survivors have faced in twelve-step groups, in one case being accused of having a sinful lifestyle, see Manlowe, *Faith Born of Seduction*, 109–10.

58. Lori Robinson, *Emerge Magazine* (May 1997): 50.

59. As quoted in Mary Pat Flaherty, "Angels Should Fear to Tread on Tyson's Rape Conviction," *Star Tribune* (Minneapolis, Minn.) 1 March 1992, 21A.

60. E. R. Shipp, "Tyson Accuser Details Offer to Drop Charges," *New York Times*, 21 February 1992.

61. Jill Nelson, *Straight, No Chaser: How I Became a Grown-Up Black Woman* (New York: Putnam, 1997), 162.

62. Reverend Calvin O. Butts, pastor of Abyssinian Baptist Church in Harlem.

63. Nelson, *Straight, No Chaser*, 163.

64. Carlson, [pseud.], interview.

65. Quina and Carlson, *Rape, Incest and Sexual Harassment*, 208.

66. Carlson [pseudo.], interview.

67. Walker, *Terrifying Love*, 206.

68. *Ibid.*, 217.

69. Williams and Holmes, *The Second Assault*, 107.

70. *Ibid.*, 183.

71. On black superwoman cultural mythology, see Michelle Wallace, *Black Macho and the Myth of the Superwoman* (New York: Dial Press, 1978).

72. Williams and Holmes, *The Second Assault*, 111.

73. *Ibid.*, 92.

74. Also see Darnell Hawkins, "Devalued Lives and Racial Stereotypes: Ideological Barriers to the Prevention of Family Violence among Blacks," in *Violence in the Black Family*, ed. Robert Hampton (Lexington, Mass.: Lexington Books, 1987): 189–205. Hawkins argues that black women and children have been historically afforded less protection from abuse within the family than any other group in society and unless persisting ideological biases are confronted and challenged, black and poor victims of violence may continue to be neglected. He asserts that stereotyped views devalue blacks by viewing violence as more normal among them, and thereby pose significant barriers to intervention and prevention of black family violence.

NOTES TO CHAPTER 6

1. Alexander Thomas and Samuel Sillen, *Racism and Psychiatry* (New York: Citadel Press, 1972). Their criticism is specifically leveled at A. Kardiner and L. Ovesey, *The Mark of Oppression* (New York: W. W. Norton, 1951). For scholars who offer a similar defense of black psychological health, focusing on black women, see Vernaline Watson, "Self-Concept Formation and the Afro-American Woman," *Journal of Afro-American Issues* 2 (summer 1974): 226–36; Jewelle Taylor Gibbs, "City Girls: Psychosocial Adjustment of Urban Black Adolescent Families," *Sage* 2, no. 2 (fall 1985): 28–36.

2. Beverly Greene, "Still Here: A Perspective on Psychotherapy with African-American Women," in *New Directions in Feminist Psychology: Practice, Theory and Research*, eds. Joan Chrisler and Doris Howard (New York: Springer, 1992), 22.

3. Ann Jones, *Women Who Kill* (New York: Holt, Rinehart and Winston, 1980), 299.

4. Jones recognizes the destruction of the will that batterers often inflict on their victims, but prefers to use descriptions of coercion techniques against state prisoners charted by Amnesty International as a model for understanding the devastating impact of the abuse on women. Jones, *Next Time, She'll Be Dead*, 90.

5. R. Emerson Dobash and Russell P. Dobash, *Women, Violence and Social Change* (New York: Routledge, 1992), especially 214–30.

6. Walker, *The Battered Woman*; Lenore E. Walker, *The Battered Woman Syndrome* (New York: Springer, 1984).

7. Walker and Browne, "Gender and Victimization by Intimates," 191.

8. For example, see Walker, "Psychology and Violence against Women," 697; "Post-Traumatic Stress Disorder in Women," 22.

9. In her introduction to *Battered Woman Syndrome* (p. 8), Walker makes it clear that changing women's sex role socialization does not stop battering.

10. Edward Gondolf, with Ellen R. Fisher, *Battered Women as Survivors: An Alternative to Treating Learned Helplessness* (New York: Lexington Books, 1988).

11. *Ibid.*, 2. For another helpful study of woman battering that compares the "learned helplessness" hypothesis of Lenore Walker and the help-seeking behavior hypothesis of Gondolf and concludes that these are not mutually exclusive or opposing traits, see Kathy Wilson, Regina Vercella, Christiane Brems, and Deborah Benning, "Levels of Learned Helplessness in Abused Women," *Women and Therapy* 13, no. 4 (1992): 53–67.

12. Gondolf, *Battered Women as Survivors*, 18.

13. *Ibid.*, 21.

14. James C. Scott, *Domination and the Arts of Resistance* (New Haven: Yale University Press, 1990), 87.

15. Martha Mahoney, "Victimization or Oppression? Women's Lives, Vio-

lence, and Agency," in *The Public Nature of Private Violence: The Discovery of Domestic Abuse*, eds. Martha A. Fieneman and Roxanne Mykitiuk (New York: Routledge, 1994), 60. For differing treatments of the issue of violence against women and the problems with analysis that requires a rigid victim/agency dichotomy, see Sharon Lamb, *The Trouble with Blame: Victims, Perpetrators, and Responsibility* (Cambridge: Harvard University Press, 1996); Jean Bethke Elshtain, *Real Politics at the Center of Everday Life* (Baltimore: Johns Hopkins University Press, 1997), especially chapter 14.

16. Mahoney, "Victimization or Oppression?" Emphasis in original, 64.

17. Ibid., 75.

18. Audre Lorde, *Sister Outsider* (Trumansburg, N.Y.: Crossing Press, 1984), 37, 38.

19. Tina Turner, with Kurt Loder, *I, Tina: My Life Story* (New York: Avon Books, 1986), 92.

20. Ibid., 167.

21. Delores Williams, *Sisters in the Wilderness: The Challenge of Womanist God-Talk* (Maryknoll, N.Y.: Orbis Books, 1993), 136.

22. Léon Wurmser, *The Mask of Shame* (Baltimore: Johns Hopkins University Press, 1981), 66.

23. Robin Quivers, *Quivers: A Life* (New York: HarperPaperbacks, 1995), 20.

24. Tom Condon and Glenda S. Buell, "A Story of Rape: One Woman's Fear, Pain, Anger and Healing," *Hartford Courant*, 2 September 1990.

25. Janice Joseph, "Woman Battering: A Comparative Analysis of Black and White Women," in *Out of Darkness: Contemporary Perspectives on Family Violence*, eds. Glenda Kaufman Kantor and Jana L. Jasinski (Thousand Oaks, Calif.: Sage, 1997), 161–69.

26. Quivers, *Quivers*, 21.

27. Tom Condon and Glenda S. Buell, "Effects of Rape Go Beyond the Crime, Beyond the Victim," *Hartford Courant*, 3 September 1990.

28. Anonymous interview by author, Washington, D.C., 13 November 1994.

29. *Ibid.*

30. Fine, "The Politics of Research Activism," 550.

31. Williams, *Sisters in the Wilderness*, 177.

32. Rushing, "Surviving Rape," 128.

33. Mary Alice Saunders, "Long Term Physical Complications of Battering: An Afro-centric Intervention of the Ancestors," *Journal of Cultural Diversity* 2, no. 3 (summer 1995): 75–82.

34. *Ibid.*, 82.

35. Ibid., 81.

36. Oya Odumidun Olufumni, "To Batter a Woman Is to Upset the Balance of Nature: A Yoruba Perspective," *NCADV Voice* (fall 1996): 10–11.

37. Ibid., 10.

38. Bernice Johnson Reagan, *We Who Believe in Freedom: Sweet Honey in the Rock—Still on the Journey* (New York: Anchor Books, 1993), 29.

39. *Ibid.*, 30.

40. Ibid., 30.

41. Ibid., 31.

42. Linda Hollies, "A Daughter Survives Incest: A Retrospective Analysis," in *The Black Woman's Health Book: Speaking for Ourselves*, ed. Evelyn C. White (Seattle: Seal Press, 1990): 88.

43. *Ibid.*

44. Ibid., 88.

45. Beverly Wildung Harrison, *Making the Connections: Essays in Feminist Social Ethics*, ed. Carol S. Robb (Boston: Beacon Press, 1985), 14–15.

46. bell hooks, *Killing Rage, Ending Racism* (New York: Henry Holt, 1995), 14.

47. See further description by hooks of how blacks who pursue and attain economic status surrender their rage, in ibid., 16–17.

48. Nancy J. Ramsay, "Sexual Abuse and Shame: The Travail of Recovery," in *Women in Travail and Transition*, eds. Maxine Glaz and Jeanne Stevenson Moessner (Minneapolis: Fortress Press, 1991), 115.

49. Herman, *Trauma and Recovery*, 214.

50. Anderson [pseud.], interview.

51. Carlson [pseud.], interview.

52. Nancy Boyd-Franklin, "Recurrent Themes in the Treatment of African American Women in Group Psychotherapy," *Women and Therapy* 11, no. 2 (1991): 25–40. For a discussion of the ways that social oppression can fuel anger and mistrust between black women see Audre Lorde, "Eye to Eye: Black Women, Hatred, and Anger," in *Sister Outsider*, 145–75.

53. Boyd-Franklin, "Recurrent Themes," 36.

54. Interview by author, New York City, N.Y., June 1993.

55. Also see Crenshaw, "Mapping the Margins," 95. With regard to women who have been battered, Crenshaw describes how many women of color are laden with burdens that are the result of gender and class oppression, which are compounded by racially discriminatory employment and housing practices. She argues that shelters must confront the routinized forms of domination that often converge in these women's lives, hindering their ability to create alternatives to abusive relationships.

56. Herman, *Trauma and Recovery*, 160. For a discussion of the reestablishment of safety and trust that is central to healing victim-survivors, see also Pellauer, "A Theological Perspective on Sexual Assault," 94.

57. Herman, *Trauma and Recovery*, 160.

58. In their study on women and the fear of rape, Margaret Gordon and Stephanie Riger conducted several thousand interviews in Chicago, Philadelphia,

and San Francisco. They point out the prevalence of the fear of assault among blacks living in those cities, especially for black women, noting that: "Blacks whether male or female, feel the least safe of any ethnic or racial subgroup, but about half as many black females report feeling safe as black males." Gordon and Riger, *The Female Fear*, 9.

59. Wilson, *Crossing the Boundary*, 160.

60. Ibid.

61. Linda Gordon, *Pitied but Not Entitled: Single Mothers and the History of Welfare* (New York: Free Press, 1994), especially 130–31ff.

62. Rushing, "Surviving Rape," 140.

NOTES TO CHAPTER 7

1. Virginia Held, *Feminist Morality: Transforming Culture, Society, and Politics* (Chicago: University of Chicago Press, 1993), 34–35.

2. This term refers to white individuals who actively attempt to be antiracist in their attitudes and actions, while recognizing this struggle as ongoing work that can never be definitively completed under the existing conditions of white supremacy.

3. For examples of these deceptions and their dangerous implications, see Dan Fagin, Marianne Lavelle, and the Center for Public Integrity, *Toxic Deception: How the Chemical Industry Manipulates Science, Bends the Law and Endangers Your Health* (Secaucus, N.J.: Birch Lane Press, 1996); Joshua Karliner, *The Corporate Planet: Ecology and Politics in the Age of Globalization* (San Francisco: Sierra Club Books, 1997), especially chapter 6; John C. Stauber and Sheldon Rampton, *Toxic Sludge Is Good for You: Lies, Damn Lies and the Public Relations Industry* (Monroe, Maine: Common Courage Press, 1995).

4. For examples, see G. Solomon et al., "Stillbirth after Occupational Exposure to N-methyl-2-pyrrolidone," *Journal of Occupational and Environmental Medicine* 38, no. 7 (1996): 705–13; P. Vawter Klein, "'For the Good of the Race': Reproductive Hazards from Lead and the Persistence of Exclusionary Policies toward Women," in *Women, Work, and Technology*, ed. Barbara Drygulski (Ann Arbor, Mich.: University of Michigan Press, 1987); Earl M. Wysong, *High Risk and High Stakes: Health Professionals, Politics and Policy* (New York: Greenwood Press, 1992); Christopher Sellers, *Hazards on the Job: From Industrial Disease to Environmental Science* (Chapel Hill, N.C.: University of North Carolina Press, 1997); Edward H. Beardsley, *A History of Neglect: Health Care for Blacks and Mill Workers in the Twentieth-Century South* (Knoxville, Tenn.: University of Tennessee Press, 1987).

5. For many detailed examples of such inaccuracies, see Noam Chomsky, *Class Warfare: Interviews with David Barsamian* (Monroe, Maine: Common Courage Press, 1996).

6. Adrienne Rich, "Women and Honor: Some Notes on Lying," in *On Lies, Secrets and Silence: Selected Prose 1966–1978* (New York: W. W. Norton, 1979), 186.

7. Lorde, *Sister Outsider*, 37.

8. For a comprehensive analysis of the notion of "community" in moral theories, see Elizabeth Bounds, *Coming Together/Coming Apart: Religion, Community, and Modernity* (New York: Routledge, 1997), especially the summary in chapter 5.

9. See Alex Carey, *Taking the Risk Out of Democracy: Corporate Propaganda versus Freedom and Liberty* (Chicago: University of Illinois Press, 1997); Jean Stefancic and Richard Delgado, *No Mercy: How Conservative Think Tanks and Foundations Changed America's Social Agenda* (Philadelphia: Temple University Press, 1998).

10. Michael Parenti, *Inventing Reality: The Politics of News Media* (New York: St. Martin's Press, 1993), 35; Karliner, *The Corporate Planet*, 175–76.

11. W. Lance Bennett, *News: The Politics of Illusion* (White Plains, N.Y.: Longman, 1996), 28; see also Edward S. Herman and Noam Chomsky, *Manufacturing Consent: The Political Economy of the Mass Media* (New York: Pantheon Books, 1988).

12. John B. Thompson, *The Media and Modernity* (Stanford: Stanford University Press, 1995).

13. For discussions on the need to create this kind of public space, see Kathy E. Ferguson, *The Feminist Case against Bureaucracy* (Philadephia: Temple University Press, 1984), 99; Thompson, *The Media and Modernity*, 258ff.

14. For further discussion of resistance to state and corporate structures of power through social movements, see Timothy Luke, *Screens of Power: Ideology, Domination, and Resistance* (Urbana, Ill.: University of Illinois, 1989), especially 211ff. Specifically addressing the role of the church in the formation of moral communities that resist leaving morality exclusively to the control of market and state forces, see Larry L. Rasmussen, *Moral Fragments and Moral Community: A Proposal for Church in Society* (Minneapolis: Fortress Press, 1993).

15. The introduction of Channel One into high schools by the Whittle Communications Company during the early 1990s is one of the most blatant examples of this commodification. Channel One provides several minutes of "educational" programs combined with commercial advertisements in exchange for free television sets in 40 percent of U.S. high schools. Karliner, *The Corporate Planet*, 187.

16. Ferguson, *The Feminist Case against Bureaucracy*, 208.

17. Liz Kelly and Jill Radford, "'Nothing Really Happened': The Invalidation of Women's Experiences of Sexual Violence," in *Women, Violence and Male Power*, eds. Marianne Hester, Liz Kelly, and Jill Radford (Philadelphia: Open University Press, 1996), 31.

18. The term "expert" refers to an increasingly popular tactic used by attor-

neys. Professionals such as therapists or academic researchers are sometimes asked to provide expert testimony about the damaging impact of violence for women. These experts may be called in by attorneys under a variety of circumstances to help women defend themselves in litigation hearings, including divorce proceedings, child custody battles, or if a woman is being prosecuted for injuring or murdering her abuser.

19. The growing availability of internet and fax resources make the compilation of such information feasible in most communities.

20. Carole Barody Corcoran, "From Victim Control to Social Change: A Feminist Perspective on Campus Rape Prevention Programs," in *New Directions in Feminist Psychology: Practice, Theory and Research*, eds. Joan C. Chrisler and Doris Howard (New York: Springer, 1992): 130–40.

21. Oliver, "Sexual Conquest and Patterns of Black-on-Black Violence," 269. See also William Oliver, "Black Males and Social Problems: Prevention through Afrocentric Socialization," *Journal of Black Studies* 20 (1989): 15–39.

22. Jones, *Next Time, She'll Be Ready*, 213.

23. Marie Fortune, "Violence against Women: The Way Things Are Is Not the Way They Have to Be," *Drew Gateway* 58 (fall 1988): 38–50.

24. On this point about the need to expand Fortune's model of justice making, I am indebted to my conversations with Renae Scott. She is a community activist whose analysis includes insights from her experiences as a battered women's shelter worker and from having served as a staff member of the Boston-based Women's Theological Center.

25. For a discussion of the critical role of Christian faith communities in developing moral responses to contemporary social crises, see Rasmussen, *Moral Fragments and Moral Community*, especially 150–51.

26. Cornel West, *Prophesy Deliverance! An Afro-American Revolutionary Christianity* (Philadelphia: Westminister Press, 1982), 98.

27. Christine Gudorf, *Victimization: Examining Christian Complicity* (Philadelphia: Trinity Press International, 1992), 92.

28. Williams, *Sisters in the Wilderness*, 177.

29. Ibid.

30. For a resource that provides rites for women's healing from violence, see Rosemary Radford Ruether, *Women-Church* (New York: Harper and Row, 1985), especially 151–61.

31. For some examples of social justice rituals, see George D. McClain, *Claiming All Things for God: Prayer, Discernment, and Ritual for Social Change* (Nashville, Tenn.: Abingdon Press, 1998).

32. In 1983, I had the privilege of meeting men from a Christian base community in Nicaragua who described their process of coming to a greater awareness of the destructive impact that the dynamics of "machismo" can have upon women. The women of that base community also testified to the behavioral

changes taking place in their community that had resulted in increasing men's participation in child care and women's involvement in formal political leadership.

33. Paul Kivel, *Uprooting Racism: How White People Can Work for Racial Justice* (Philadelphia: New Society Publishers, 1996), 40–46. For his work on domestic violence, see *Men's Work: How to Stop the Violence That Tears Our Lives Apart* (New York: Hazelden/Ballantine, 1992).

Select Bibliography

Abney, Veronica D., and Ronnie Priest. "African Americans and Sexual Child Abuse." In *Sexual Abuse in Nine North American Cultures: Treatment and Prevention*, ed. Lisa Aronson Fontes, 11–30. Thousand Oaks, Calif.: Sage, 1997.

Adam, Barry D. *The Survival of Domination: Inferiorization and Everyday Life.* New York: Elsevier, 1978.

Adams, Carol J., and Marie Fortune, eds. *Violence against Women and Children: A Christian Sourcebook.* New York: Continuum, 1995.

Armstrong, Louise. *What Happened When Women Said Incest: Rocking the Cradle of Sexual Politics.* Reading, Mass.: Addison Wesley, 1994.

Asbury, Jo-Ellen. "African-American Women in Violent Relationships: An Exploration of Cultural Differences." In *Violence in the Black Family: Correlates and Consequences*, ed. Robert L. Hampton, 89–105. Lexington, Mass.: Lexington Books, 1987.

Bachman, Ronet, and Linda Saltzman. "Violence against Women: Estimates from the Redesigned Survey." In *Bureau of Justice Statistics, National Crime Victimization Survey* (August 1995).

Blassingame, John. "Using the Testimony of Ex-Slaves: Approaches and Problems." *Journal of Southern History* 41, no. 4 (November 1975): 473–92.

———, ed. *Slave Testimony, Two Centuries of Letters, Speeches, Interviews, and Autobiographies.* Baton Rouge: Louisiana State University Press, 1977.

Bohn, Carole R. "Dominion to Rule: The Roots and Consequences of a Theology of Ownership." In *Christianity, Patriarchy, and Abuse: A Feminist Critique*, eds. Joanne Carlson Brown and Carole R. Bohn, 105–16. New York: Pilgrim Press, 1989.

Bounds, Elizabeth. *Coming Together/Coming Apart: Religion, Community, and Modernity.* New York: Routledge, 1997.

Boyd, Julia. "Ethnic and Cultural Diversity: Keys to Power." In *Diversity and Complexity in Feminist Therapy*, eds. Laura S. Brown and Maria P. P. Root, 151–67. New York: Harrington Press, 1990.

Boyd-Franklin, Nancy. *Black Families in Therapy: A MultiSystems Approach.* New York: Guilford Press, 1989.

Boyd-Franklin, Nancy. "Recurrent Themes in the Treatment of African American Women in Group Psychotherapy." *Women and Therapy* 11, no. 2 (1991): 25–40.

Brent, Linda. *Incidents in the Life of a Slave Girl*, ed. L. Maria Child. New Introduction and notes by Walter Teller. New York: Harcourt Brace Jovanovich, 1973.

Brooks, Sara. *You May Plow Here: The Narrative of Sara Brooks*, ed. Thordis Simonsen. New York: W. W. Norton, 1986.

Brown, A., et al. "A Review of Psychology of Women Textbooks: Focus on the Afro-American Woman." *Psychology of Women Quarterly* 9 (March 1985): 29–39.

Brown, Joanne C., and Carole Bohn, eds. *Christianity, Patriarchy and Abuse*. New York: Pilgrim Press, 1989.

Brown, Joanne C., and Rebecca Parker. "For God So Loved the World?" In *Christianity, Patriarchy and Abuse*, eds. Joanne C. Brown and Carole Bohn, 1–30. New York: Pilgrim Press, 1989.

Brown, Karen Strauch, and Marjorie Ziefert. "Crisis Resolution, Competence, and Empowerment: A Service Model for Women." *Journal of Primary Prevention* 9, nos. 1 and 2 (fall/winter 1988): 92–103.

Browne, Angela. *When Battered Women Kill*. New York: Free Press, 1987.

Brownmiller, Susan. *Against Our Will: Men, Women and Rape*. New York: Simon and Schuster, 1975.

Bunch, Charlotte. *Violence against Women*. New York: Ford Foundation Women's Program, 1991.

Burns, Maryviolet C., ed. *The Speaking Profits Us: Violence in the Lives of Women of Color*. Seattle: Center for the Prevention of Sexual and Domestic Violence, 1986.

Burt, Martha R. "Cultural Myth, Violence against Women, and the Law." *Drew Gateway* 58 (fall 1988): 25–37.

Burt, Martha R., and Rochelle Semmel Albin. "Rape Myths, Rape Definitions, and Probability of Conviction." *Journal of Applied Social Psychology* 11, no. 3 (1981): 212–30.

Bussert, Joy M. K. *Battered Women: From a Theology of Suffering to an Ethic of Empowerment*. New York: Kutztown Publishing Co., 1986.

Caputi, Jane. "Advertising Femicide: Lethal Violence against Women in Pornography and Gorenography." In *Femicide: The Politics of Woman Killing*, eds. Jill Radford and Diana E. H. Russell. New York: Twayne, 1992.

———. *The Age of the Sex Crime*. Bowling Green, Ohio: Bowling Green State University Popular Press, 1987.

Carbonell, Dina, et al. "Violence against Women." In *The New Our Bodies, Ourselves, Updated and Expanded for the 1990s*, ed. Boston Women's Health Collective, 131–50. New York: Simon and Schuster, 1992.

Children's Defense Fund. *Report on the Costs of Child Poverty:Wasting America's Future*. Boston: Beacon Press, 1994.

Collins, Patricia Hill. *Black Feminist Thought: Knowledge, Consciousness and the Politics of Empowerment*. Boston: Unwin Hyman, 1990.

Comer, James P. *Maggie's American Dream: The Life and Times of a Black Family*. New York: New American Library, 1988.

Cooper-White, Pamela. *The Cry of Tamar: Violence against Women and the Church's Response*. Minneapolis: Augsburg Fortress, 1995.

Copeland, Elaine J. "Counseling Black Women with Negative Self-Concepts." *Personal Guidance Journal* 55 (March 1977): 397–400.

Corcoran, Carole Barody. "From Victim Control to Social Change: A Feminist Perspective on Campus Rape Prevention Programs." In *New Directions in Feminist Psychology: Practice, Theory and Research*, eds. Joan C. Chrisler and Doris Howard, 130–40. New York: Springer, 1992.

Crenshaw, Kimberlé Williams. "Mapping the Margins: Intersectionality, Identity Politics, and Violence against Women of Color." In *The Public Nature of Private Violence: The Discovery of Domestic Abuse*, eds. Martha A. Fineman and Roxanne Mykitiuk, 93–118. New York: Routledge, 1994.

Cross, William E. *Shades of Black: Diversity in African American Identity*. Philadelphia: Temple University Press, 1992.

Curtis, Lynn A. *Violence, Race, and Culture*. Lexington, Mass.: Lexington Books, 1975.

Davis, Angela. *Violence against Women and the Ongoing Challenge to Racism*. Latham, N.Y.: Kitchen Table Press, 1985.

———. *Women, Race and Class*. New York: Random House, 1981.

Dill, Bonnie Thornton. "The Dialectics of Black Womanhood." In *Black Women in America*, eds. Micheline R. Malson, Elisabeth Mudima-Boyi, Jean F. Barr, and Mary Wyer, 65–77. Chicago: University of Chicago Press, 1988.

Dobash, R. Emerson, and Russell P. Dobash. *Violence against Wives*. New York: Free Press, 1979.

———. *Women, Violence and Social Change*. New York: Routledge, 1992.

Douglas, Mary. *Purity and Danger: An Analysis of Concepts of Pollution and Taboo*. New York: Routledge, 1991.

Equiano, Olaudah. *The Life of Olaudah Equiano, or Gustavus Vassa, the African*. Boston, 1837. As quoted in *Black Voyage: Eyewitness Accounts of the Atlantic Slave Trade*, ed. Thomas Howard. Boston: Little, Brown, 1971.

Escott, Paul D. "The Art and Science of Reading WPA Slave Narratives." In *The Slave's Narrative*, eds. Charles T. Davis and Henry Louis Gates, Jr., 40–47. New York: Oxford University Press, 1985.

Eugene, Toinette M. "'Swing Low, Sweet Chariot!': A Womanist Response to Sexual Violence and Abuse." In *Violence against Women and Children: A Christian*

Theological Sourcebook, eds. Carol J. Adams and Marie Fortune, 185–200. New York: Continuum, 1995.

Fanon, Frantz. *Black Skin, White Masks*. New York: Grove Press, 1967.

Ferguson, Kathy E. *The Feminist Case against Bureaucracy*. Philadelphia: Temple University Press, 1984.

Fine, Michelle. "The Politics of Research Activism: Violence against Women." *Gender and Society* 3, no. 4 (December 1989): 549–58.

Forrester, John. "Rape, Seduction and Psychoanalysis." In *Rape: An Historical and Social Inquiry*, eds. Sylvana Tomaselli and Roy Porter, 57–83. New York: Basil Blackwell, 1986.

Fortune, Marie. "The Nature of Abuse." *Pastoral Psychology* 41, no. 5 (1993): 286–87.

———. *Sexual Violence: The Unmentionable Sin*. New York: Pilgrim Press, 1983.

———. "Violence against Women: The Way Things Are Is Not the Way They Have to Be." *Drew Gateway* 58 (fall 1988): 38–50.

Fortune, Marie, and Judith Hertze. "A Commentary on Religious Issues in Family Violence." In *Sexual Assault and Abuse: A Handbook for Clergy and Religious Professionals*, eds. Mary D. Pellauer, Barbara Chester, and Jane Boyajian, 67–83. San Francisco: HarperCollins, 1987.

Frankenberg, Ruth. *The Social Construction of Whiteness: White Women, Race Matters*. Minneapolis: University of Minnesota Press, 1993.

Frazier, Franklin. *The Negro Family in the United States*. Chicago: University of Chicago Press, 1939.

Fullilove, Mindy Thompson et al. "Violence, Trauma, and Post-Traumatic Stress Disorder Among Women Drug Users." In *Journal of Traumatic Stress* 6, no.4 (1993): 533–543.

Garna, Joann M. "A Cry of Anguish: The Battered Woman." In *Women in Travail and Transition*, eds. Maxine Glaz and Jeanne Stevenson Moessner, 126–45. Minneapolis: Fortress Press, 1991.

Gelles, Richard, and Murray Straus. *Intimate Violence*. New York: Simon and Schuster, 1988.

Gibbs, Jewelle Taylor. "City Girls: Psychosocial Adjustment of Urban Black Adolescent Families." *Sage* 2, no. 2 (fall 1985): 28–36.

Giddings, Paula. *When and Where I Enter: The Impact of Black Women on Race and Sex in America*. New York: William Morrow, 1985.

Gilkes, Cheryl Townsend. "The 'Loves' and 'Troubles' of African-American Women's Bodies: The Womanist Challenge to Cultural Humiliation and Community Ambivalence." In *A Troubling in My Soul: Womanist Perspectives on Evil and Suffering*, ed. Emilie M. Townes, 232–49. Maryknoll, N.Y.: Orbis Books, 1993.

Gondolf, Edward, with Ellen R. Fisher. *Battered Women as Survivors: An Alternative to Treating Learned Helplessness*. New York: Lexington Books, 1988.

Gordon, Linda. *Pitied but Not Entitled: Single Mothers and the History of Welfare.* New York: Free Press, 1994.

Gordon, Margaret T., and Stephanie Riger. *The Female Fear.* New York: Free Press, 1989.

Greene, Beverly. "Still Here: A Perspective on Psychotherapy with African-American Women." In *New Directions in Feminist Psychology: Practice, Theory and Research,* eds. Joan C. Chrisler and Doris Howard, 13–25. New York: Springer, 1992.

Grier, William, and Price Cobbs. *Black Rage.* New York: Basic Books, 1968.

Griffin, Susan. "Rape: The All-American Crime." In *Forcible Rape,* eds. Duncan Chappell et al., 47–66. New York: Columbia University Press, 1977. Reprint from *Ramparts* (September 1971).

Gudorf, Christine. *Victimization: Examining Christian Complicity.* Philadelphia: Trinity Press International, 1992.

Gullattee, Alyce C. "Psychiatric Factors to Consider in Researchon the Black Woman." *Journal of Afro-American Issues* 2 (summer 1974): 199–203.

Guthrie, R. V. *Even the Rat Was White: A Historical View of Psychology.* San Diego: Dunbar Press, 1976.

Gutman, Herbert G. *The Black Family in Slavery and Freedom: 1750–1925.* New York: Pantheon, 1976.

Hamilton, Jean. "Emotional Consequences of Victimization and Discrimination in 'Special Populations.'" *Psychiatric Clinics of North America* 12 (March 1989): 35–51.

Hampton, Robert, ed. *Black Family Violence.* Lexington, Mass.: Lexington Books, 1991.

———, ed. *Violence in the Black Family: Correlates and Consequences.* Lexington, Mass.: Lexington Books, 1987.

Hampton, Robert L., and Richard Gelles. "Violence toward Black Women in a Nationally Representative Sample of Black Families." *Journal of Comparative Family Studies* 25, no. 1 (spring 1994): 105–19.

Harris, Angela P. "Race and Essentialism in Feminist Legal Theory." *Stanford Law Review* 42, no. 3 (February 1990): 581–616.

Harrison, Beverly Wildung. *Making the Connections: Essays in Feminist Social Ethics,* ed. Carol S. Robb. Boston: Beacon Press, 1985.

Hawkins, Darnell. "Devalued Lives and Racial Stereotypes: Ideological Barriers to the Prevention of Family Violence among Blacks." In *Violence in the Black Family: Correlates and Consequences,* ed. Robert L. Hampton, 189–205. Lexington, Mass.: Lexington Books, 1987.

Held, Virginia. *Feminist Morality: Transforming Culture, Society, and Politics.* Chicago: University of Chicago Press, 1993.

Herman, Judith Lewis. *Trauma and Recovery.* New York: Basic Books, 1992.

Herman, Judith, with Lisa Hirshman. *Father-Daughter Incest.* Cambridge: Harvard University Press, 1981.

Hernton, Calvin. *Coming Together: Black Power, White Hatred, and Sexual Hang-Ups.* New York: Random House, 1971.

———. *Sex and Racism in America.* New York: Grove Press, 1965.

Hester, Marianne, Liz Kelly, and Jill Radford, eds. *Women, Violence and Male Power.* Philadelphia: Open University Press, 1996.

Holiday, Billie, with William Dufty. *Lady Sings the Blues.* New York: Doubleday, 1956. Reprint, New York: Penguin Books, 1992.

Hollies, Linda. "A Daughter Survives Incest: A Retrospective Analysis." In *The Black Woman's Health Book Speaking for Ourselves,* ed. Evelyn C. White, 82–91. Seattle: Seal Press, 1990.

hooks, bell. *Ain't I a Woman.* Boston: South End Press, 1981.

———. *Black Looks: Race and Representation.* Boston: South End Press, 1992.

———. *Feminist Theory: From Margin to Center.* Boston: South End Press, 1984.

———. *Killing Rage, Ending Racism.* New York: Henry Holt, 1995.

———. *Talking Back: Thinking Feminist, Thinking Black.* Boston: South End Press, 1989.

Imam, Hyatt, and Spring Redd. "The Elizabeth Stone House: A Residential Mental Health Program for Women." *Sage* 2, no. 2 (fall 1985): 65–68.

Jacobs, Janet Liebman. "Victimized Daughters: Sexual Violence and the Empathetic Female Self." *Signs* 19, no. 11 (1993): 126–45.

James, Stanlie, and Abena P. A. Busia, eds. *Theorizing Black Feminisms: The Visionary Pragmatism of Black Women.* London: Routledge, 1993.

Jones, Ann. *Next Time, She'll Be Dead.* Boston: Beacon Press, 1994.

———. *Women Who Kill.* New York: Holt, Rinehart and Winston,1980.

Jones, Jacqueline. *Labor of Love, Labor of Sorrow: Black Women, Work and the Family, from Slavery to the Present.* New York: Vintage Books, 1986.

Joseph, Janice. "Woman Battering: A Comparative Analysis of Black and White Women." In *Out of Darkness: Contemporary Perspectives on Family Violence,* eds. Glenda Kaufman Kantor and Jana Jasinski, 161–69. Thousand Oaks, Calif.: Sage, 1997.

Kardiner, A., and L. Ovesey. *The Mark of Oppression.* New York: W. W. Norton, 1951.

Keckley, Elizabeth. *Behind the Scenes: Or Thirty Years a Slave, and Four Years in the White House.* 1868. Reprint, New York: Oxford University Press, 1988.

Kivel, Paul. *Uprooting Racism: How White People Can Work for Racial Justice.* Philadelphia: New Society Publishers, 1996.

Ladner, Joyce A. *Tomorrow's Tomorrow.* New York: Doubleday, 1971.

Ledner, Caryl. *Ossie: The Autobiography of a Black Woman.* NewYork: W. W. Norton, 1971.

Leifer, Myra, et al. "Roschach Assessment of Psychological Functioning in Sexually Abused Girls." *Journal of Personality Assessment* 56 (February 1991): 14–28.

Lockhart, Lettie. "Methodological Issues in Comparative Racial Analyses: The Case of Wife Abuse." *Social Work Research and Abstracts* 21 (1985): 35–41.

———. "A Re-examination of the Effects of Race and Social Class on the Incidences of Marital Violence: A Search for Readable Differences." *Journal of Marriage and Family* 49 (August 1987): 35–41.

Loftus, Elizabeth F., Sara Polonsky, and Mindy Thompson Fullilove. "Memories of Childhood Sexual Abuse: Remembering and Repressing." *Psychology of Women Quarterly* 18 (1994): 67–84.

Lorde, Audre. *Sister Outsider*. Trumansburg, N.Y.: Crossing Press, 1984.

MacKinnon, Catharine A. *Feminism Unmodified*. Cambridge: Harvard University Press, 1987.

———. *Toward a Feminist Theory of the State*. Cambridge: Harvard University Press, 1989.

Mahoney, Martha. "Victimization or Oppression? Women's Lives, Violence, and Agency." In *The Public Nature of Private Violence: The Discovery of Domestic Abuse*, eds. Martha A. Fineman and Roxanne Mykitiuk, 59–92. New York: Routledge, 1994.

Manlowe, Jennifer. *Faith Born of Seduction: Sexual Trauma, Body Image, and Religion*. New York: New York University Press, 1995.

Marsh, Clifton E. "Sexual Assault and Domestic Violence in the African American Community." *Western Journal of Black Studies* 17, no. 3 (1993): 149–55.

Matthews, Nancy A. *Managing Rape: The Feminist Anti-Rape Movement and the State*. New York: Routledge, 1994.

———. "Surmounting a Legacy: The Expansion of Racial Diversity in a Local Anti-Rape Movement." *Gender and Society* 3, no. 4 (December 1989): 518–32.

Mellon, James, ed. *Bullwhip Days: The Slaves Remember*. New York: Weidenfeld and Nicolson, 1988.

Miller, Alice. *Thou Shalt Not Be Aware: Society's Betrayal of the Child*. Translated by Hildegarde and Hunter Hannum. New York: Meridian, 1984.

Morton, Patricia. *Disfigured Images: The Historical Assault on Afro-American Women*. Westport, Conn.: Praeger, 1991.

Moynihan, Daniel Patrick. *The Negro Family: The Case for National Action*. Washington, D.C.: Government Printing Office, March 1965.

Oliver, William. "Black Males and Social Problems: Prevention through Afrocentric Socialization." *Journal of Black Studies* 20 (1989): 15–39.

———. "Sexual Conquest and Patterns of Black-on-Black Violence: A Structural-Cultural Perspective." *Violence and Victims* 4, no. 4 (1989): 257–73.

Olufumni, Odumidun Oya. "To Batter a Woman Is to Upset the Balance of Nature: A Yoruba Perspective." *NCADV Voice* (fall 1996): 10–11.

O'Meally, Robert. *Lady Day: The Many Faces of Billie Holiday.* New York: Little, Brown, 1991.

Omolade, Barbara. "Hearts of Darkness." In *Powers of Desire: The Politics of Sexuality,* eds. Ann Snitow, Christine Stansell, and Sharon Thompson, 350–67. New York: Monthly Review Press, 1983.

———. *It's a Family Affair: Real Lives of Black Single Mothers.* Latham, N.Y.: Kitchen Table Press, 1986.

Paglia, Camille. *Vamps and Tramps.* New York: Vintage Books, 1994.

Patterson, Orlando. *Slavery and Social Death.* Cambridge: Harvard University Press, 1982.

Pellauer, Mary D. "A Theological Perspective on Sexual Assault." In *Sexual Assault and Abuse: A Handbook for Clergy and Religious Professionals,* eds. Mary D. Pellauer, Barbara Chester, and Jane Boyajian, 84–95. San Francisco: Harper-Collins, 1987.

Pellauer, Mary D., with Susan Brooks Thistlethwaite. "Conversation on Grace and Healing: Perspectives from the Movement to End Violence against Women." In *Lift Every Voice: Constructing Christian Theologies from the Underside,* eds. Susan Brooks Thistlethwaite and Mary Potter Engel, 169–85. San Francisco: HarperCollins, 1990.

Plass, Peggy S. "African American Family Homicide: Patterns in Partner, Parent, and Child Victimization, 1985–1987." *Journal of Black Studies* 23, no. 4 (June 1993): 515–38.

Poling, James N. *The Abuse of Power.* Nashville: Abingdon Press, 1991.

Prothrow-Stith, Deborah. *Deadly Consequences.* New York: HarperCollins, 1991.

Quina, Kathryn, and Nancy Carlson. *Rape, Incest and Sexual Harassment: A Guide for Helping Survivors.* New York: Greenwood Press, 1989.

Ramsay, Nancy J. "Sexual Abuse and Shame: The Travail of Recovery." In *Women in Travail and Transition,* eds. Maxine Glaz and Jeanne Stevenson Moessner, 109–25. Minneapolis: Fortress Press, 1991.

Rasmussen, Larry. *Moral Fragments and Moral Community: A Proposal for Church in Society.* Minneapolis: Fortress Press, 1993.

Rawick, George P. "General Introduction." In *The American Slave.* Supplement series 1, vol. 1. Westport, Conn.: Greenwood Press, 1977.

———, ed. *The American Slave: A Composite Autobiography.* 41vols., Series 1, Supplement Series 1 and 2. Westport, Conn.: Greenwood Press, 1972, 1978, 1979.

Rhodes, Jean F., Lori Ebert, and Adena B. Meyers. "Sexual Victimization in Young, Pregnant and Parenting, African-American Women: Psychological and Social Outcomes." *Violence and Victims* 8, no. 2 (1993): 153–63.

Rice, Sara. *He Included Me: The Autobiography of Sara Rice,* ed. Louise Westling. Athens: University of Georgia Press, 1989.

Richie, Beth E. *Compelled to Crime: The Gender Entrapment of Battered Black Women.* New York: Routledge, 1996.

Robinson, Tracy, and Janie Victoria Ward. "A Belief in Self Far Greater than Anyone's Disbelief: Cultivating Resistance among African American Female Adolescents." *Women and Therapy* 2, no. 3/4 (1991): 87–103.

Rosewater, Lynne B. "Diversifying Feminist Theory and Practice:Broadening the Concept of Victimization." In *Diversity and Complexity in Feminist Therapy,* eds. Laura Brown and Maria Root, 299–311. New York: Harrington Park Press, 1990.

Rouse, Linda P. "Abuse in Dating Relationships: A Comparison of Blacks, Whites and Hispanics." *Journal of College Student Development* 29 (July 1988): 312–19.

Rushing, Andrea Benton. "Surviving Rape: A Morning/Mourning Ritual." In *Theorizing Black Feminisms: The Visionary Pragmatism of Black Women,* eds. Stanlie M. James and Abena P. A. Busia, 127–40. New York: Routledge, 1993.

Russell, Diana E. H. *Rape in Marriage.* New York: Macmillan, 1982.

———. *Sexual Exploitation: Rape, Child Sexual Abuse and Workplace Harassment.* Beverly Hills: Sage, 1984.

Sampson, R. J. "Urban Black Violence: The Effect of Male Joblessness and Family Disruption." *American Journal of Sociology* 93, no. 2 (1987): 348–82.

Schecter, Susan. *Women and Male Violence.* Boston: South End Press, 1982.

Schneider, Elizabeth M. "The Violence of Privacy." In *The Public Nature of Private Violence: The Discovery of Domestic Abuse,* eds. Martha A. Fineman and Roxanne Mykitiuk, 36–58. New York: Routledge, 1994.

Scott, James C. *Domination and the Arts of Resistance.* New Haven: Yale University Press, 1990.

Scott, Kesho Yvonne. *The Habit of Surviving.* New York: Ballantine Books, 1991.

Scully, Diana. *Understanding Sexual Violence: A Study of Convicted Rapists.* Boston: Unwin Hyman, 1990.

Shapiro, Jeremy, et al. "Multimethod Assessment of Depression in Sexually Abused Girls." *Journal of Personality Assessment* 51 (fall 1990): 234–48.

Stanko, Elizabeth A. *Intimate Intrusions: Women's Experience of Male Violence.* London: Routledge and Kegan Paul, 1985.

Staples, Robert. *The Black Woman in America.* Chicago: Nelson Hall, 1973.

———. "The Political Economy of Black Family Life." *Black Scholar,* 17 (1986): 2–11.

T., "Manner of 'De Light'—a New Kind of Talk." Unpublished paper, 1994.

Thomas, Alexander, and Samuel Sillen. *Racism and Psychiatry.* New York: Citadel Press, 1972.

Thurston, Linda P. "Women Surviving: An Alternative Approach to 'Helping' Low-Income Urban Women." *Women and Therapy* 8, no. 4 (1989): 109–27.

Townes, Emilie M., ed. *A Troubling in My Soul: Womanist Perspectives on Evil and Suffering.* Maryknoll, N.Y.: Orbis Books, 1993.

Turner, Tina, with Kurt Loder. *I, Tina: My Life Story.* New York: Avon Books, 1986.

Uzzell, Odell, and Wilma Peebles-Wilkins. "Black Spousal Abuse: A Focus on Relational Factors and Intervention Strategies." *Western Journal of Black Studies* 13, no. 1 (1989): 10–16.

Viano, Emilio C. "Violence among Intimates: Major Issues and Approaches." In *Intimate Violence: Interdisciplinary Perspectives,* ed. Emilio C. Viano, 3–12. Washington, D.C.: Hemisphere Publishing, 1992.

Walker, Lenore E. *The Battered Woman.* New York: Harper and Row, 1979.

———. *The Battered Woman Syndrome.* New York: Springer, 1984.

———. "Battered Women: Sex Roles and Clinical Issues." *Professional Psychology* 12, no. 1 (February 1981): 81–91.

———. "Feminist Therapy with Victim/Survivors of Interpersonal Violence." In *Handbook of Feminist Therapy: Women's Issues in Psychotherapy,* eds. Lynne Bravo Rosewater and Lenore E. A. Walker. New York: Springer, 1985.

———. "Post-Traumatic Stress Disorder in Women: Diagnosis and Treatment of Battered Woman Syndrome." *Psychotherapy* 28, no. 1 (spring 1991): 21–29.

———. "Psychology and Violence against Women." *American Psychologist* 44, no. 4 (April 1989): 695–702.

———. "Response to Mills and Mould." *American Psychologist* 45, no. 5 (1990): 676–77.

———. *Terrifying Love: Why Battered Women Kill and How Society Responds.* New York: Harper and Row, 1989.

———. "Victimology and the Psychological Perspectives of Battered Women." *Victimology* 8, nos. 1–2 (1983): 82–104.

Walker, Lenore, and Angela Browne. "Gender and Victimization by Intimates." *Journal of Personality* 53, no. 2 (June 1985): 179–95.

Wallace, Michelle. *Black Macho and the Myth of the Superwoman.* New York: Dial Press, 1978.

Watson, Vernaline. "Self-Concept Formation and the Afro-American Woman." *Journal of Afro-American Issues* 2 (summer 1974): 226–36.

Welch, Sharon. *Communities of Resistance and Solidarity: A Feminist Theology of Liberation.* New York: Orbis Books, 1985.

West, Cornel. *Prophesy Deliverance! An Afro-American Revolutionary Christianity.* Philadelphia: Westminister Press, 1982.

White, Deborah Gray. *Ar'nt I a Woman.* New York: W. W. Norton, 1985.

White, Evelyn. *Chain, Chain, Change: For Black Women Dealing with Physical and Emotional Abuse.* Seattle: Seal Press, 1985.

Williams, Delores. "African-American Women in Three Contexts of Domestic Violence." In *Violence against Women, Concilium,* eds. Elizabeth Schüssler

Fiorenza and M. Shawn Copeland, 34–43. Maryknoll, N.Y.: Orbis Books, 1994.

————. *Sisters in the Wilderness: The Challenge of Womanist God-Talk.* Maryknoll, N.Y.: Orbis Books, 1993.

Williams, Joyce. "Confronting Public Attitudes about Rape." *Victimology* 9, no. 1 (1984): 66–81.

Williams, Joyce, and Karen Holmes. *The Second Assault: Rape and Public Attitudes.* Westport, Conn.: Greenwood Press, 1981.

Wilson, Kathy, Regina Vercella, Christiane Brems, and Deborah Benning. "Levels of Learned Helplessness in Abused Women." *Women and Therapy* 13, no. 4 (1992): 53–67.

Wilson, Melba. *Crossing the Boundary: Black Women Survive Incest.* Seattle: Seal Press, 1994.

Wood, Frances E. "'Take My Yoke upon You': The Role of the Church in the Oppression of African-American Women." In *A Troubling in My Soul: Womanist Perspectives on Evil and Suffering,* ed. Emilie M. Townes, 37–47. Maryknoll, N.Y.: Orbis Books, 1993.

Wriggins, Jennifer. "Rape, Racism, and the Law." *Harvard Women's Law Journal* 6 (1983): 103–41.

Wurmser, Léon. *The Mask of Shame.* Baltimore: Johns Hopkins University Press, 1981.

Wyatt, Gail. "The Aftermath of Child Sexual Abuse of African American and White Women: The Victim's Experience." *Journal of Family Violence* 5, no. 1 (March 1990): 66–81.

————. "The Sexual Abuse of Afro-American and White American Women in Childhood." *Child Abuse and Neglect* 9 (1985): 507–19.

————. "Sexual Abuse of Ethnic Minority Children: Identifying Dimensions of Victimization." *Professional Psychology: Research and Practice* 21, no. 5 (1990): 338–43.

Wyatt, Gail Elizabeth, Michael D. Newcomb, and Monkia H. Riederle. *Sexual Abuse and Consensual Sex: Women's Developmental Patterns and Outcomes.* Newbury Park, Calif.: Sage, 1993.

Wyatt, Gail Elizabeth, Cindy M. Notgrass, and Michael Newcomb. "Internal and External Mediators of Women's Rape Experiences." *Psychology of Women Quarterly* 14 (1990): 153–76.

Index

Against Our Will (Brownmiller), 93–94

Baraka, Amiri, aka Leroi Jones, 126, 129
Battered women's shelter: and racism, 144;
  and women's spiritual needs, 80, 188,
  204
Battering, 64, 66, 71–71, 79–80, 87, 108,
  115; and acquiesent/pleasing behavior,
  61, 64–65, 163–64; and anger, 145; and
  Black Panthers, 127–29; and church/
  religious response, 120–21, 141–42; and
  community resistance, 196, 204; as domestic violence, 101–5; fighting back,
  74, 166; and male domination, 132; and
  oppressed black male, 83, 85, 102–5;
  and police response, 123, 139–40; and
  woman-blaming, 117, 136; and women's
  agency, 117–19, 154–61. *See also* Inti-
  mate violence
Battering victim-survivors: disbelieved,
  123–24, 144; and honorable families,
  81–82
Bender, Lauretta, 124
Bible, 61–62, 69, 74–75, 81, 171. *See also*
  Christian faith
Black Panther Party, 127–29
The Black Woman in America (Staples), 97
Boyd-Franklin, Nancy, 176
Brent, Linda, aka Harriet Brent Jacobs,
  21–22
Brinkley-Kennedy, Rhonda, 84
Brooks, Sara, 24–25
Brown, Elaine, 128–29
Browne, Angela, 65
Brownmiller, Susan, 93–95. *See also* Davis,
  Angela; hooks, bell; Rape
Burt, Martha, 123–4
Bussert, Joy, 220n. 57
Byrd, Senator Robert, 133–34

Caputi, Jane, 117
Carlson, Nancy, 144
Carter, Lawrence, 142
Child sexual abuse/assault, 64; and groups,
  175–77; and spiritual resources, 168–69.
  See also Incest
Child sexual abuse victim-survivors, 124,
  141; and resistance, 162, 164, 196; and
  self blame, 71. *See also* Incest
Christian ethics, 1, 3, 181–82, 184–85, 203;
  feminist, 1, 68, 172; womanist, 119–20
Christian faith: communal ethics, 203;
  community truth-work, 198–99; crisis,
  59–60; Eve, 62, 74; and forgiveness,
  75–76, 171–72; homophobia in, 73; is-
  sues of race, 113; Latin American base
  communities, 201; and resistance work,
  167–68, 171–72; and shame, 74–76. *See
  also* Bible; God
Church: response to rape, 142–43; self-critique, 199; work ethic, 140–41
Cleaver, Eldridge, 127–28
Clinton, President Bill, 134
Comer, Maggie, 24, 29
Coming Together (Hernton), 96
Crenshaw, Kimberlé, 216n. 60, 228n. 55
Curtis, Lynn, 92

Davis, Angela, 95, 224n. 50
Dobash, R. Emerson, 156
Dobash, Russell P., 156
Dollard, John, 137
Dyson, Michael Eric, 223n. 34

Equiano, Olaudah, aka Gustavus Vassa, 16
Eugene, Toinette, 119–20

Feminist resistance-building, 189–91, 206
Feminist theorists: of cultural obstruction,

Feminist theories *(continued)*
116–19; of cultural victimization, 110–12, 131–32; early "second wave," 91–95; of intimate violence, 55–56, 68; and racism in theories of, 112–16; and women's agency, 154–61
Ferguson, Kathy, 191
Fine, Michelle, 138
Fortune, Marie, 55, 56, 113, 130; justice-making, 197; women abandoned by God, 59–60
Frazier, E. Franklin, 137

Gelles, Richard, 101–2, 104–7
Gender: and breach with community, 58; fused with racial meanings, 76–88, 145–47, 153–54, 175, 179, 206; issues in black communal life, 96–100, 102–5, 126–29, 136, 142–43; and patriarchy, 5; socialization, 62, 65; stereotypes, 69–70, 71–72, 198; and theories about intimate violence, 108–12, 116–19, 131–33, 154–61; theorizing and race, 55–56
Geto Boys, 131
Gilkes, Cheryl, 119
God: anger at, 171, 72; disconnection from, 59–60, 75, 80; disfavor/disapproval of, 28, 74; forgiving of, 172; as helpful resource, 29, 165, 167–70, 198; maleness of, 61; pleasing of, 61; righteous anger of, 172. *See also* Christian faith; Church
Goldberg, David Theo, 59
Gondolf, Edward, 158–59
Gone with the Wind, 130
Gordon, Margaret, 67
Gray, Fredrica, 166–67
Greene, Beverly, 153–54
Griffin, Susan, 92
Group therapy, 174–78
Guffy, Ossie, 26–28

The Habit of Surviving (Scott), 80
Hampton, Robert, 101–2, 104
Harrison, Beverly, 1, 172–73
Hawkins, Darnell, 225n. 74
Held, Virginia, 182
Herman, Judith, 55; dishonor of victims, 124; group therapy, 174; studying whites, 114; victim isolation, 57–58. *See also* Incest

Hernton, Calvin, 96–97
Hill, Anita, 125
Holiday, Billie, 25–26, 28, 92
Hollies, Linda, 170–71
Holmes, Karen, 92; 146–47
hooks, bell: "battered woman," 220n. 58; on black rage, 173; on Brownmiller, 217n. 5; "talking-back," 62

Incest: and women's anger, 170–72; and lesbianism, 86; and shame, 87; study of white women, 114–15. *See also* Herman, Judith
Incest victim-survivor, 81; breaking silence, 178–79; and Christian forgiveness, 75–76, 170–72; stereotypes of, 144–45
Intimate violence: acquiescent behavior, 61, 64–65; definition of, 4; dissociating, 63; splitting behavior, 65; statistics, 209n. 5; victim-survivor, 5. *See also* Battering; Incest; Rape

Jemison, T. J., 142
Jones, Ann: community networks, 196; victim-blaming, 116–17, 134, 155, 220n. 58
Joseph, Janice, 166

Keckley, Elizabeth, 20
Kivel, Paul, 202

Ladner, Joyce, 98–99
Laney, Lucy, 179
"Learned helplessness," 154–59. *See also* Walker, Lenore
Lesbian, 4; Christian homophobia, 73; self-suppression, 66, 86; woman to woman attraction, 141–42. *See also* Incest
Little, Joan, 169–70
Long, Senator Russell, 134
Lorde, Audre, 162, 187

MacKinnon, Catharine, 110–11, 131–32
Madheart (A Morality Play) (Baraka), 126, 129
Mahoney, Martha, 160–61
Miller, Sherman, 125
Morehouse College, 142
Morton, Patricia, 137
Moynihan, Senator Daniel Patrick, 135

Moynihan Report (*The Negro Family: The Case for National Action, 1965*), 135

National Baptist Convention, 142
Nelson, Jill, 143
Newton, Huey, 129
N.W.A. [Niggaz With Attitude], 131

Oliver, William, 102–4
Olufumni, Oya Odumidun, 169
O'Meally, Robert, 211n. 21

Paglia, Camille, 219n. 49
Patriarchy, definition of, 5
Peebles-Wilkins, Wilma, 218n. 29
Pellauer, Mary, 68, 69
"Personal Responsibility Act" (1995), 135
"Personal Responsibility and Work Reconciliation Act" (1996), 134
Peters, Mary, 17
Police: and support teams, 206; distrusted, 167; skepticism of, 123, 147; unreliable, 139–40
Poling, James N., 22n. 57, 213n. 18
Prine, Ila B., 16–17
Prothrow-Stith, Deborah, 106–7, 140
Psycho, 130

Quina, Kathryn, 144
Quivers, Robin, 165–66

Race/racial: accomodation, 62; analysis of rape, 92–100; anxieties, 183; assumptions about, 194; and community visibility, 58–59; education, 195–96, 202, 206; ideology, 122; pathology, 135, 153, 190; perceptions of victim-survivors, 144–47; and rituals, 200–1; and self-blame, 72; and shame, 70, 82, 84–87, 125, 183, 189; theorizing, 56; and therapy groups, 174–77
Racism, 2, 67, 188, 191; and battered women's shelter, 144; and black men, 83–85; and Christian faith, 60; and poverty, 138–39; recovering racists, 183; splitting the self, 65; and women's agency, 156, 161. *See also* Race/racial; White supremacy
Ramsay, Nancy, 174
Rape, 57, 70, 131, 166, 180; charge against

black men, 83; charge by white women, 93–95, 125; and church response, 142–43; by Eldridge Cleaver, 127–28; and community resistance, 189, 192, 196, 204; cultural permission for, 117, 121; and male dominance, 111, 132; and poor women, 138; and shame, 67–71, 73–74; and spirituality, 167, 168; social theories about, 92–100, 107–8; and Mike Tyson, 142–43; of white women, 126–27. *See also* Brownmiller, Susan; Intimate violence
Rape victim-survivors: disbelieved, 58, 147; myths/stereotypes about, 123–24, 144–46; responses of, 78–79, 84–85, 138
Rasmussen, Larry, 230n. 14
Reagan, Bernice Johnson, 169–70
Rice, Sara, 22–24, 28–29
Rich, Adrienne, 186
Richie, Beth, 87
Riger, Stephanie, 67
Roiphe, Katie, 123
Rushing, Andrea Benton, 84, 168, 179–80

Sapphire, 14
Saunders, Mary Alice, 168
Schecter, Susan, 118–19
Scott, James, 159, 179
Scott, Kesho Yvonne, 80
Self-blame, 71–74, 111, 136–37
Sex and Racism in America (Hernton), 96
Sexual/sexuality: distortedness of black women, 96, 137; and heterosexual relations, 107; hierarchy, 111, 131–32; and race, 114; sinfulness, 75; and "uncleaness," 75; and violence, 111, 117, 127–28, 130–31. *See also* Rape
Shame: and black single moms, 135; and blameworthy women, 82, 133; and cleansing self, 68–69; resistance, 161, 165, 203; self-blame, 111, 71–74
Sharpton, Al, 142
Sillen, Samuel, 153
Slave/slavery: about, 14–16, 164; testimonies, 16–22
Smith, Henrietta Evelina, 19–20
Snoop Doggy Dogg, 131
Soul on Ice (Cleaver), 127
Spellman College, 142

Spirituality, 80; ancestors, 168–69; defintion of, 4; and life-threatening violence, 66; and politics, 188; and resistance, 168–70. *See also* Christian faith
Stanko, Elizabeth, 109
Staples, Robert, 97–99
Straus, Murray, 105–6, 107

"T.," 64, 79–80
Terrell, Mary Church, 179
Thomas, Alexander, 153
Thomas, Altamese, 167
Till, Emmett, 93, 95
Turner, Ike, 163–64
Turner, Tina, 163–64
Tyson, Mike, 142–43

Uzzell, Odell, 218n. 29

Viano, Emilio, 110–11
Violence, Race, and Culture (Curtis), 92

Walker, Lenore, 55, 85, 112–13; about angry black women, 145; and compliant behavior, 65; cycle theory of battering, 56, 85; and "learned helplessness," 155–57; studying racial/ethnic groups, 115. *See also* Battering
Walker, Theodore, 218n. 32
Washington, Desiree, 142
"Welfare," 134–35, 202
Welsing, Frances Cress, 136
White, Evelyn, 83
White supremacy, 5, 156. *See also* Racism
Williams, Delores, 164, 167; about domestic violence, 120; and resistance rituals, 200
Williams, Joyce, 92, 146–47
Williams, Monica, 78
Williams, Rose, 18–19
Wilson, Melba, 87, 178–79
Womanist approaches, 109, 119–21
Wriggins, Jennifer, 224n. 46
Wyatt, Gail Elizabeth, 79

Young, Annie, 17–18
Young, Clara C., 17

About the Author

Traci C. West was born and raised in Connecticut. She is an ordained United Methodist minister who has served in campus and parish ministries.

She is currently an assistant professor of Ethics and African American Studies at Drew University Theological School in Madison, New Jersey.